D1471391

00092260

Football Hooliganism

Steve Frosdick and Peter Marsh

WILLAN
PUBLISHING

Published by

Willan Publishing
Culmcott House
Mill Street, Uffculme
Cullompton, Devon
EX15 3AT, UK
Tel: +44(0)1884 840337
Fax: +44(0)1884 840251
e-mail: info@willanpublishing.co.uk
website: www.willanpublishing.co.uk

Published simultaneously in the USA and Canada by

Willan Publishing
c/o ISBS, 920 NE 58th Ave, Suite 300,
Portland, Oregon 97213-3786, USA
Tel: +001(0)503 287 3093
Fax: +001(0)503 280 8832
e-mail: info@isbs.com
website: www.isbs.com

First published 2005

ISBN 1-84392-129-4

British Library Cataloguing-in-Publication Data

A catalogue record for this book is available from the British Library

Project managed by Deer Park Productions, Tavistock, Devon
Typeset by GCS, Leighton Buzzard, Bedfordshire.
Printed and bound by T.J. International, Padstow, Cornwall

Contents

Preface   *ix*
About the authors   *xi*
Acknowledgements   *xiii*
Foreword by Jim Chalmers (President, Football Safety Officers' Association)   *xv*

Part I   Introduction   **1**

1   **Introduction**   **3**
         Overview of the book   6
         Aims of the book   7
         Chapter summary   9

2   **Football violence in history**   **10**
         Folk-football: the origins of the violence   10
         Development and codification   13
         A history of disorder   16
         A history of disaster   23
         Chapter summary   24

Part II   Defining Football Hooliganism   **25**

3   **The nature and extent of British football hooliganism**   **27**
         Introduction   27
         The nature of 'football hooliganism'   27
         Empirical approaches?   31
         The extent of British football hooliganism   34
         England disorder overseas   43
         Chapter summary   45

4   **Levels of football violence in Europe**   **46**
         Introduction   46

| | Levels of violence | 47 |
| | Chapter summary | 55 |

5	**European fan profiles and behaviour**	**57**
	Introduction	57
	Germany	57
	Italy	58
	France	61
	The Netherlands	63
	Austria	65
	Scandinavia	65
	Stages of development	69
	Chapter summary	70

| **Part III Explaining Football Hooliganism** | | **73** |

6	**An overview of British theories of football hooliganism**	**77**
	Introduction	77
	Populist explanations	80
	'Hooligan porn'	80
	British academic explanations	81
	Who are the hooligans?	84
	Chapter summary	85

7	**British theoretical perspectives in detail**	**86**
	Introduction	86
	The Harrington Report	87
	The Lang Report	88
	Ian Taylor	89
	Subculture theories	90
	Media amplification	92
	Ethogenic approach	93
	The Leicester School	94
	Ethnographic approaches	97
	Chapter summary	101

8	**Theoretical approaches from Europe and beyond**	**102**
	Introduction	102
	Italy	102
	Germany	106
	The Netherlands	108
	Other European research	109
	Conclusions on European theoretical approaches	109
	Towards a world understanding of football hooliganism?	111

Chapter summary   112

9   The media and football hooliganism   113
      Introduction   113
      History   114
      Theory   115
      The role of the media in other European countries 119
      Conclusion   121
      Chapter summary   123

10   Football violence and alcohol   125
      Introduction   125
      The 'alcohol–violence connection'   125
      Anomalies in alcohol controls   128
      The effectiveness of the controls?   129
      Culture and alcohol   130
      The roligans   131
      The police view   132
      Unexpected consequences of alcohol bans   132
      The case of the Scots   134
      Conclusion   135
      Chapter summary   136

11   Racism and football fans   138
      Introduction   138
      Forms of racism   139
      Is football hooliganism motivated by racism?   141
      Anti-racism initiatives   142
      The European dimension   146
      Conclusion   148
      Chapter summary   150

Part IV Tackling Football Hooliganism   153

12   Policing football hooliganism   155
      Introduction   155
      Policing prior to Euro '96   155
      Policing Euro '96   161
      Developments in policing since Euro '96   164
      Chapter summary   167

13   Repressive social controls   169
      Introduction   169
      Legal provisions   169

New and refurbished grounds 172
Technology 173
Government reports 174
Chapter summary 176

14   More proactive and preventive measures   178
Introduction 178
'Friendly but firm' policing 178
Risk and safety management 180
Fan culture and coaching 182
New directions in tackling football hooliganism 186
Chapter summary 188

References and selected bibliography   189
Useful websites   204
Index   205

Preface

In 1984, Manchester United travelled to Turin to play Juventus in the semi-finals of the European Cup-Winners' Cup. To discourage people from travelling, the Manchester club did not sell any tickets for the match – a sort of unofficial ban. But some supporters went anyway, hoping to get their tickets in Italy. The journalist Bill Buford went with them, fascinated as to why a club would want to ban its own supporters:

> There was a roar, everybody roaring, and the English supporters charged into the Italians. In the next second I went down. A dark blur and then smack: I got hit on the side of the head by a beer can – a full one – thrown powerfully enough to knock me over. As I got up, two policemen, the only two I saw, came rushing past, and one of them clubbed me on the back of the head. Back down I went. I got up again, and most of the Italians had already run off, scattering in all directions. But many had been tripped up before they got away.
>
> Directly in front of me – so close I could almost reach out to touch his face – a young Italian, a boy really, had been knocked down. As he was getting up, an English supporter pushed the boy down again, ramming his flat hand against the boy's face. He fell back and his head hit the pavement, the back of it bouncing slightly.
>
> Two other Manchester United supporters appeared. One kicked the boy in the ribs. It was a soft sound, which surprised me. You could almost hear the impact of the shoe on the fabric of the boy's clothing. He was kicked again – this time very hard – and the sound was still soft, muted. The boy reached down to protect himself, to guard his ribs, and the other English supporter kicked him in the face (Buford 1991: 86).

Buford graphically describes the social phenomenon we shall be examining in this book. Why is it that sports spectators and football fans engage in violent behaviours? What type of people get involved? How much violence is there? What kinds of violence are we talking about? And what do the authorities and other interested parties do both to prevent the violence starting and to deal with it if it does break out?

This book provides a broad analysis of football hooliganism. Unlike previous books on the subject it is not concerned with a single theoretical perspective but rather to provide a critical overview, discussing the various historical, criminological, sociological, psychological and social policy approaches to the subject. Three fallacies provide themes which run through the book: the notion that football hooliganism is new, that it is a uniquely football problem and that it is an English phenomenon. The book examines the long history of football-related violence, the problems in defining the nature of football hooliganism, the data available on the extent of football hooliganism across Europe, a detailed review of the various theories about who the hooligans are and why they behave as they do, and an analysis of policing and social policy in relation to tacking football hooliganism.

The book is intended to appeal to a wide readership, whether the academic, the student or the lay reader. We hope you enjoy it – and that you understand something more about football hooliganism as a result.

Steve Frosdick and Peter Marsh
June 2005

About the authors

Peter Marsh, a chartered psychologist, is a director of the Social Issues Research Centre and of MCM Research Ltd. Peter studied at Ruskin College, Oxford where he obtained a Diploma in Social Studies, and subsequently at University College, Oxford where he gained his BA in psychology and doctorate.

He is still known for his early work on football hooliganism, conducted in the late 1970s and early 1980s. His first book, *Rules of Disorder* published in 1978, is still a set text on the subject. This was followed by work on problems in pubs and the connections between drinking and disorder, begun in 1977 when he was Co-director of the Contemporary Violence Research Centre in Oxford University. Further work on aspects of aggression and violence has included research with youth gangs in New York and Chicago and with youth groups in France and Italy.

His other main research interests have been in the field of non-verbal behaviour, leading to a number of books. *Gestures*, written with Desmond Morris and others, won a Choice 'academic book of the year' award in the USA. Books such as *Eye to Eye* (Book of the Month Club in the USA) and *Tribes* were the subject of extensive promotional tours in the UK and USA. His most recent 'popular' book, *Lifestyle*, is concerned with people's relationship to their homes and their environments. Other works include *Aggro: The Illusion of Violence*. A further, continuing research interest is in the role of the motorcar and driving behaviour. With Peter Collett he is the author of *Driving Passion: The Psychology of the Car*.

Between 1979 and 1990 Peter was a senior lecturer in psychology at Oxford Brookes University and was made an honorary senior research fellow on his departure from full-time teaching. Since 1987 he has been a director of MCM Research – a research and consultancy company which specializes in applications of social psychology to the workplace and public contexts. In 1997 he co-founded the Social Issues Research Centre with Kate Fox. This not-for-profit organization is primarily concerned with positive aspects of lifestyles and social behaviour.

Peter is a frequent contributor to radio and TV programmes. He has presented a number of videos and is regularly invited to speak at conferences and meetings on a range of subjects.

Steve Frosdick has been Director of IWI Associates Ltd since 1996. He has an MSc in strategic risk management and is a Member of the International Institute of Risk and Safety Management. He is a founder member of the Football Safety Officers' Association and has held affiliations with several universities and consultancies.

Since January 2000 he has held a part-time academic post in the Institute of Criminal Justice Studies at the University of Portsmouth, where he teaches courses on safety and security at sports grounds and pursues his interests in the broad field of risk. Through IWI Associates, Steve has completed a wide variety of consultancy, research and training projects. His strategic risk management experience includes safety at sports grounds, events management, policing, programme and project management, strategic management, community and race relations, information security and general business risk. Clients have included the football authorities, various police organizations, conference organizers, universities and publishers.

From 1979 to 1995, Steve worked as a police officer in a wide variety of operational and support posts. Operationally, he served as patrol officer, custody officer, shift manager and operations manager. In other roles he gained experience in corporate strategy, project management, the management of risk, information management, quality improvement, performance measurement and cognitive assessment. He retired following a career break during which he successfully developed a consultancy and academic career.

Steve has an international reputation as an expert in stadium and arena safety and security. He has lectured and given conference presentations in the UK, USA, France, Portugal, Switzerland, Italy and Mauritius and has published over 50 articles, book chapters and other papers. He was the principal author and co-editor (with Lynne Walley) of the 1996 textbook *Sport and Safety Management* and is co-author (with Jim Chalmers) of the 2005 book on *Safety and Security at Sports Grounds*. He is a frequent contributor to *Stadium and Arena Management* magazine and has spoken at six of the annual 'Stadium and Arena' conferences since 1998. He is also the editor of the UK football authorities' *Training Package for Stewarding at Football Grounds*. Although now a Southampton season ticket holder, he is a lifelong fan of Brentford.

Acknowledgements

Some of this book is derived from research undertaken for the *Football Hooliganism in Europe* report to the Amsterdam Group. Peter Marsh therefore wishes to acknowledge the substantial contributions of his colleagues at the Social Issues Research Centre in Oxford. Particular thanks go to Kate Fox, James Marsh and Giovanni Carnibella – and to Simon Bradley.

Steve Frosdick wishes to thank the many members of the Football Safety Officers' Association who have granted him research access over the years: particularly John Beattie at Arsenal; Leon Blackburn at Norwich City; Ken Chapman, Colin Sayer and Simon Clayton at Millwall; Mel Highmore and John Newsham at Blackburn Rovers; Mike Holford (sadly deceased) and John Sidney at Nottingham Forest; Mick Coleman at Portsmouth; and Brendan McGlinchey at Southampton. Thanks also to Bryan Drew at the National Criminal Intelligence Service and to John Rutherford at the Football Safety Officers' Association for privileged access to important data sources, and to John de Quidt at the Football Licensing Authority. Steve also acknowledges the contributions from his dissertation students at the University of Portsmouth – particularly Alex Arthur, Robert Broomhead, Kelly Faulkner, Robert Newton and Paul Williamson.

We are grateful to Jim Chalmers – former Police Match Commander at Aston Villa, Football Licensing Authority Inspector, Assistant Safety Officer at Kidderminster Harriers and now the President of the Football Safety Officers' Association (as well as being one of Steve Frosdick's students) – for agreeing to write the Foreword and for the contribution from his own dissertation to Chapter 3 of this book.

Finally, we would both wish to thank Brian Willan, Jim Clancy, Emma Gubb and their colleagues at Willan Publishing for supporting this venture and helping us see it through to publication.

Foreword

by Jim Chalmers
(President, Football Safety Officers' Association)

When I was approached to write the Foreword to this book my first reaction was 'Oh no, not another academic study of football hooliganism'. As a former police officer, an Inspector with the Football Licensing Authority and currently as a safety manager at Kidderminster Harriers FC, I have experienced at first hand the growth and decline of the phenomenon in the UK from the 1960s to the present day. As a very mature student who has recently completed a BSc in risk and security management, a good part of my studies, including my dissertation, focused on the topic of football-related violence and disorder.

In my studies, I soon discovered how over the years there has been a plethora of books, articles, studies, judicial and government inquiries with numerous diverse opinions on the causes and cures of football hooliganism. It is a topic that everyone seems to have an opinion on. So it was with a sense of foreboding that I started to read the book. How wrong I found I was. My concerns were soon allayed since as each chapter unfolds, so does another dimension of the subject to grip the reader's attention.

One of the aims of the book is to provide a 'course reader' to support the teaching of the subject in schools, colleges and universities. As the members of my association and I know, we regularly receive questionnaires or requests for interviews from students of all ages who are studying the topic of football hooliganism, which confirms the popularity of the subject as a field of study. I wish this book had been available to me during my own studies since for the first time all the threads of the debate have been pulled together in a concise yet comprehensive publication. The book is structured in a logical and readable style, with personal and practical experiences included to support and explain the academic theories.

The strength of the book lies in the balanced, unbiased yet critical review of all that has been written about the subject from the very early days of the sport to the present time. It is not another study where academics try to score points off each other merely because they disagree on the causes and cures of football hooliganism. Instead the authors present the arguments, the debates, the evidence and opinions from the widest of sources without judging who is right or wrong. Having presented the theories and the facts they leave the final judgement to the reader.

The authors suggest that this book is aimed principally at the world of education. Yet having viewed the book from both a practical and an academic perspective, I find that there is much to commend it to a far wider audience. It will interest members of my association, the police, regulatory bodies and the genuine fan concerned with the harm which hooliganism does to what Pele described as 'The Beautiful Game'.

Part I

Introduction

Sports spectator behaviour has been for many years a major cause for concern, not only in the UK but also throughout Europe. Violent supporter behaviour has been labelled as 'football hooliganism' and is sometimes referred to as 'the English disease'. Chapter 1 examines three popular fallacies about such behaviour: that football hooliganism is new, that it is a uniquely football problem and that it is an English phenomenon. These fallacies are refuted with examples from history, from other sports and from countries around the world. Examples are also given to illustrate that football hooliganism remains a contemporary problem.

Chapter 1 concludes with an overview of the remainder of the book, which is structured in fourteen chapters in four main parts. Part I is the introduction and Part II deals with defining football hooliganism. Part III is about explaining the phenomenon, whilst Part IV looks at tackling it. The book has three clear aims: to provide the first holistic view of football hooliganism and so provide a 'course reader' to support the teaching of the subject; to present a clear, unbiased but critical review of the literature on football violence in Europe; and to examine and evaluate the various approaches to tackling such violence.

Chapter 2 shows how spectator violence has its origins in medieval folk-football. The game of football has been associated with violence since its beginnings in thirteenth-century England. Medieval football matches involved hundreds of players, and were essentially pitched battles between the young men of rival villages and towns – often used as opportunities to settle old feuds, personal arguments and land disputes. Forms of 'folk-football' existed in other European countries (such as the German 'Knappen' and Florentine 'calcio in costume'), but the roots of modern football are in these violent English rituals.

Chapter 2 continues by looking at the historical development of modern ball games, particularly soccer, emphasizing the ongoing link between sport and violence. The much more disciplined game of football introduced to continental Europe in 1900s was the reformed pastime of the British aristocracy. Other European countries adopted this form of the game, associated with Victorian values of fair-play and restrained enthusiasm. The chapter then considers the different phases through which football-related violence has evolved. Only two periods in British history have been relatively free of such violence: the interwar years and the decade following the Second World War. The behaviour now known as 'football hooliganism' originated in England in the early 1960s, and has been linked with the televising of matches (and of pitch-invasions, riots, etc.) and with the 'reclaiming' of the game by the working classes. In other European countries, similar patterns of behaviour emerged about 10 years later, in the early 1970s. Some researchers argue that a similar 'proletarianization' of the game was involved, but there is little consensus on this issue, and much disagreement on the extent to which continental youth were influenced by British hooligans. Finally, Chapter 2 concludes by noting the lack of direct causal connection between spectator violence and stadium disasters.

1. Introduction

Football fan behaviour has been for many years a major cause for concern throughout Europe, particularly in Germany, Holland, Italy and Belgium, as well as in the UK. Substantial disturbances at football matches have also been witnessed in Greece, the Czech Republic, Denmark and Austria and Eastern Europe. Debates in the European Parliament and at national government level in many European Community countries have highlighted a growing sense of frustration about our apparent inability to curb or redirect the anti-social behaviour of a minority of football supporters which constitutes the problem.

The popular media in Britain, with their unique penchant for hysteria and sensationalization, have waged a war of words on the 'mindless thugs' and 'scum' who have populated the soccer terraces since the mid-1960s – reserving their most extreme vitriol for the reporting of events involving English fans abroad. Violent and anti-social behaviour amongst football fans is referred to as 'football hooliganism', or sometimes as the 'British disease' or 'English disease'. These populist terms have been used by the media and by politicians (see Dunning 2000) to label the deviant behaviours which have become associated with (particularly) English football from the 1960s onwards. But these labels are based on three popular fallacies: that the violence is something relatively new; that it is found only at football matches; and that it is an English phenomenon. None of these claims stands up to scrutiny.

Spectator violence is nothing new. On the contrary it is an ancient and historical problem, going back at least to when there was disorder between the 'Blues' and the 'Greens' – the supporters of different chariot-racing teams in Ancient Rome. As we shall see in Chapter 2, many modern ball games – such as rugby, hurling, American football, Gaelic football and Australian Rules football – are derived from the medieval folk-football played in England since the thirteenth century. This was an excuse for fighting which regularly featured violence, death, injury and damage (see Elias and Dunning 1971).

Whilst they may not be as widely reported in the media, incidents of spectator violence have occurred with some regularity at sports such as rugby league in England, rugby in France, cricket worldwide and baseball, basketball, ice hockey and American football in the USA. In fact the USA has a substantial history of spectator violence (see Murphy *et al.* 1990). Whatever examples we cite from our scrapbooks will be quickly out of date; however, in March 2002, a rugby league Challenge Cup match between Leigh and Wigan was 'in danger of being abandoned after the bottles were thrown in the second half, with the crowd being warned three times' (*Daily Telegraph*, 19 March 2002). In October 2001, at French rugby side Montferrand, 'three Scottish match officials were physically and verbally abused by French fans' (*Daily Telegraph*, 8 October 2001).

American football saw serious disorder at a Cleveland Browns match in December 2001, when sustained missile throwing forced the players to leave the field (*Daily Telegraph*, 18 December 2001). In Columbus, Ohio, police used tear gas and made 50 arrests from a 50,000 crowd as rioting continued all night after a College American football game (*Daily Telegraph*, 6 December 2002). In November 2004, Indiana Pacers players and Detriot Pistons fans were involved in a mass fight in the stands at a basketball – rather neatly described as 'basketbrawl' – match (*Daily Telegraph*, 22 November 2004). Even at the Winter Olympics in Salt Lake City in February 2002, the police fired tear gas to disperse disorderly crowds after the finals of the bobsleigh competition!

In English cricket, the 2001 tour by Pakistan was marked by crowd problems at several grounds. The *Daily Telegraph* (8 June 2001) reported how one match 'ended in utter chaos last night after a crowd invasion by several hundred Pakistan followers'. At a second match, *The Times* (18 June 2001) told how 'Pakistan supporters flooded onto the pitch at Headingly attacking a steward who was kicked in the head and stomach'. In 2003, Lancashire County Cricket Club launched an inquiry after 'more than 1,000 people ran onto the Old Trafford pitch to celebrate Pakistan's day-night victory against England' (*Football and Stadium Management* August/September 2003). In January 2002 in Melbourne, Australia, a one-day cricket international was held up whilst more than 200 cricket fans were ejected and about 10 arrested after objects were thrown at the New Zealand players (*Daily Telegraph*, 12 January 2002). On the very day of writing this chapter, the *Daily Telegraph* (21 February 2005) reported that 'The New Zealand cricket authorities are to review security after Australia's captain stopped the match several times when his players were pelted with plastic bottles and debris during the one-day international in Wellington'.

Even minor sports are not exempt from hooliganism. *Yahoo News* (16 June 2003) reported at least 20 persons injured when 'rampaging Serb water polo fans stoned the Croatian embassy in Belgrade and tore down its flag after a violent European championship final'.

Disorder has also affected virtually every country in which football has been played. Again our examples will be quickly out of date, so a few cases from 2002 to 2005 must suffice to make the point. In Scotland, an Aberdeen v. Rangers match in January saw missile-throwing and fighting inside the ground (*Sunday Telegraph*, 20 January 2002). An Internet news items reported that the 2002 UEFA Cup Final between Feyenoord and Dortmund involved fighting outside the ground and in the city of Rotterdam; whilst the close of Spain's end of the 2001/2 season saw fighting inside and outside grounds, together with attacks on players and officials.

Also in Spain, Barcelona fans stormed the directors' box and broke windows after losing to Valencia (*Daily Telegraph*, 20 January 2003). Notwithstanding that their team was playing thousands of miles away in Osaka, Russian fans rioted in Moscow after they were beaten by Japan in the World Cup (*Daily Telegraph*, 10 June 2002). In a European championship qualifier, Macedonian players were pelted with missiles by Turkish supporters (*Daily Telegraph*, 12 June 2003). The UEFA website (8 December 2004) also reported how missile-throwing marred a Valencia v. Werder Bremen match. As a final example, AS Roma were required to play their remaining homes games in the 2004/5 Champions League behind closed doors after their game against Dynamo Kiev was abandoned at half-time, the referee having been hit in the face by a coin (*The Times*, 22 September 2004).

But the problems are not confined to the countries included in the above examples. As the Head of the Sports Department at the Council of Europe put it, 'Spectator violence and misbehaviour is still a problem all over Europe' (Walker 2000). And the problems are not confined to Europe either. For example, following the previous suspension of the Argentinean League because of crowd violence, renewed problems in the 2001/2 season included the abandonment of a derby match between Boca Juniors and River Plate. The worst incident the authors have heard of came from the island of Mauritius on 23 May 1999. Following a soccer match between two teams named 'Scouts Club' and 'Fire Brigade', there were riots in the capital, Port Louis, during which seven people were burned to death (Vuddamalay 2002).

So right up through history, we find clear examples of spectator violence in sports other than football and in countries other than England. But it is right to say that the sorts of behaviours we shall be examining in this book have particularly come to prominence since the 1960s, particularly in a football context, and particularly involving the English – at home and abroad. It is 'football hooliganism' rather than spectator violence in general which has received academic attention, which has provoked special policing and has led to specific legislation. So 'football hooliganism' inevitably provides the focus for our book. And there is no doubt that spectator violence – or 'football hooliganism' – remains a current concern in English football. Co-author Steve Frosdick keeps large scrapbooks of press cuttings and media reports on football hooliganism, adding to them on an almost daily basis. By way of illustration, we shall begin by giving three examples from the 2001/2 season. In January 2002, an FA Cup-tie between Cardiff and Leeds was played in a very hostile atmosphere. The match was disrupted by persistent missile-throwing and concluded with a large-scale pitch incursion (*Independent*, 7 January 2002). In May 2002, serious fighting outside the ground marred the end of season play-off between Millwall and Birmingham City. Some 47 police officers and 26 police horses were injured by fans throwing paving stones, bricks and explosives in disturbances which lasted an hour and a half (*Guardian*, 4 May 2002). Notwithstanding the absence of problems at the 2002 World Cup in Japan and South Korea, English fans were reported as involved in trouble abroad on at least one occasion. In May 2002, 123 Manchester United fans were deported from Germany after clashes with police in the old town area of Cologne (*Daily Telegraph*, 2 May 2002).

And the reports of English football hooliganism continue to the present day, with two widely reported incidents during the week when this chapter was being written. In the FA Cup fifth round, 'Wayne Rooney's return [to Everton] in Manchester United colours prompted angry supporters to throw coins, a mobile phone and a bottle' (*Sunday Telegraph*, 20 February 2005), as a result of which Manchester United's goalkeeper needed treatment to a head wound. Outside the ground, fighting between rival fan groups resulted in 33 arrests. Also in the FA Cup, the Burnley v. Blackburn Rovers match featured 'three separate pitch invaders and a coin thrown' (*Daily Telegraph*, 21 February 2005). Again in the FA Cup but not reported in the national media, co-author Steve Frosdick (being both a lifelong Brentford fan and a Southampton season ticket holder) attended the Southampton v. Brentford match at which the three final scores were two–two (goals), seven–six (arrests) and 12–69 (ejections). Some of the Brentford ejections involved fans seated in the Southampton areas and whose goal celebrations provoked disorder.

Overview of the book

This book is derived from two existing sources. First is a report to the Amsterdam Group prepared by co-author Peter Marsh and his colleagues (see Carnibella *et al.* 1996). Secondly is a distance learning course unit, prepared by co-author Steve Frosdick in 2003, which draws on, updates and expands upon the Peter Marsh report. The two texts have been updated and merged seamlessly together. This book takes a holistic view of the whole phenomenon of football hooliganism: namely, the history of football-related violence; the problems in defining football hooliganism; a detailed analysis of the data available on the extent of football hooliganism in the UK and Europe; a detailed review of the various theories about who the hooligans are and why they behave as they do; and an analysis of policing and social policy in relation to tackling football hooliganism in Europe.

The book is structured in fourteen chapters in four main parts. To assist the casual reader, each part has its own introduction and each chapter closes with a short summary. Part I is the introduction and contains two chapters. This chapter is the general introduction and an overview of the remaining chapters. Chapter 2 takes a historical perspective and examines football-related violence from medieval times to the present day. Part II – 'Defining football hooliganism' – contains three chapters. Chapter 3 examines the nature and extent of British football hooliganism. Chapter 4 then looks at the levels of football violence found in various other European countries, whilst Chapter 5 profiles the behaviour of fans in different European countries.

Part III – 'Explaining football hooliganism' – contains six chapters. Chapter 6 takes a first pass at the various British theoretical explanations, which are then more critically reviewed in a detailed second pass in Chapter 7. Chapter 8 then looks at theoretical approaches from Europe and beyond. The particular issues with the media, alcohol and racism are then addressed individually in Chapters 9, 10 and 11. Part IV – 'Tackling football hooliganism' – contains three chapters. Chapters 12 and 13 cover the repressive nature of historical and most contemporary social policy in relation to football hooliganism – Chapter 12 dealing specifically with policing policy and practice and Chapter 13 with other social controls such as government inquiries and legal provisions. Chapter 14 then examines the more recent and more preventive approaches such as the 'firm but friendly' policing style, 'fan coaching' projects and other changes in the culture of fan support.

Aims of the book

Sports-related studies have grown considerably in popularity and most universities now offer degree courses in sports and leisure-related subjects. Within this general area, the study of football is of particular interest and 'soccerology' has emerged as an academic subject within social science. Within both the general area and the specific context of football, the study of football hooliganism has become attractive for three reasons. First it is 'sexy' and interesting. Secondly there is a wealth of populist and academic literature available. Thirdly, the subject is large enough to form a course unit in its own right. Previous academic books have expounded a variety of rival theoretical explanations of football hooliganism. But there is no previous text which takes a holistic view of the whole phenomenon. There is thus a significant gap in the market. This book is thus the only academic text on football hooliganism aimed particularly at the student market. It is the first book to examine the whole topic of football hooliganism from a broad social science perspective (e.g. history, sociology, psychology, social policy and criminology). The book has been written to appeal directly to students and others interested in understanding football hooliganism in all its aspects, and thus we have included within the chapters various references for further study, together with a list of useful websites and an extensive list of references and selected bibliography. The first aim of this book, then, has been to provide a 'course reader' to support the teaching of football hooliganism in schools, colleges and universities.

A further principal aim of this book has been to present a clear, unbiased, but critical review of the literature on football violence in Europe. This we have attempted to do by standing back from the vested interests, academic or otherwise, of the individuals and research groups from whom the literature emanates. This detachment has been difficult at times because co-author Peter Marsh established a fairly significant theoretical perspective on football hooliganism in the late 1970s. In keeping with the traditions of this field, he has also been soundly attacked by a number of other authors whose work is reviewed within these pages. None the less, the research from which this book is derived has been a collective effort and we would claim that a high degree of balance has been maintained. The input to the research of a number of consultants and colleagues throughout Europe has added significantly to this objectivity.

A third aim has been to examine and evaluate approaches to tackling the problems of football hooliganism. To this end we have considered European and national governmental and police initiatives, the guidelines and recommendations of football lead bodies, the proposals of organizations representing supporters and the various schemes run by football clubs. Many of the extant initiatives are modest in scope and not widely reported. Some are purely reactive control measures, such as bans on travel and the availability of alcohol etc. These, whilst temporarily curbing some of the violence, do little to tackle the root causes of football hooliganism and, in some cases, lead to tragic consequences. The deaths of fans at Hillsborough, for example, were a direct consequence of the introduction of fences in the UK to prevent pitch invasions and other disorderly behaviour. These were removed following the Taylor Reports (Home Office 1989, 1990), with no apparent increase in disturbances at matches.

Chapter summary

Together with the Preface, this chapter introduces the social phenomenon of 'football hooliganism' and poses the questions the book seeks to address. Why is it that football fans engage in violent behaviours? What type of people get involved? How much violence is there? What kinds of violence are we talking about? And what do the authorities and other interested parties do both to prevent the violence starting and to deal with it if it does break out?

Three popular fallacies were examined: that football hooliganism is new, that it is a uniquely football problem and that it is an English phenomenon. These fallacies were refuted with examples from history, from other sports and from countries around the world. Examples were also given to illustrate that football hooliganism remains a contemporary problem.

The chapter concluded with an overview of the remaining chapters. The book has three clear aims: to provide the first holistic view of football hooliganism and so provide a 'course reader' to support the teaching of the subject; to present a clear, unbiased but critical review of the literature on football violence in Europe; and to examine and evaluate the various approaches to tackling such violence.

2. Football violence in history

I protest unto you that it may rather be called a frendly kind of fyghte than a play or recreation – a bloody and muthering practice than a fellowly sport or pastime. For dooth not everyone lye in waight for his adversarie, seeking to overthrowe him and picke him on his nose, though it be uppon hard stones? In ditch or dale, in valley or hill, or whatever place it be hee careth not so he have him down. And he that can serve the most of this fashion, he is counted the only felow, and who but he? (Stubbs 1583).

Folk-football: the origins of the violence

Medieval origins

Football has been associated with violence ever since its early beginnings in thirteenth-century England. The original 'folk' form of the game, most often played on Shrove Tuesdays and other Holy Days, involved only slightly structured battles between the youth of neighbouring villages and towns. The presence of a ball, in the form of a leather-bound inflated pig's bladder, was almost incidental to this semi-legitimized opportunity for settling old scores, land disputes, and engaging in 'manly', tribal aggression. Parallels existed in other European countries, such as the German 'Knappen' and the Florentine 'calcio in costume', but the roots of the modern game are to be found firmly in these ancient English traditions.

These calendrical rituals, often accompanied by extended bouts of drinking, quite regularly resulted in serious injuries and even death to the participants. To a large extent, however, they constituted what Elias and Dunning (1986) have described as 'an equilibrating type of leisure activity deeply woven into the warp and woof of society'. Whilst the sporadic outbursts of violence at contemporary football matches in Europe give rise to almost hysterical sanction, our ancestors found nothing particularly strange or sinister in these far bloodier origins of the modern game.

This sanguine tolerance of football violence was not, however, universal and as early as the fourteenth-century there were calls for controls on the game. These stemmed not so much from moral disquiet about the violent consequences of football but from the fact that, by driving ordinary citizens away from the market towns on match days, it was bad for business. When the game spread to London, played out by rival groups of apprentices, orders forbidding the sport were swift. Nicholas Farndon, the Mayor of London, was the first to issue such a proclamation in 1314:

> And whereas there is a great uproar in the City through certain tumults arising from the striking of great footballs in the field of the public – from which many evils perchance may arise – which may God forbid – we do command and do forbid, on the King's behalf, upon pain of imprisonment, that such games shall not be practised henceforth within this city.

The effect of this proclamation, however, was limited and, despite numerous arrests, the games continued. Fifteen further attempts to control the sport were made by 1660 and elsewhere in England and Scotland similar, largely ineffective, bans were issued. The Scots were no less passionate about their warring game. According to Marples (1954), at the turn of the seventeenth century Scottish football was characterized by 'its association with border raids and forays and with violence generally. Often a football match was the prelude to a raid across the Border, for the same hot-headed young men were game for both, and the English authorities learnt to keep their eyes on the footballers'.

Throughout the seventeenth-century we find reports of several hundred football players destroying drainage ditches and causing mayhem in the towns. By the eighteenth-century the game took on a more overt political significance. A match in Kettering, for example, consisting of 500 men per side, was a scarcely disguised food riot in which the object was to loot a local grain store. The authorities became, not unnaturally, rather nervous.

The transformation of the game itself from an unregulated battle on an ill-defined field of play to one of a number of modern rule-governed sports came largely as a result of urbanization and industrialization which corralled the traditional battlefield game into smaller and smaller arenas. Soon, the disorder of the game itself aroused harsh judgement. Walvin (1994) reported that 'In 1829, a Frenchman who saw a football match in Derby asked "If this is what they call football, what do they call fighting?"'

Folk-football and violence in modern sports

We have seen that folk-football was a violent spectacle. But the game was not the same everywhere. Games were played with different sizes and shapes of balls, which were propelled using different combinations of feet, hands and sticks:

> But the elementary characteristics, the character of the game as a struggle between different groups, the open and spontaneous battle-enjoyment, the riotousness and the relatively high level of socially tolerated physical violence, as far as one can see, were always the same. And so was the tendency of the players to break whatever customary rules there were, if the passions moved the players (Elias and Dunning 1971: 125).

Thus we can see that modern ball games such as rugby, hurling and the various types of football played in America and Australia, together with the modern game of soccer, are all violent sports with the same violent origins. Such sports are violent for the players and for the supporters.

Referring to football, Finn (1994: 95) claims that 'All matches, from the best behaved to the least disciplined, are aggressive events which incorporate varying levels of violence. To play soccer is to be involved in acts of aggression and violence'. Whilst Poulton (2001: 129) argues that football, 'is a sport that emphasises a very competitive, very aggressive, and very masculine style of play, especially in England. It is therefore unsurprising that there should be connections between the values that underpin the game of football and the values that underpin football-related violence'. Finn goes on to argue that the supporters may be seen as participants in the match itself. The match is violent. The spectators are involved in the match. There is thus a culture of violence associated with football supporting. And the same can be said – at least to some extent – for other sports too.

Further study

If you want to read more about folk-football, read the book chapter ('Folk football in medieval and early modern Britain') by Elias and Dunning (1971). Alternatively (or in addition), you might want to read Chapter 1 ('Pre-industrial football') of James Walvin's history of football, *The People's Game* (1994).

Development and codification

The four-stage development of modern football has been succinctly summarized by Dunning (1971: 133–4). The first stage was the folk-football we have already discussed:

> The approximate duration of the second stage was from 1750 to 1840, when the game in its rough, relatively simple folk-forms was taken up by the public schools, elaborated in certain respects and adapted to their characteristic forms of social organisation, particularly to their systems of authority.
>
> The third stage lasted from about 1840 to about 1860 when the game in the public schools began to be subjected to more formal organisation, when the rules were written down for the first time, and when the players were required to exercise a higher degree of self-control in their play than had previously been demanded of them.
>
> The fourth stage occurred when football in its public school forms was diffused into society at large and when organisations began to be set up to promote its further development and to organise and regulate it on a national level. In the course of this stage, the game began to develop as a mass spectator following for the first time and the possibility emerged of men working as full-time professional players. This was the last stage in the development of the game. It lasted from about 1850 to about 1890.

It was during the third and fourth stages that other sports such as rugby also evolved in their own distinctive forms. Walvin (1994, 53–54) notes the continuing link between spectator sports and violence during this time:

> Even in mid-Victorian Britain there was a pronounced association between certain recreations, violence and illegality. It was of course to this sphere of sport that the older tradition of football belonged and it continued to be a truism that spectator sports and violence went hand in hand. Indeed public executions, arguably one of the most popular of spectator sports, were only finally outlawed in 1868.

Taming the game

It was in the arena of the public schools that the unruliness of ball games became a cause for alarm amongst the educators of England's privileged sons. The older boys exercised complete power over the younger 'fags' and would enlist them into the game on their behalf whereupon: 'the enemy tripped, shinned, charged with the shoulder, got you down and sat upon you ... in fact might do anything short of murder to get the ball from you' (Dunning 1971).

Where countless other masters had been terrorized by their pupils, Dr Thomas Arnold, the headmaster at Rugby from 1828, succeeded in tempering the wild and brutal football so avidly played by the boys. First he ensured the masters' control over the barbaric 'prefect-fagging' system by formalizing the older boys' right to power through appointments. Then, rather than attempting to ban football as other masters had done, he legitimized the game and encouraged the pupils to formalize a set of rules to govern it. As the fight for dominance amongst the pupils was pacified through delegation of power, the real violence on the football field was ritualized by regulation. Much of the emphasis on the gentlemanly qualities of the game and the evangelical promotion of the sport as an alternative to idle evils such as alcohol can be traced to this period when the game flourished in the public schools. Gradually, the newly refined and 'respectable' game of football permeated the rest of society. It was in this form that football was exported to the continent.

Export of the new game

In France, Germany and Italy, the unrestrained character of English team sports came to be regarded as superior to the regimented exercises of gymnastics for, as one of the founders of the Ecole des Roches said, the 'gradual emancipation and self-revelation of youth'. The French aristocracy in particular, sought to exemplify the ideals of the great Imperial power by adopting the sporting values of the British gentleman.

To the north, the Scandinavians also modelled their behaviour on the 'ideal British gentleman'. In Denmark, for example, football matches in the early 1900s were attended by large but well mannered crowds, often including royalty. Betting was absent as were police. Unruly spectator behaviour was considered to be a southern continental problem.

In Sweden, local rivalries were more pronounced as were class distinctions in this era. Spectators were largely segregated into the decorous upper-classes and the more boisterous working-class sections. The press positively encouraged their extroverted behaviour (so long as it stayed within the bounds of decency) as it added atmosphere to the game. Official cheer squads debuted during the 1912 Olympics in imitation of the Americans. It was during competition between Sweden and Denmark that outdoing the other team's cheer or banner squad became a kind of sport in itself. Combined with drinking, these 'organized expressions of feeling' gave some cause for concern. The cause of unruly spectator behaviour was invariably traced to incidents on the field itself such as poor refereeing or fights between players which 'inflamed' the public. Whilst the justification for such behaviour was not contested, by 1914 the propriety of these excessive verbal displays of support began to be questioned.

In France, the noble nature of the British import was soon sold out for reinterpretation by the masses. By the early 1900s, the number of aristocratic players diminished as the sport gained popularity amongst the middle class. The liberating nature of football once praised by the elite now came to symbolize middle-class, working industrial values antagonistic to the aristocracy and the church. Thus football became 'an allegory of liberalism'. The new French clubs set themselves squarely at odds with the elitist, exclusive shooting and gymnastics clubs. At the turn of the century English-style football clubs were springing up all over Europe. But, as Pierre Lanfranchi (1994) points out, the founding members of these clubs were largely members of white-collar practical professions – engineers, technicians, traders, doctors – or university students.

The interwar period saw a rise in nationalist sentiment on the continent and, tangentially, an amplification of public enthusiasm for football. Thus in 1938, an Italian newspaper reported Bologna's victory over Chelsea as 'a brilliant victory for Fascist Italy'. In this 20-year interwar period, continental football teams distinguished themselves with their own style, technique, and strong national allegiances ready to challenge the British dominance of the sport.

Return to the working class

In England, the spectator passion of the new century began to perturb the defenders of Victorian standards. For despite the middle-class administration and refinement of the game, football in the early 1900s remained a working-class pastime with most of the new grounds built close to the heart of working-class communities. Descriptions of crowd behaviour at these urban matches varied greatly depending on the background of the writer. Thus, 'the old-guard defenders of an upper-class amateur, Corinthian ideal of the game could vent their spleen at the take-over of football by the industrial workers of the north by depicting crowds as dirty, fickle and degenerate' (Taylor 1992).

Certainly, the new rule-centred football was not free from violence. However limited the number of actual players, the commonly held feeling that football was a participatory game had not been dispelled. Whilst the upper classes continued their tradition of polite disassociation from the jousting rivalries on the fields of sport, the working man merged his heart and soul with the effort and staked his reputation on the outcome of the game.

Further study

If you want to read more about the development of modern football, read the book chapter ('The development of modern football') by Dunning (1971). Alternatively (or in addition), you might want to read Chapters 2, 3 and 4 ('The public schools and football', 'The rise of working-class football' and 'Football to 1914') in Walvin (1994).

A history of disorder

Football-related violence also seems to have evolved through a series of stages. Prior to the First World War, the violence was spontaneous rather than organized, involving attacks on players, referees and opposing supporters. There was then a relative calm between the wars. Thereafter, the decade following the end of the Second World War was particularly peaceful, with crowd control being 'largely a case of dealing with the occasional pub fight or with individual offenders whose inclinations to fight may have had no football-related basis at all, or, finally, of dealing with the sorts of problems which were occasionally produced simply by the sheer size of football crowds' (Williams 1991a: 165).

From around the 1950s to the early 1970s, the phenomenon began to emerge of young men attending football matches for the specific purpose of engaging in violence, whether by wrecking the trains conveying them or by fighting the fans of opposing teams. The late 1970s and 1980s then saw the emergence of more organized 'firms' or 'crews', together with the exporting of the violence to the continent. According to Elliott *et al.* (1999: 17), 'a new trend of disorder as stylized viciousness rather than emotional overreaction seemed to emerge. Fighting, throwing missiles and obscene and racist chanting became perceived as more commonplace. Drunken groups of rival supporters seemed to be forever running rampage through town centres and on public transport'.

The 1970s 'firms' or 'crews' had some association with the skinhead style, but the 1980s saw the emergence of the high-earning and snappily dressed 'soccer casual'. During the 1990s, intensive policing coupled with the extensive use of closed circuit television (CCTV) largely displaced the violence from inside the grounds.

Disorder before the First World War

Invasions of the pitches in Britain occurred even in the 1880s, but were more often caused by simple overcrowding than organized assaults. And whilst other violent disturbances in the terraces were not uncommon they were usually regarded as understandable outbursts of collective feeling. This Scandinavian lenience soon hardened to anxious castigation as the crowds and 'incidents' multiplied. In 1909 a riot that even today would merit bold headlines broke out after officials declined the fans' demand for extra play time to settle a draw between Glasgow and Celtic. The ensuing riot involved 6,000 spectators and resulted in injury to 54 policemen, serious damage to the grounds, emergency equipment and 'the destruction of virtually every street-lamp around Hampden' (Hutchinson 1975).

Although no accurate figures are available on the frequency of such episodes, the reported levels of violence and mayhem should be enough to dissolve any romantic nostalgia for the gentlemanly behaviour of prewar football fans. A survey of the reports led Hutchinson to the conclusion that 'Riots, unruly behaviour, violence, assault and vandalism, appear to have been a well-established, but not necessarily dominant pattern of crowd behaviour at football matches at least from the 1870s'.

The disturbances mostly revolved around the activity on the field and perceived injustices to either the players or the crowd as in the Hampden case above. Reports of fighting between fans on the terraces are relatively few. Some historians suspect that the relative paucity of crowd misbehaviour reports, relative to the abundance of reported assaults on players and officials, points not to the absence of such violence but rather to the lenient attitude towards crowd disturbances that did not actually interfere with the game. This may be explained by the fact that, within the stadium, it was the referee who reported incidents to the Football Association. If violence tipped on to the field he would consider it a problem; if it spilled on to the streets it became the problem of the town police; but if it was contained within the stands it largely went unreported. Television, of course, would turn the spotlight on these inconsequential scuffles.

Calm between the wars

Whilst no period in the history of English football has been completely free of incident, the interwar years saw a decline in the intensity of the occurrences. Official rebukes harped on tamer misdemeanours such as 'ungentlemanly conduct'. Moral degeneration was a favourite topic of editorials. This discontent about deteriorating standards of behaviour in the terraces was precipitated by dismay at 'un-English' and excessively violent play on the field. In 1936 the FA issued a stern memorandum regarding 'rough play' to the players. A *Reynolds Times* report sardonically called for the FA to issue another to the fans, stigmatized in the *Times* as 'altogether too vocal and biased in their opinions on the conduct of the referee' (Pearson 1983).

Whilst a few street-battle style clashes were reported in the interwar years, most incidents of crowd misbehaviour involved vocal protests against administrative rulings insensitive to the fans such as the sale of top players, or abuse of the referee, an offence considered so monstrous that Bradford Park closed its boys' section for three months after the referee had been 'pelted with rubbish'.

Not only was there a decline in football-related violence in these postwar years, several newspapers even saw fit to report on the good behaviour that distinguished the crowds attending cup finals. The number of women attending football matches increased significantly during this period, some even considering the environment wholesome enough to bring infants (Dunning *et al*. 1982). Even the Scots ritualized the Border raids of old by way of the tamer, albeit no less high-spirited, biannual trip to Wembley.

The new hooligans

High levels of national solidarity may have helped to continue this pacific trend after the Second World War and into the 1950s, but by 1960 a new form of zealous patriotism became violently directed at immigrants – an attitude also reflected by many hard-core football hooligans (see also Chapter 11).

Many sociologists place television at the graph intersection of the decline in match attendance from the 1950s onwards and the rise in spectator violence. Television not only allowed fans to watch games at home, it graphically publicized fan violence. One such pioneering broadcast televised a major riot after an equalizing goal during a Sunderland v. Tottenham game in 1961. That the hooligans were seen on television, the *Guardian* later said 'provided ... encouragement to others.'

The rise of counter-culture youth protest movements seemed to need no encouragement. The Teddy Boys, Mods, Rockers, Skinheads and the Bovver Boys all added to the increasingly stereotyped Football Hooligan. The term 'Hooligan' was coined in the 1890s as an alternative to 'street Arab' or 'ruffian.' Now readily applied to the 'wild and unruly' football fan of the 1960s, the term and the on-screen images of undisciplined 'toughs' rekindled a Victorian-style 'moral panic' vocalized by the Conservative Party and fanned by the press. According to the Chester Report (Department of Education and Science 1968), incidences of football violence doubled in the first five years of the 1960s compared with the previous 25 years.

Hooliganism in Europe

The prevailing consensus that postwar permissiveness was precipitating the decline and fall of the 'British way of life' led to calls for the birch, the stocks, military service and other such disciplines for the football rowdies (see Taylor 1992). Nation-wide preparations for hosting the 1966 World Cup highlighted the need to solve the 'problem' before such bad British behaviour was internationally broadcasted. Although in the next decade football hooliganism would be dubbed 'the British disease' that infected the civilized continental spectators, several reports may reveal earlier strains of the illness in Europe. In Yugoslavia, for instance, a mid-1950s wave of football disorder known as 'Zusism' put terror into vogue. The origin of the word stems from 'ZUS', an acronym of the Serbo-Croat words for 'slaughter, kill, annihilate'. The communist newspaper *Borba* carried reports of two incidents near Belgrade involving fans armed with 'hammers, mallets and metal bars'. On one occasion knife-wielding spectators rushed on to the field seriously injuring the referee. And not long after in Turkey, 'fans of the Kayseri and Sivas clubs fought with pistols, knives and broken bottles for days after the end of a match between the two sides. Before troops restored order, cars were burned out, 600 spectators injured and 42 of them killed, 25 by stab wounds' (Dunning *et al.* 1981).

Several reports contradict an Italian sociologist's claim that hooliganism was an unknown problem before the 1970s when Italian youths began imitating the British (Roversi 1991). Dunning *et al.* (1981) cite an incident at a match in Vialoggio in 1920 when police had to intervene to quell fighting between opposing fans. The referee in charge was killed. In 1955, 52 people were injured during a riot at a match between Naples and Bologna, and four years later 65 injuries resulted from a pitch invasion when Naples played Genoa. These contradictory reports may simply indicate a divergent definition of hooliganism. The Roversi Report makes a clear distinction between 'spectator disorderliness' which may include unintentionally violent acts – 'peaceful' invasion of the pitch and the throwing of fire-crackers as being 'simply the expression of joy'– and intentional violence on the part of hooligans. He claims that the 'intentional violence' is a new phenomenon at football matches.

Still, in England it was the increase in local television coverage of incidents which some historians claim precipitated the 'amplification spiral' of violence (see also Chapter 9). Whether due to television coverage or not, the 1960s witnessed a colourful change in the style of fan support. Football supporters became more organized with carefully orchestrated waving displays, chants and slogans; and more mobile. Regular support of away games helped to disperse the varying styles across the country. It also increased the incidences of vandalism to trains. Liverpool and Everton supporters held the record for the worst cases of train-wrecking to and from matches in the early 1960s.

By 1964, the core of troublemakers was perceived to concentrate in groups with 'no allegiance to either team' (Maguire 1986), and could no longer be characterized simply as overly ardent supporters. These groups identified and named themselves separately from the teams, and used match days as venues for confrontations with rival groups. By 1967 the sport of 'taking ends' emerged as the favourite pastime of young male supporters. The object was to charge at supporters of the rival team thus driving them away from their viewing area behind the goal, capture as much of their team gear as possible (flags, scarves, etc.), and land a few good kicks and punches before police stepped in. Although on film these charges looked menacingly aggressive, in reality, serious injuries were rare. However intimidating the threats and waved fists, the blows inflicted were, according to commentators such as Marsh (1978a), largely symbolic.

By the 1970s these groups became increasingly sophisticated in their cohesiveness, organization and 'scoring' systems that, amongst other means, used press coverage to determine which group was on top in the hierarchy of hooligan 'firm' rivalries. In other European countries hooligan groups emerged that, whilst accused of mimicking the British fans, had distinct styles all of their own. These groups are discussed in Chapter 5.

Historical examples of violent incidents in Britain

1314, 1315	Edward II bans football.
1349, 1388, 1410	Football was banned from the city of London due to complaints from merchants.
1364	Synod of Ely bans clergy from playing football due to the violent nature of the game.
1477	Edward IV issues edict against football.
1496	Henry VII issues edict against football.
1539	Annual match in Chester abolished due to violence.
1555	Football banned in Liverpool due to mayhem.
1576	Middlesex County Records reports that 100 men assembled unlawfully to play football. There was a 'great affray.'
1579	After the start of a match against the students of Cambridge, the townsmen of Chesterton proceeded to assault their opponents with sticks, driving them into the river.
1581	Evanses Feld at Southemyms. One yoeman killed by two others during a football match.
1608	Football banned in Manchester due to the mayhem caused by 'a company of lewd and disordered persons'.
1638	Football crowd destroys drainage ditches on Isle of Ely.
1694	Fenland drainage destroyed during football match.
1740	Football match in Kettering turns into a food riot and local mill is destroyed and looted.

1768	Football matches held to tear down enclosure fences at Holland Fen and West Haddon.
1797	Kingston-upon-Thames. Traditional Shrove Tuesday match turned into a riot after three participants were arrested by magistrates.
1843	200 soldiers and 50 policemen were needed to patrol the ropes at a Preston North End versus Sunderland match.
1846	A match was stopped in Derby, the Riot Act was read and two troops of dragoons called in. The Mayor was injured by the crowd.
1881	At Wigan station two railway officials were knocked unconscious by a group travelling to a Newton Heath versus Preston North End game.
1884	Preston North End fans attacked Bolton Wanderers players and spectators at the end of the game.
1885	Aston Villa v. Preston. A mob of 'roughs' attacked the visiting team with sticks stones and other missiles.
1886	A railway station battle occurred between Preston North End and Queens Park fans.
1888	Report of 'a continuous hail of bottles' on to the pitch at an unspecified match.
1889	Small Heath v. West Bromwich Albion. Small Heath fans molest strangers.
1889	At Middlewich station a fight broke out between Nantwich and Crewe fans. Nantwich men stormed the platform occupied by Crewe. Many sustained injuries.
1893	During a match between Nottingham Forest and West Bromwich Albion spectators invaded the field and fought with the Albion players.
1896	Whilst returning from a football match, three young men attacked and murdered a police sergeant and injured a constable.
1899	After a match at Shepshed between Albion and Loughborough Corinthians the Loughborough players were stoned and struck.
1905	Preston North End v. Blackburn. Several fans tried for hooliganism including a 'drunk and disorderly' 70-year-old woman.
1906	Tottenham v. Aston Villa cup tie had to be abandoned after spectators swarmed on to the pitch at the interval.
1909	Six thousand spectators involved in a riot at Hampden Park, Glasgow. The pitch was destroyed, 54 police constables were injured and much damage done to the town.

1920	Birmingham City football fans use bottles as clubs and missiles.
1921	Bradford Park closes the boys' section for three months after the referee was pelted with rubbish.
1924	After a match in Brighton the pitch was invaded, the referee chased by the crowd and a policeman knocked unconscious.
1930	Rangers ground closed after unruly conduct of spectators during match against Northampton Town.
1930	Clapton Orient v. Queens Park Rangers. Police called in to stop fighting between rival spectators behind the Rangers' goal.
1934	Leicester City fans vandalized a train returning from a match in Birmingham.
1935	Police lead a baton charge against stone-throwing fans during a match between Linfield and Belfast Celtic.
1936	During a match at Wolverhampton Wanderers spectators attacked visiting Chelsea players. Later the crowd protested outside the officials' entrance over the sale of top players.
1949	Millwall v. Exeter City. Referee and linesmen attacked with blows and projectiles from the crowd.
1951	At the Queens Park Rangers ground missiles were thrown at the Sheffield Wednesday goalkeeper.
1954	Several hundred spectators came on to the field during a match between Everton Reserves and Bolton Wanderers Reserves. Fireworks were thrown and a linesman was kicked.
1955–6	Liverpool and Everton fans involved in several train-wrecking exploits.
1946–60	An average of 13 incidents of disorderly behaviour by spectators per season reported to the Football Association.
1961–8	An average of 25 such incidents per season reported.

Historical examples of violent incidents in Europe

1908 Hungary	After a match between Manchester United and an unnamed Hungarian team, the Manchester players were attacked by Hungarian fans as they left the ground.
1933 France	Gendarmes were needed to quell a disturbance in the crowd during a match between Nice and the Wolves. The Wolves were taken off the field by their manager.
1931 Germany	Hertha Berlin v. Fuerth. A pitch invasion by the Hertha fans resulted in severe injury to a Fuerth player.
1946 Sweden	Hundreds of angry Malmo supporters pelted a bus carrying the rival team's players.

Further study

If you want to learn more about the history of English football violence, read the book chapter ('Having an away day: English football fans and the hooligan debate') by John Williams (1991a). This is a particularly good chapter, since it also provides a thorough critique of the academic theories set out in Chapters 6 and 7. Alternatively (or in addition), you might want to read the book *The Roots of Football Hooliganism: An Historical and Sociological Study* by Dunning *et al.* (1988). Although the book is out of print, it is stocked by many libraries. Used copies are also quite readily available through online bookstores such as Amazon.

A history of disaster

This history of disorder has evolved in parallel with a history of disaster. This, like the violence, has itself had a particular association with football. Research by Elliott *et al.* (1999) shows evidence of at least 44 UK-related incidents involving deaths and multiple injuries, 41 of which took place in UK football grounds. Two took place in rugby league grounds and one involved Liverpool supporters at Heysel in Belgium. Compare this history with the position outside the UK, where the Elliott *et al.* research shows evidence of only 26 football disasters, all bar two of which occurred in what might be described as developing countries. As Elliott *et al.* conclude, British football has a unique history of disaster and disorder.

These two phenomena – disaster and disorder – are not as directly inter-related as one might suppose. It is a common fallacy that stadium disasters are largely caused by spectator violence. Consider the 1989 Hillsborough disaster in Sheffield, when 96 Liverpool fans were crushed to death against a pitch perimeter fence. The subsequent reports by Lord Justice Taylor (Home Office 1989, 1990) set out in considerable detail the complex range and chain of causal factors leading up to the disaster. Yet in a newspaper article in 1996, Bernard Ingham (Margaret Thatcher's Press Officer) claimed 'that the Hillsborough soccer disaster was caused by tanked up yobs who arrived late, determined to force their way into the ground' (*Daily Mail* 20 June 1996). The research by Elliott *et al.* shows that crowd pressure – either direct or leading to structural collapses – was the immediate cause of all except three of the 44 tragedies they list. There was one fire (at Bradford in 1985). But for only two of the disasters (at Birmingham and Heysel, both in 1985) could the immediate cause be said to be the disorderly behaviour of the fans. Even then, the underlying cause of Heysel was bad planning rather than hooliganism (see Home Office 1985, 1986).

Further study

If you want to learn more about the history of football stadium disasters, read the book chapter ('The failure of legislation by crisis') by Elliott *et al.* (1999).

Chapter summary

In this chapter, we have seen how spectator violence has its origins in medieval folk-football. The game of football has been associated with violence since its beginnings in thirteenth-century England. Medieval football matches involved hundreds of players, and were essentially pitched battles between the young men of rival villages and towns – often used as opportunities to settle old feuds, personal arguments and land disputes. Forms of 'folk-football' existed in other European countries (such as the German 'Knappen' and Florentine 'calcio in costume'), but the roots of modern football are in these violent English rituals.

We have looked at the historical development of modern ball games, particularly soccer, emphasizing the ongoing link between sport and violence. The much more disciplined game of football introduced to continental Europe in 1900s was the reformed pastime of the British aristocracy. Other European countries adopted this form of the game, associated with Victorian values of fair-play and restrained enthusiasm.

We have considered the different phases through which football-related violence has evolved. Only two periods in British history have been relatively free of such violence: the interwar years and the decade following the Second World War. The behaviour now known as 'football hooliganism' originated in England in the early 1960s, and has been linked with the televising of matches (and of pitch-invasions, riots, etc.) and with the 'reclaiming' of the game by the working classes.

In other European countries, similar patterns of behaviour emerged about 10 years later, in the early 1970s. Some researchers argue that a similar 'proletarianization' of the game was involved, but there is little consensus on this issue, and much disagreement on the extent to which continental youth were influenced by British hooligans.

Finally, we have noted the lack of direct causal connection between spectator violence and stadium disasters.

Part II

Defining Football Hooliganism

In Chapter 3 we see how difficult it is to name, let alone define, the phenomenon we are studying in this book. There is a wide range of behavioural and other variables involved in 'football hooliganism', 'spectator violence' (or whatever we choose to call it) and it is difficult to divorce the violence (whatever it is) from the wider social context in which it takes place. There are also considerable difficulties in defining the extent of spectator violence. In relation to British football, Chapter 3 notes the considerable shortcomings in the available empirical and statistical data, but is able to conclude that the phenomenon appears to be both declining and changing. Violence has become irregular rather than routine and has been displaced away from the stadium. Different types of behaviours, including racist 'hate speech', have become characterized as football-related violence. Chapter 3 closes by looking at the problem of boorish England supporters abroad, introducing the concepts of media amplification and moral panic.

Chapter 4 shows how there has been no systematic recording of football-related violent incidents in any other European country. The lack of quantitative or reliable empirical data on football-related violence, and particularly the lack of comparable data, makes assessment of the variations and similarities between European countries very difficult, but some general conclusions can be drawn from the available evidence. It is clear that some form of disorderly behaviour has occurred in virtually every country in which football is played. Disorder of some kind appears to be a near-universal and seemingly inevitable accompaniment to the game. Football-related disorder is not, however, necessarily of the same nature, or influenced by the same causal factors, in all of the cultures in which it occurs. Even the most dogmatic academics have come to admit that 'universal' explanations cannot accommodate all cross-cultural variations.

Both the extent and the nature of football-related violence are influenced by different historical, social, economic, political and cultural factors in different European countries. Social class has been a significant factor in England, for example, religious sectarianism in Scotland and Northern Ireland, subnationalist politics in Spain, historical regional antagonisms in Italy, etc. There are, however, significant cross-national similarities in the 'stages of development' of the problem. Most countries experience an initial stage of sporadic violence directed mainly at referees and players, followed by a second stage involving violence between opposing groups of fans and against police/security officers inside the stadium and a third stage involving an increase in violent encounters between these groups outside the stadium.

Apart from Britain, the nations who have experienced the most significant problems of football-related violence are Italy, Germany, the Netherlands and Belgium. The available data indicate that levels of football-related violence in these countries are roughly similar, with incidents occurring at around 10 per cent of matches (or around 10 per cent of supporters classifiable as 'violent'). Austria, Sweden and Denmark also experience some problems with football-related violence, although these appear to be on a smaller scale. Sporadic violence has also been reported in Greece, the Czech Republic, Albania and Turkey. France, Spain, Portugal and Switzerland have also experienced episodes of violence.

In Chapter 5 we see that, in most European countries, football-related violence is a predominantly internal problem, with the majority of incidents occurring at club-level matches, whilst supporters of the national team abroad are generally better behaved. The English are an obvious exception to this rule, and rivalries between some other nations (e.g. Germany and the Netherlands) have led to violence, but these incidents seem to have diminished. Internally, however, fans tend to cause more trouble at 'away' matches than when supporting their team at home. This is a common pattern across Europe. In Denmark, a new style of non-violent, carnivalesque fan-culture, promoted by the 'roligans' (a pun on 'hooligans', from 'rolig' meaning 'peaceful'), has gained popularity. In France and Switzerland, the theatrical, flamboyant Italian style of support (but largely without the passionate hostilities) has superseded the dour, and more violent, English style.

Football hooliganism is clearly not an exclusively 'British' or 'English' disease'. Nor can the British hooligans be held entirely responsible for 'spreading' the disease in Europe. Research findings show that whilst some of the more violent European fans regard the English hooligans as role models, others – including the Scottish 'Tartan Army' and the Danish roligans – have quite deliberately adopted a very different style of behaviour.

3. The nature and extent of British football hooliganism

Introduction

This chapter is presented in two main sections, both of which are concerned with problems of definition. We begin with the question of nomenclature, noting the wide range of variables which might be involved in any definition. We then consider the difficulties inherent in seeking to separate the phenomenon from its wider social context. In the second main part, we go on to examine how much football hooliganism there actually is – and has been – in Britain. We critique the problems inherent in the trying to interpret the official statistics, noting that the phenomenon appears to be both declining (from what was anyway a low base) and changing. We then consider the issue of disorder involving England fans abroad.

The nature of 'football hooliganism'

What do we call it?

Notwithstanding the long history set out in Chapter 2, there are real difficulties in defining the phenomenon which forms the subject of this book. In the first place, what do we call it? As we saw in Chapter 1, the particular association with football caused the media to invent the label 'football hooliganism'. But the three popular fallacies we refuted might lead us to conclude that 'spectator violence' would be a more accurate name. However 'spectator violence' implies something done whilst spectating (i.e. watching an event). Yet, as we shall see, much of the violence takes place away from the stadium. So we might perhaps say 'sports-related violence' instead, only this could then include violence committed by the players themselves.

Since, as we shall see in Part III, the academic literature is focused entirely on football, the academic discussions of definition deal only with 'football hooliganism'. Taking three samples from the literature in chronological order, we find that Canter *et al.* (1989: 108) described 'football hooliganism' as 'a term which covers many behaviours, both simple and complex'. More recently, Dunning (2000: 142) noted that, 'the label "football hooliganism" … lacks precision and is used to cover a variety of forms of behaviour which take place in more or less directly football-related contexts'. Whilst Williams (2002: 45) argues that 'there is no useful precise definition of "football hooliganism" available'. Thus we find ourselves in the interesting position of writing a book about something we're not sure what to call!

So many variables

The second problem of definition is that there are so many variables around the phenomenon:

- *The sport involved* We saw in Chapter 1 the range of sports in which incidents of spectator violence take place.
- *Criminal offence categories* If we think about the categories of Home Office Recordable Offences, are we talking about offences against the person (e.g. assaults), offences against property (e.g. vandalism) or offences against the state (e.g. disorder)? As Gary Armstrong suggests in the video *Trouble on the Terraces*, everything from throwing a crisp packet on to the pitch up to homicide could potentially be included.
- *Extent of criminalization of behaviours* Do we limit the definition to acts which are recorded as crimes, or do we include 'misdemeanours' (non-recordable offences such as drunkenness) or even plain anti-social behaviour, e.g. urinating in someone's front garden?
- *Location* Where do the behaviours take place? Is it inside, outside or even well away from the venue?
- *Extent of organization* Are we only counting organized violence, e.g. a pre-planned fight between two 'crews'? Or do we include the spontaneous, e.g. a pitch incursion to celebrate a goal? Do we include 'contagious' acts (see Le Bon 1896) where crowds 'go mad' because they catch the bad behaviour off each other?
- *Whether arrests were made or not* Do we only count incidents for which arrests are made? There are several offences, e.g. unlawful pitch incursion, which are only counted in the official statistics when they are detected as a result of a person being arrested by the police.
- *Extent of injuries sustained and/or extent of damage caused* Should we use the outcomes of the violence as a means of categorization? On the one hand, a relatively minor incident may result in a few broken

windows. On the other hand, a fairly serious affray may result in no actual injury or damage but in considerable numbers of people being afraid for their personal safety.

- *The league or division from which the team's fans were drawn* Was it a Premier League team, a Football League team or a non-League team?
- *When the violence took place* Was it before, during or after the match; or even not on a match day at all?
- *Provocation* Whether the behaviour was 'provoked' by the actions of the players or the decisions of the match officials.

The key point is that the range of variables adds considerably to the problems of definition. We don't know what to call it and we don't know what 'it' is! Consider the variables involved in this further quotation from Dunning (2000: 142–3):

> the politicians and media personnel who employ the term are liable to use 'football hooliganism' in a 'cover-all' sense which includes *inter alia*: forms of verbal as well as physical violence; the throwing of missiles at players, match and club officials and other fans; the vandalising of club and private property; fist fights, fights involving kicking, and fights involving weapons such as knives and even guns. It is also important to realise that such behaviour takes place, not only at or in the immediate vicinity of football grounds, but also involves fights between groups of males who share a claimed allegiance to opposing football clubs and which take place on days other than as well as on match days and in contexts, e.g. pubs, clubs, railway and bus stations, which are sometimes far removed from football stadia *per se*. In terms of these political and media usages, the label 'football hooliganism' is also sometimes loosely used to cover politically orientated behaviour, e.g. that of groups on the political right. It is also used in relation to protests against the owners and managers of clubs and in the condemnation of racist behaviour in football-related contexts as well as of more or less directly football-related fighting. As one can see, 'football hooliganism' is a complex and many-sided phenomenon.

The wider social context

Consider the following newspaper report from the *Sunday Telegraph* on 23 June 2002, the day following Turkey's victory over Senegal in the World Cup in South Korea and Japan:

> Turkey's World Cup success was marred last night as scores of football fans clashed with rival Kurds on the streets of *London* [our

emphasis]. A group of more than 100 Turks were celebrating their team's victory in the Haringey area when they encountered about 50 Kurdish men. During a two-hour stand off, there were heated exchanges and reports of thrown missiles from both sides of the road. Police intervened and arrested two men before dispersing the crowds. One man, aged 25, was hurt in the fracas and was taken to a north London hospital with head injuries.

Here we have an incident involving street fighting by Turkish football fans against persons quite unconnected from the football match in question, which in any event had been played thousands of miles away. One might well ask to what extent this incident could be said to be an instance of 'football hooliganism'?

It's difficult to divorce the incident from its wider social context, isn't it? We know that there is a long history of violence between Turks and the Kurdish ethnic minority in Turkey. We know that this enmity has spilled over into London, where there are many residents of both Turkish and Kurdish origin. So could we argue that the violence in this incident was simply another Turkish/Kurdish clash and that the connection with football was ancillary?

It is similarly difficult to consider English football hooliganism in isolation. In 2001 a Home Office Working Group on Football Disorder commented that:

> English football disorder cannot be removed from its wider social context. In many ways it is a manifestation of a wider social problem of alienated young males demonstrating their frustration in an anti-social and violent way. It occurs in high streets up and down the country every weekend. Mediterranean holiday resorts are equally at risk (Home Office 2001: 15).

We might perhaps construct similar arguments in respect of the young Pakistanis who invaded cricket pitches during the Test Match series in 2001. Might we argue that such actions represented the same sorts of protest against the Establishment as the riots which occurred in northern towns such as Bradford and Oldham the same summer?

Having first discussed the problems involved in defining the *nature* of football hooliganism violence, we shall now go on to examine its actual *extent*. So how extensive a problem is football hooliganism? We shall see that there are similar definitional problems here, arising particularly from the paucity and inadequacy of the empirical data available.

Empirical approaches?

The problem faced by all researchers on football hooliganism is that of the interpretation and labelling of the patterns of behaviour under study. For one investigator, a specific incident involving rival fans might be classed as 'serious violence'. A second observer may describe the same behaviour as 'relatively harmless display'. A journalist at the same event might use terms such as 'mindless thuggery' or 'savagery'. And there is no objective way of choosing between these descriptions. Even video recordings of events at football matches are of little help here since the action in question still has to be interpreted and placed within some conceptual framework which renders it intelligible and meaningful.

This lack of objective facts in theory and research on football hooliganism has bedevilled the debate since the 1960s. Football intelligence has been part of the remit of the National Criminal Intelligence Service (NCIS) since its inception in 1992. Prior to that date, however, there were no accessible data concerning frequencies and levels of football hooliganism in Britain (see Trivizas 1980a). Such data as did exist had to be obtained from local police forces, individual football clubs or from sources such as the St John Ambulance Brigade who attend to injuries at football matches. Even here, however, problems of comparability arose since there was no specific offence of football hooliganism. Arrests of fans were usually made for 'behaviour likely to cause a breach of the peace' and later under the Public Order Act 1986. From these figures it was impossible to glean any indication of the seriousness of violence involved, in terms of physical injury, etc. With the advent of specific offences under the Football (Offences) Act 1991 in Britain it became easier to determine levels of problem in different areas. Here, however, the scope of the Act went beyond offences of violence, for example, including chanting in an 'indecent' or 'racist' manner. Police forces also varied in terms of the rigour with which the Act was enforced.

The introduction of the NCIS into the UK has gradually provided a little more consistency in the ways in which statistics are collated and analysed, and the recent appointment of analysts as well as police officers within the NCIS Football Unit has improved matters still further. Up until 2000/1, statistics on what were described as 'football-related' arrests were published annually by the NCIS. Since 2001/2, the Home Office have published the figures. These NCIS and Home Office statistics provide us with the only 'official' statistics on the nature and extent of football hooliganism. On the basis of these figures, it is generally agreed that football hooliganism, however defined, has been declining in the UK since the mid-1990s. In 1995, the Head of the Football Unit of the NCIS commented:

Figures for the 1994/95 season suggest that the number of arrests in league games has been reduced where stewarding has replaced policing at grounds. However, the overall situation has also been improved through the increasing use of intelligence which shows that pockets of organised hooligans, who are often involved in a wide range of criminal activities, chose to cause trouble at predetermined locations away from grounds. Nevertheless the arrest figures confirm that closed circuit television, all-seater grounds and improvements in the stewarding and policing of games are all helping to effectively combat [sic] the hooligan problem.

It is not surprising that a senior police officer should wish to reinforce the continuing need for his own unit, even in the light of a significant reduction in the problems which this unit was designed to tackle. We must also wonder how much has really changed on the football terraces – what do the figures actually reflect? It is interesting to compare this use of statistics with a study conducted back in 1976 in Scotland by the Strathclyde Police – a time when football hooliganism is generally thought to have been at its peak throughout the UK. The report in which the study was published included a strong comment about the way in which arrests at football matches were often reported:

We would like … to comment on reports in some sections of the press about arrests made during or after the match. There is on these occasions seldom any reference made to the nature of these arrests – we understand many are unconnected with hooliganism as such. If there are only a few arrests e.g. there were only five arrests out of a 50,000 crowd at a Celtic Rangers match in January 1997 (or one for every 10,000 spectators present) too little credit is given to the efforts of the clubs, stewards, the police and above all else the crowd themselves for their good behaviour. We recognise that much depends on the way in which this information is relayed to the press by the police. We think that if arrests were categorised the media would co-operate in presenting a true picture of events at matches (Scottish Education Department 1977).

This wish expressed by McElhone in 1977 was clearly never fulfilled. Detailed arrest statistics of the kind he proposed have rarely been available from the police, and the press, by and large, have tended not to let the facts, on the few occasions on which they have been available, get in the way of a good story. This was the case in 1977 with the figures provided by the Strathclyde Police. Their study was the most obvious one to conduct – a comparison of arrests for various offences at football matches with levels of such offences throughout the country. In other words, were levels of crime and violence at matches significantly higher than throughout the 'normal' population? Their calculations indicated that: 'the incidence of Breaches of the Peace and Assaults can be calculated as … 7.32 per 100 hours per 100,000 spectators'. (Less detailed figures obtained by Peter Marsh from local police forces in England in the same year produced a result of similar magnitude.) Comparing these figures with the country as a whole, taking into account the locations and times of football games, the Strathclyde Police showed that the level of offences at football matches was only marginally higher than would be predicted. They commented:

> The fact that there are 1.67 per cent more crimes committed when football matches are played than when they are not hardly seems a cause for concern … concern about hooliganism should be aimed at activities on Friday and Saturday evenings rather than at football matches … The conclusion to be drawn from this report is that concern expressed by the media about hooliganism is out of proportion to the level of hooliganism which actually occurs at these matches.

We deal in some detail with the McElhone report here, despite the fact that it was produced nearly 30 years ago and is rarely considered in contemporary discussion of football hooliganism, for three reasons. First, it is the kind of calm, objective analysis which has not been repeated since 1977 but for which there is a clear need in the present. The only study which comes close to the scale and objectivity of the Strathclyde Police analysis is that of Eugene Trivizas in 1980. Using Home Office data for England and Wales he came to significantly the same conclusion:

> According to the findings of this study, the commonly held stereotypes concerning 'football hooliganism' and 'football hooligans' (i.e. the popular image of the football hooligan as a juvenile vandal) do not coincide with police statistics. That means that either: (a) The stereotypes are wrong or (b) arrests for the typical offence and of the typical offender are not made by the police (Trivizas 1980a: 287).

Secondly, the Strathclyde study highlights with great clarity the fact that the fear of football hooliganism was, and probably still is, a more significant phenomenon than football hooliganism itself. Thirdly, it is a reminder that in place of endless theorizing, much of it undoubtedly misplaced – as Armstrong and Harris (1991) have argued – we need to focus much more closely on the facts of hooliganism.

Contemporary social scientists with an interest in the subject will, of course, argue, that much has changed since the late 1970s. Whilst some will concede that in its early years football hooliganism in Britain had a more benign, ritual quality, the nature of the phenomenon has now changed. This is, at least in part, true. The implicit social rules which might once have constrained the activities of fringe members of the football fan culture are now less in evidence. But we still have all too little information about what is actually happening apart from the relative small-scale ethnographic studies discussed above. Even here the processes of selective focus and interpretation make generalizations very difficult. But we shall see what we can do with the data which we have got.

The extent of British football hooliganism

Three key points emerge from our discussion of empirical approaches above. First, there has been a historical absence of useful statistical data on violence in British football. Secondly, such data as there were seemed to suggest that 'football hooliganism' was a declining problem. Thirdly, the only two decent empirical studies undertaken suggested that 'football hooliganism' was not much of a problem in the first place anyway. To try to unpack these points a little further, let us start with the usefulness of the statistical data, then look at the second and third points together.

Troublesome data sources

For 2003/4 the Home Office statistics are set out in 11 tables covering numbers of banning orders, international arrests and various combinations of arrests by club supported, place of arrest and type of offence. As were the NCIS before them, the Home Office are careful to emphasize the caveat that 'Statistics for football-related arrests tell only part of the story and need to be placed in context' (Home Office 2004). As we shall see in Chapter 9, this caveat is frequently ignored by the media, including the broadsheets, who are content to take the figures as a 'league table' of the extent of football hooliganism.

Our discussion of the statistics will be confined here to illustrating the importance of this Home Office caveat; thus our analysis in this section is limited to extracts from the figures for the four seasons from 2000/1. Table 3.1 shows attendances and arrests in League matches only for arrestable offences that are football offences under Schedule 1 of the Football Spectators Act 1989 (as amended). To illustrate the problems in interpreting the figures, look at the arrests by division. We see that the Premiership accounts for between 38 per cent and 48 per cent of arrests across all four divisions. For each of the four seasons, the percentage share of the arrests decreases as we go down the divisions. The correlation is clear. But what does this tell us? Are the spectators in the Premiership the worst behaved? Or is it simply that there are more spectators at these

Table 3.1 Attendances and arrests for football offences in league matches

League matches	2000/1 No.	%	2001/2 No.	%	2002/3 No.	%	2003/4 No.	%
Total attendances	26,030,167	–	27,756,977	–	28,346,386	–	29,197,510	–
Total arrests	3,391	100	2,977	100	3,355	100	3,010	100
1.1 Premiership	1,623	48	1,192	40	1,460	44	1,137	38
1.2 Division One	816	24	929	31	945	28	849	28
1.3 Division Two	601	18	595	20	641	19	616	20
1.4 Division Three	351	10	261	9	309	9	408	14
Arrest Rate	1 in 7,676	–	1 in 9,324	–	1 in 8,449	–	1 in 9,700	–

Source: Home Office (2004).

35

matches? Perhaps there are more police in attendance? Or the policing is more stringent? It is salient to note that the Home Office (2004) report that '25% of matches [are] completely police free'. These are generally lower-division matches where there are simply no police present to make any arrests.

Turning to banning orders, the Home Office (2004) figures show that these have increased dramatically from 1,794 on 14 August 2003 to 2,596 on 18 October 2004. Does this mean that more football violence is occurring? Or is it that a different policing approach is being applied – particularly given that in 2003 an extra £5 million was provided for intelligence-led policing operations to obtain more banning orders (Home Office 2003a)?

Delving into the statistics for individual clubs, all sorts of problems of interpretation arise. Two examples will serve to illustrate the issues. First, Kidderminster Harriers in Division Three had no arrests at all for the two seasons 2002/3 and 2003/4. Does this mean they have the best-behaved fans? Or are there no police in attendance? Secondly, for the two seasons 2002/3 and 2003/4, Sunderland had the highest numbers of arrests in division One. Does this tell us that Sunderland have the most hooliganism in that Division? Or does it demonstrate the impact of the Sunderland Ground Safety Officer's zero-tolerance policy on spectator misconduct?

Difficulties in interpreting these arrest and banning order statistics add considerably to the problems of definition. Further problems arise from the fact that, as with other crime statistics (see, for example, Coleman and Moynihan 1996: 32–9), the figures are socially constructed. Not all the offences committed will get discovered or reported to the police, who are then selective about what they record. Of those recorded only a small percentage will result in an arrest. Even fewer will result in a clear-up or conviction at court. From the authors' considerable experience in and around football grounds, we can say with confidence that many offences are either ignored, result in a word of warning or at worst in ejection from the ground. So we can be fairly sure that only a small proportion of offences make it into the arrest statistics.

In addition to this 'attrition rate', there is a problem with what then does get counted. The NCIS figures previously included 'ticket touting', 'drugs offences', 'theft' and a range of other non-violent offences. The Home Office figures now cover defined 'football offences' but these include 'ticket touting', 'breach of banning order' and 'miscellaneous'. So if we read that 'City' had 50 fans arrested, 'United' had 20 and 'Rovers' had 10 arrests, we might be tempted to conclude that 'City' had the most hooligan fans. However if most of the 'City' arrests were for ticket touting, most of the 'United' arrests for a pitch incursion to celebrate a goal and most of the 'Rovers' arrests for violent disorder, then we might draw rather different conclusions.

The statistics are also more a reflection of police tactics than of the extent of spectator violence. Both the NCIS and Home Office have acknowledged that the figures are an unreliable indicator of extent. Sometimes the police will make large numbers of arrests to intervene and prevent disorder, whilst at other times they will disperse a disorderly crowd and make few or no arrests (see NCIS 2000a; Home Office 2004).

Turning from the arrest statistics to an alternative data source, we find that for the 1999/2000 and 2000/1 seasons, the NCIS published on the Internet a log of incidents of football-related disorder compiled from the post-match reports submitted by Police Football Intelligence Officers (see NCIS 2000b, 2001a). The logs are available to download from the NCIS website at http://www.ncis.gov.uk. Because of irresponsible media reporting, the logs since 2001/2 have no longer been published and are 'restricted' documents.

For 2000/2001, for example, the log contains information on 152 separate incidents. For each incident, the log shows the fixture (if any) with which it was associated, the date and a short summary of what happened. In class, Steve Frosdick has set students the exercise of going through the log and coding it to try to answer the following questions:

- What percentage of the incidents took place outside the ground?
- In what percentage of the incidents do the police appear to have made arrests?
- In what percentage of the incidents does injury or damage appear to have resulted?
- What percentage of the incidents involved supporters of a Premier League team?
- What percentage of the incidents merit the label 'football hooliganism'?

Students tend to come to the following conclusions:

- The vast majority of incidents took place outside or away from the ground.
- The teams involved tended to come from the lower divisions.
- There is quite a focus on reporting the effective intervention of the police.
- There are few reports of incidents involving injury, damage or arrests.

The first point suggests the idea of displacement, which we will examine below. The third point may perhaps suggest that the police are keen to report incidents which they feel they handled well; whilst the last point further undermines the usefulness of arrest statistics as a measure of the extent of football hooliganism.

It needs to be made quite clear that the published figures on arrests and banning orders do not provide more than a small part of the overall picture. Additional data sources are required if we are to discover more about the extent of British football hooliganism. However, at least one of these – the NCIS Football Disorder Logs – are no longer in the public domain. This was a topic which appealed to Robert Newton, one of Steve Frosdick's dissertation students (see Frosdick and Newton 2004; Newton 2004). In addition to analysing the official statistics, Newton used privileged access to four data sources relating to the four football seasons 1999/2000 to 2002/3. Data were obtained from the 'restricted' Football Disorder Logs compiled by the NCIS. Data were also obtained from the post-match reports recorded by ground safety officers in a private database held by the Football Safety Officers' Association (FSOA 2004). This includes information on ejections, which have become more significant in view of the increased numbers of matches at which there is no police presence. An incident of spectator violence can just as easily be dealt with by a steward ejecting the offender from the ground as by a police officer making an arrest. Finally, data were taken from a database of football-related disorder incidents compiled by the BBC (2002) and published on the Internet.

These data sources have their own shortcomings. The BBC database does not purport to be a census. The FSOA database was only started during the 2001/2 season and, by August 2002, only about half the clubs were using it to file reports. Thus the FSOA database is incomplete. Only those incidents which the police football intelligence officers chose to report are included in the NCIS disorder logs. Thus the data sources, whilst adding to the story, have limitations in themselves.

Newton concluded that football hooliganism does not appear to be a very extensive social phenomenon. Hooligan incidents recorded by the police are associated with about one match in 20 and only 0.011 per cent of spectators are arrested for a football-related offence. Ground safety officers report more incidents than the police but these tend to involve minor disorder and sanctions short of arrest.

Between 50 per cent and 60 per cent of reported incidents of football hooliganism take place away from the ground. And between 43 per cent and 50 per cent of incidents take place after the match. These findings support the notion that intensive social controls during the pre-match period and at the stadium have displaced the phenomenon to town centres, licensed premises and public transport systems – more of this later in this chapter.

The more passive consumerist fans of Premiership teams engage in less hooliganism than those of Division One. Cup matches have a higher arrest rate than League matches. However some 19 per cent of football hooliganism involves encounters between fans of teams that have not played each other that day. Football hooliganism involves public disorder, sometimes with the use of missiles, but it does not generally result in injuries. It is thus not a particularly violent phenomenon.

We might conclude that, the more we examine the official statistics and other available data sources, the more their usefulness is called into question. Or rather, they pose as many questions as they purport to answer about the extent of football hooliganism.

A declining problem?

The Football Industry Group at the University of Liverpool (FIG) suggest that 'football hooliganism' peaked during the 1970s and 1980s (see FIG 2002). So what data do we have on the extent of the phenomenon during these peak years? How much of a problem was 'football hooliganism'?

The 1977 McElhone Report (Scottish Education Department 1977), which we discussed earlier, showed that, in 1976, there were nearly four million spectator visits to Scottish football matches. Of these four million people, 1,079 people were arrested – an average of four arrests per match – which represents an arrest rate of 0.028 per cent. In his discussion of the 1977 figures, Bale (1993) noted that these compared very favourably with the number of arrests for assaults and breaches of the peace in leisure activities on Saturday nights. They also represented only one thirteenth of arrests for drink-driving offences. Bale also noted that, 11 years later in 1988, arrests inside Scottish grounds had reduced to 0.017 per cent of attendance figures. He cited a *Guardian* newspaper report from 17 January 1989 which suggested that this figure was not very different from England.

At first sight, these figures suggest that, even at its peak, football hooliganism was less extensive than one might have supposed from media coverage and police attention. Certainly McElhone in 1977 and Bale in 1993 drew this conclusion. McElhone concluded that 'concern expressed by the media about hooliganism is out of proportion to the level which actually occurs at matches' (Scottish Education Department 1977). Whilst Bale concluded that 'given such low figures, which predate the most serious forms of containment, the measures used to control spectators seem draconian in the extreme' (1993: 29).

Thinking back to the problems of definition and to the troublesome statistics we have just looked at, to what extent can we say McElhone's and Bale's conclusions were justified? We may feel that there are shortcomings in the figures. They only measured arrests, so incidents of violence for which no arrests were made did not get counted. And they only measured arrests at matches, so football-related arrests away from the stadium were probably not included.

Moving into the early 1990s, Frosdick noted that historical data from the NCIS (1992) suggested that, 'at worst during the early 1990s, only one in every 2500 spectators [0.040 per cent] has been either ejected from the ground or arrested either inside or outside the ground. In terms of arrests, this data indicated a slight reduction on the 1977 Scottish Education Department survey finding' (Frosdick 1999: 5). Note that the NCIS data also included persons ejected from the stadium – a sanction short of arrest – together with football-related arrests outside and away from the stadium.

There is fairly wide support for a perceived decrease in the early 1990s. Redhead (1991a: 479) commented that 'discourses on football hooliganism seemed to have proliferated just as the phenomenon itself appears to have disappeared from public view; at least in Britain'. The Football Industry Group (FIG 2002) suggests that football hooliganism decreased subsequent to the Hillsborough disaster in 1989. Whilst the Sir Norman Chester Centre for Football Research (SNCCFR) at the University of Leicester concluded that 'There has been a long term decline in hooliganism since the mid-1980s' (SNCCFR 2001: 3).

Later on in the 1990s, the NCIS stopped including ejections in their statistics. This was unfortunate in terms of providing a fuller picture of sanctions against errant spectators, but understandable in terms of post-Hillsborough changes such as higher-profile stewarding and the narrowing of the police role at football matches, including many 'police-free' games (see Frosdick and Sidney 1999 for a fuller discussion of these changes).

One of Steve Frosdick's dissertation students – Jim Chalmers (President of the Football Safety Officers' Association and the author of the Foreword to this book) – chose to investigate the question of ejection statistics (see Chalmers 2004). With no national code of practice on spectator ejections, Chalmers found that variations in policy, procedures and recording practices made it difficult to quantify the true extent of ejections and to make comparisons between clubs:

> There is no guarantee that every ejection will find its way into the statistics or that every breach of a ground regulation will in fact lead to an ejection. Many breaches will result in a warning by Stewards, which will never be recorded. Mass disobedience by fans, such as persistent standing in seated areas will not find its way into the statistical data (Chalmers 2004).

Chalmers' questionnaire survey of ground safety officers achieved a response rate of 82.6 per cent. He found that there had been about 4,000 reported ejections inside stadiums during the 2003/4 season – considerable more that the 3,010 arrests reported in Table 3.1 above – but that there were no data to say why these ejections had occurred:

Ejection figures will also be influenced by the way the Safety Officer or individual Stewards enforce Ground Regulations or the criminal law in 'police free' games. Club policy is another variable or as one Safety Officer put it 'We eject for smoking in a no-smoking area and how can this be compared with a Club that does not have a no-smoking policy?' Another said 'We eject for persistent standing in a seated area whilst other Clubs ignore this'. The attitude of the Safety Officer will have a bearing as one said 'Ejections are for us a last resort. I feel ejecting them admits defeat. The fewer we get the better it shows we are managing our fans'. One Safety Officer saying 'Low ejection figures could be the result of good behaviour or lax stewarding whilst high numbers could indicate bad behaviour or an attempt to enforce ground regulations' summed up the issue of using numbers as an indicator of spectator behaviour (Chalmers 2004).

Chalmers concluded that the formal publication of statistics on ejections could help our understanding of spectator behaviour inside football grounds, and so would add a little more to the partial picture we have through the current official sources.

The NCIS and Home Office statistics in Table 3.1 above show that the average arrest rate over the four seasons was one in 8,787 or 0.011 per cent, which represents a further reduction on the previous figures we have discussed. So it seems fairly clear that arrest rates have been declining from a fairly low base. Adding the ejections discovered by Chalmers to the arrest figures we already have still only gives us an arrest and ejection rate of 0.024 per cent, which itself represents a decrease on the 0.040 per cent reported by Frosdick (1999) above. However, given the shortcomings in the statistical data, how far can we claim that this decline represents a real decrease in the extent of football hooliganism in Britain?

Inside the grounds, there seems to be some good supporting evidence for a reduction. Following an upwards blip in media interest in reporting incidents in January 2002, the Premier League undertook a snapshot survey which showed that 'Of the 306,595 people who attended the 10 elite matches, only 20 were arrested and 58 ejected' (*Daily Telegraph*, 16 January 2002). This represents an arrest rate on the day of 0.007 per cent – extremely low – and we should note that, of the 20 arrests, 15 were for drunkenness, two were for ticket touting, one was for criminal damage and one for running on to the pitch.

Fan surveys also support the idea of a reduction inside the ground, with only 7 per cent of fans thinking that hooliganism is increasing and seven out of ten fans reporting that they never see fighting or missile throwing (see Williams 2002). Football writer Simon Inglis claims that 'I've been going to football more or less every week since 1967 and cannot recall witnessing a single serious outbreak of fighting, off the pitch that is, either in or around a British football stadium since, I don't know when' (2002: 87). Whilst Williams (2002: 40–1) concludes that:

> the *routine* place of the serious hooligan encounter, as an obvious and intrusive part of the main football event, on a near-weekly basis at larger football grounds in England 20 years ago, now seems ruptured, possibly for good … Today, specific smaller clubs or matches, usually involving well-known offenders, or particular club combinations based on geography, or on some other source of rivalry, seem to be the main (if more irregular) hooligan focus.

So it seems fair to conclude that there has been a reduction in the extent of football hooliganism inside our football grounds, and that serious violence is rare and irregular rather than frequent and routine. But does this mean that the phenomenon has largely disappeared?

A changing problem?

NCIS (2001b) suggests that 'Dealing with football hooliganism within and in the close vicinity of stadiums has been increasingly successful but it has displaced the problem'. This idea of displacement is a key point. The stadiums may be more peaceful, but police resources are stretched dealing with 'increasingly mobile "football gangs" who more frequently engage in violence at pubs, railway stations and on the streets before and after matches' (Evans 2001).

Certainly the British Transport Police (BTP) reports an increase in displaced football-related violence. Their Annual Report for 2002 'highlights an increase in disorder amongst travelling football fans'. 'Football disorder has grown, is more organised and, where it does occur, is more serious. Day in, day out, officers are dealing with potentially critical public order situations,' says the report. 'BTP spends around 8% of its total budget and a third of the overtime budget on football policing' (BTP 2002).

Developing the displacement theme, Garland and Rowe (2000) suggest that, together with the more organized violence, the experience of watching football has also been displaced from the stadium. Given the rising admission prices and more muted atmosphere, many people now choose to watch live football on large-screen televisions in public houses and clubs – and incidents of more spontaneous disorder do break out in such establishments. So the problem is changing because its traditional nature has been displaced from inside the stadium to the public transport network and to other locations.

But the problem is also changing inside the stadium because, as Carlton

Brick suggests, 'Football-related deviancy has not disappeared as such; rather it has become something else' (2000: 159). We saw earlier how difficult it was to define the nature of football hooliganism. What Brick is arguing is that there has been a redefinition of what is deviant inside the stadium. Traditional fan behaviour has involved the frequent use of 'hate speech' – general and racist abuse. This is an escape from the restrictions of everyday life. As Perryman puts it, 'We all want to get out of control, be unruly, shout words and behave in a way unacceptable at work or at home. This doesn't have to involve intimidation, offence or violence and for the vast majority of us it never does' (2001: 23).

Brick demonstrates that this type of behaviour has, for 'new morality' reasons, become less acceptable to the authorities and indeed to the new types of fan. Referring to recent football-related legislation, he argues that 'Distinctions between football-related offences and other forms of anti-social behaviour are significantly blurred, as are definitions of violence and harm which now include acts of speech' (2000: 165–6). It is this type of definitional change which has brought the question of racism into the hooliganism debate and we discuss this in more detail in Chapter 11.

We have now looked in some detail at the extent of spectator violence associated with British football at home. To conclude this chapter, we shall now look briefly at the issue of England fans overseas.

England disorder overseas

Historically, the problem of violence was associated with English teams playing in European competitions (for example, see Williams *et al.* 1984). English football clubs were banned from European competitions between 1985 and 1990 following the contributory behaviour of Liverpool supporters to the Heysel stadium disaster in Belgium. But there have been few serious problems with English club sides since 1990 (SNCCFR 2001: 4). The more recent perceived problem is rather with supporters of the national team.

The Bassam Report suggests that 'England supporters are more likely to become embroiled in disorder than the followers of other national teams' (Home Office 2001: 18). But to what extent? To some extent certainly, since most of us will be able to think of at least one incident of spectator violence involving England supporters. One notorious incident, which we mention elsewhere, was the forced abandonment of an Ireland v. England match after 27 minutes in 1995 after England supporters threw missiles on to the crowd below them.

We should, however, stop to reflect on what it is that gets construed as 'disorder'. According to Poulton, 'What may be considered – or at least tolerated – as normal, high-spirited, "laddish" behaviour in this country, such as heavy drinking, singing and chanting, may be deemed to be anti-social, aggressive posturing that is deeply offensive in some cultures and societies' (Poulton 2001: 132–3). Whilst Sugden, in his study of Leeds United fans abroad, notes that 'just having a laugh can be deeply offensive to those not sharing the joke, particularly in sensitive cross-cultural settings' (Sugden 2001: 101). But the key point in considering England fans abroad is to examine the issues of media amplification. We shall be looking in more detail at this concept in Chapter 9. However it is worth making some brief observations here.

Murphy *et al.* (1990) have undertaken a detailed analysis of press reporting of soccer crowd disorder. They show, from a historical perspective, how the media played a de-amplifying role during the interwar years and up until the 1950s. Thereafter, through amplification of the extent of the problem, the press 'played a part of some importance in directing hooligan behaviour into the football context' (Murphy *et al.* 1990: 126).

For example, the arrest of English supporters outside an Oslo public house before the England v. Norway match on 1 June 1993 drew banner headlines and widespread 'outraged' coverage in the national press (for example, *Evening Standard*, 2 June 1993; *Daily Telegraph*, 3 June 1993). Yet, interviewed on BBC Radio News, Johnny Birmingham, the disc jockey working at the pub, reported that the boisterousness was no different from any ordinary Friday or Saturday night, except that there were over one hundred riot police waiting outside!

Frosdick (1999) has argued that the treatment of football hooliganism bears all the hallmarks of the type of moral panic described by Cohen (1971). Like the mods and rockers before them, the football hooligans are folk devils, labelled as deviant by the middle-classes, in order to bolster middle class perceptions of the correctness of their own way of life. The media reinforce this with over-reporting of incidents that do occur and the creation of 'non-stories' where nothing has happened (Frosdick 1999: 6–39). For example, Buford has shown that during the seven days of the final build-up to the 1990 World Cup in Italy, although nothing untoward was happening, the *Guardian* newspaper carried 471 column inches devoted to football supporters – 'nearly forty feet of reports that said: there is nothing to report' (1991: 276).

This moral panic can become a self-fulfilling prophesy. Media reporting suggests the likelihood of hooliganism. Football therefore becomes more attractive to the type of person disposed to violence. The police plan for the trouble anticipated and may be inclined to over-react to minor incidents (see Stott and Reicher 1998 for a fuller discussion of this issue). Nobody is surprised when serious disorder breaks out, since it was what everybody expected in the first place. And the press – who started it all – feign outrage at 'England's shame'. What Frosdick is arguing, then, is that the extent of disorder involving England supporters abroad is perceived to be higher than it really is. The perception is driven by media amplification and, as we shall see in Part IV, is itself a driver of repressive and quite draconian social policy.

Chapter summary

In this chapter we have seen how difficult it is to name, let alone define, the phenomenon we are examining in this book. There is a wide range of behavioural and other variables involved in 'football hooliganism' (or whatever we choose to call it) and it is difficult to divorce the violence (whatever it is) from the wider social context in which it takes place.

We also saw that there were considerable difficulties in defining the extent of spectator violence. We noted the considerable shortcomings in the available empirical data, examining in detail the football disorder logs and arrest statistics produced by the NCIS and Home Office. This analysis reinforced the limitations in the reports and statistics. We were able, however, to conclude that the phenomenon appears to be both declining and changing. Violence has become irregular rather than routine but has been displaced away from the stadium. Different types of behaviours have become characterized as football hooliganism.

Finally, the chapter looked at the problem of boorish England supporters abroad, introducing the concepts of media amplification and moral panic.

4. Levels of football violence in Europe

Introduction

If there is a lack of empirical data about football violence in the UK, then the dearth of data in other European countries is even greater, despite the fact that social scientists in these countries tend to be more empirically oriented than their British colleagues. Despite the extensive research literature on the subject, empirical information on cross-cultural variations in the scale and nature of football-related violence elsewhere in Europe has been hard to come by.

In their Introduction to *Football, Violence and Social Identity*, Giulianotti *et al.* (1994) ask: 'What commonalities or differences exist between … supporters in different cultural contexts?' This is immediately followed by: 'Are the bases for these overlaps and distinctions found in actual behaviour or secondary interpretation?' In accordance with academic etiquette, the contributors to this edited volume of essays do not feel obliged to answer the questions raised in the Introduction. Yet the need for the second question indicates that the most striking 'commonality' between football supporters of different European nations is the number of social scientists engaged in interpreting, analysing and explaining their behaviour.

These academics are themselves divided into mutually hostile factions supporting rival explanations of the nature and causes of football violence. The divisions are along theoretical, rather than national lines, such that an Italian or Dutch sociologist may be a supporter of, for example, the British 'Leicester School' or the French 'postmodernist' approach – resulting in very different interpretations of his or her own nation's football culture.

In addition to the inevitable distortions of 'secondary interpretation', the ritual chanting and aggressive displays of the rival theoretical schools often obscure our view of the behaviour that is the subject of their debate. The participants in the debate all accept that cross-national differences in the behaviour of football fans in Europe exist – and the contributors to Giulianotti *et al.*'s 'cross-cultural, interdisciplinary, pluralist' volume reach the unremarkable conclusion that a nation's football culture is 'indicative of a given society's cognition of existential, moral and political fundamentals'. Yet none of the many writers on this subject has provided any clear indication of exactly what the differences are.

At the 1987 European Conference on Football Violence, the Dutch researcher Dr J.P. van de Sande commented that, in terms of research on hooliganism, 'In Holland the situation is very much like that in other countries, many opinions but few facts'. In 1996, co-author Peter Marsh reported that 'Nearly ten years later, we must sadly report that while opinions are still plentiful, facts remain scarce' (Carnibella *et al.* 1996: 60).

As the domestic element of the so-called 'English (or British) disease' has been covered in depth in Chapter 3 we will now focus in this chapter on the scale and nature of football hooliganism in other European countries.

Levels of violence

The available literature we have seen has not included any quantitative comparisons of levels of football-related violence in European countries. This may be because there have been very few quantitative data available on the incidence of football-related violence in individual countries. Even in Britain, where the problems have been recognized and researched for over two decades, systematic recording of incidents has only been undertaken in the last few years, as we saw in Chapter 3. Empirical data on football-related violence in other European countries have been sketchy, often out of date and difficult to compare as different sources do not define terms such as 'violent incident' or 'serious incident' in the same way – and in many cases do not define these terms at all. The lack of data, and specifically the lack of directly comparable data, has clearly hindered any attempt to assess variations in the scale of the problem within Europe.

In addition to these difficulties, patterns of football-related violence in Europe have been constantly changing, and levels of violence cannot be relied upon to remain stable for the convenience of researchers and publishers. Even newspapers, with the benefit of daily publication, cannot always keep up with the changing trends. On Saturday 5 May 1990, for example, the *Independent* reported a significant improvement in crowd behaviour in England, going so far as to claim that 'hooliganism is not fashionable any more'. Only hours after the paper reached the news-stands, 3,000 Leeds United fans rioted in Bournemouth, and football-related disorder was reported in no less than nine other towns.

There is enough evidence, however, to show that football-related violence is by no means an exclusively 'British disease', and that some European countries – the Netherlands, Belgium, Germany and Italy in particular – have experienced problems of football-related disorder comparable with those found in the UK.

Italy

According to official data, there were 123 arrests of football fans, 513 injuries and 2 deaths in the 1988/9 season. From unofficial data (newspaper reports), researchers found evidence of around 65 violent incidents during the 686 Serie A and B League matches that season – i.e. violent incidents occurred at around 9.5 per cent of matches in this category. Government sources gave a slightly higher estimate of 72 incidents – 10.5 per cent – for this season. This compares with just two reported incidents during the 620 matches of the 1970/1 season (0.3 per cent), indicating a significant increase in football-related violence over these two decades, although an increase in press coverage of the problem during this period may have distorted the picture to some degree.

For the 1990s, the figures available come from a different source – the police – and refer not to violent incidents *per se* but to cautions and arrests, which may be for a variety of offences, and to injuries. The various sets of figures are therefore not directly comparable – and the numbers of cautions and arrests may tell us more about changes in policing methods than about actual variation in levels of violence – but these statistics may provide a rough indication of recent changes in levels of football-related 'trouble'.

The number of football fans 'cautioned' by the police rose from 636 in the 1988/9 season to 2,922 in the 1994/5 season. The number actually 'detained' by the police increased from 363 to 778. Data on injuries were only available for the 1990/1 season, when football-related disorder was at its peak, probably due to the World Cup. In this season the records show 1,089 injuries, compared to 513 during the 1988/9 season, but all other evidence indicates a decline in levels of violence during the following years. Nearly 2,000 fans were 'detained' by the police during the 1990/1 season, for example, compared to 778 in 1994/5 – less than half the 1990/1 figure.

Even if we ignore the unrepresentative peak in 1990/1, these police data would appear to have indicated an overall increase in levels of disorder since 1989. There was also a spread of fan problems to southern Italy, including Sicily, and to the lower football divisions. On closer examination, however, we find that 1989 saw an increase in the powers given to the police and the judiciary regarding the control of football crowds. It is well known that changes in policing methods and policy can have a dramatic effect on crime figures of any kind. In particular, increases in police powers and activity may result in massive increases in numbers of cautions and arrests, not necessarily associated with equally significant increases in the number of offences committed.

Reporting from newspaper sources, Roversi and Balestri (2000) confirm a peak of incidents in 10.6 per cent of matches in 1990/1, steadily reducing in subsequent years to 3.6 per cent by 1997/8. Italian football violence thus appears to have been in decline. And, in line with a common trend throughout Europe, the most significant change has been the shift from violent incidents inside the stadiums (during the 1970s) to more incidents occurring outside the stadiums (from the early 1980s).

Belgium

A study conducted in 1987 (Walgrave *et al.*) reported 'serious' incidents (defined as those resulting in large numbers of arrests and people seriously injured) at 5 per cent of football matches (8 out of 144 matches), with 'less serious' incidents (the term was not defined) at 15 per cent of matches.

Four groups of supporters were identified as causing the most trouble: Anderlecht, Antwerp, Club Brugge and Standard Liege. These supporters were involved in all the 'serious' incidents and in four out of five of the 'less serious' incidents. When two of these clubs met, there were always serious incidents (except when matches were played in Brugge, where drastic security measures had been introduced, including heavy police escorts to, from and during the match). These four groups caused trouble considerably more often at away-matches than when playing at home – a pattern which seems to have been common in most European countries. From the early 1980s violence occurred more often outside the stadium, either before or after the match, rather than inside the stadium and during the match – again a common pattern throughout Europe. The list of key troublemakers later expanded to include Beerschot, Charleroi and RWDM, but the basic patterns of disorder remained unaltered.

The Belgian research project concluded that there are 'distinct differences' between what happens in the UK and on the European continent, although the authors did not specify what these differences are. The researchers noted that violence seemed to be a traditional and now intrinsic element of football culture in the UK. They claimed that this was not the case in Belgium, as football violence had only become a 'systematic' problem on the European continent since the early 1970s, but expressed concern that 'the acquired tradition for violence could lead to the same result' (Walgrave *et al.* 1987). According to Interior Minister Johan van de Lanotte, this prophecy was not fulfilled. There was a significant decline in violence at Belgian League matches, with violent incidents down by about 25 per cent in the 1994/5 season.

Post-Heysel panic initially led to some excessive precautions – such as a match against Scotland where 600 policemen were brought in to watch over just 300 Scottish supporters – and the Belgian authorities have sometimes been criticized for heavy-handedness in dealing with visiting fans, for example during the 2000 European Championships.

Van de Lanotte claimed that the reduction in violent incidents had been due to somewhat less extreme security measures such as the obligatory use of closed-circuit television cameras by all first-division clubs, a doubling in the number of bans on troublemakers from stadiums, better ticketing systems to keep rival fans apart and more stewards. Evidence from other countries, however, suggests that periodic fluctuations in levels of football-related violence can occur for a variety of reasons, and that premature complacency over 'proven effective' security measures may precede a re-escalation of violence.

In an attempt at a detailed statistical analysis, albeit with reservations about his data sources, de Vreese (2000) agreed that there had been a lull in incidents during the 1994/5 season. This he attributed to three similar factors to van de Lanotte, namely: the installation of CCTV, the new legal ability to take photographs of subjects and an increased willingness by clubs to exclude troublemakers from the stadiums. However, following the July 1995 announcement that Euro 2000 would be jointly hosted by Belgium, de Vreese found that incident levels returned to their former levels for the next three seasons. There was then a further lull in 1998/9, which could not be explained.

The Netherlands

No reliable data have been available on levels of football-related violence in the Netherlands. Calculations from the available information in 1996 indicated that, out of approximately 540 matches in a football season, 100 were defined as 'high risk'. The 'risk' was not defined, and may not have referred specifically or exclusively to actual violence: other problems such as 'damage to property' and 'general disorderliness' were mentioned in the report from which these figures were drawn, which also stated that 'large-scale, riot-like incidents are scarce' (Sande 1987).

Of the 80,000 people who attended professional football matches, only around 230 to 270 were defined as 'hard-core' hooligans, although a further 2,000 were considered to be 'potential' hooligans. Taken together, these data suggested levels of football-related disorder similar to those found in the Italian and Belgian research, with aggressive or violent incidents – or at least the potential for some form of disorder – at around 10 per cent of matches. These figures were from 1987, since when there had been, according to van der Brug (1994), a slight drop in football hooliganism, although he noted that 'events at a number of games played recently indicate that these outbreaks of football violence are far from being kept under control'.

Researchers have become more cautious in their assessments of apparent declines in football-related violence, having discovered that their confident explanations of downward trends tend to be followed by embarrassing re-escalations. Also, many are understandably reluctant to suggest that there may be no further need for their services.

As elsewhere, the consensus amongst researchers is that football violence in the Netherlands has steadily increased since the early 1970s, with the 1980s seeing a massive increase in violence outside the stadiums. There was some evidence of a slight reduction in levels of violence in the 1990s. However, concerns about spectator misbehaviour remained. These resulted in the COTASS (Club-Oriented Ticketing and Authorization System for Stadiums) project, which used database and networking technology to encourage Dutch football clubs to introduce an integrated approach to access control, customer service, ticketing and marketing. A previous attempt to introduce an access control card had been scuppered on day one by concerted supporter action. But there was a view that requiring all supporters to possess some kind of card to gain access to a football ground would act as a curb to soccer violence. This was a questionable assumption since, as we have seen, much of the fighting in Holland happens away from the ground.

Hooliganism is concentrated in the top division of the sport, and even here only some teams have violent supporters. Certain groups of fans (known as 'Siders') are responsible for a disproportionate amount of the football-related violence that occurs in the Netherlands, and the 'high-risk' matches mentioned above invariably involve one or more of the teams with violent 'Siders'. The main troublemakers have been Ajax (F-Side), Den Bosch (Vak-P), Den Haag (North-Side), Feyenoord (Vak-S/Vak-R), Groningen (Z-Side), P.S.V. (L-Side) and Utrecht (Bunnik-Side).

Germany

No quantitative data have been available on levels of football-related violence in Germany, and there have been very few empirical data on fans or their behaviour. Some indication of levels of violence was provided by the German police, who expected a contingent of 1,000 'category C' (violent) fans to attend the Euro 96 championships, out of a total 10,000 supporters travelling to Britain (*The Times* 21 May 1996). This suggested that around 10 per cent of German fans were regularly involved in violent incidents – indicating levels of football-related violence roughly comparable with those in Italy, Belgium and the Netherlands.

The main hooligan groups have been Bayern Munich (Munich Service Crew), Braunschweig (Braunschweiger Jungs), Bielefeld (Blue Army), Duisburg, Dussledorf (First Class), Essen, Frankfurt (Alderfront), Hamburg, Hertha Berlin (Endsig/Wannsee Front), Karlsruhe (Karlsruhe Offensive/Blau-Weiss Brigaten), Koln, Rostock, St Pauli and Schalke 04 (Gelsen Szene).

Internationally, the German fans' arch-enemy has traditionally been Holland, although predicted violent clashes between German and Dutch fans at Euro 96 did not occur, indicating that levels of violence at international matches may be in (possibly temporary) decline.

France

Again, factual data on levels of football-related violence were not available. Mignon (1994) claims that the first 'hooligan incidents' (the term is not defined), excluding those provoked by English visitors, occurred during the 1978–9 season, and the first groups of 'kops' and 'ultras' were formed in the early 1980s. What he calls the 'ultra phenomenon' did not expand nationally until after the Heysel disaster in 1985, when the main supporters' associations of Paris, Marseilles and Bordeaux were founded. Acts of vandalism, fights and ambushes became more frequent during the latter half of the 1980s, some of which were associated from the start with the use of fascist symbols and racist slogans.

Paris Saint-Germain supporters, in particular the group known as the 'Boulogne kop', and Marseilles Olympique supporters have been the most numerous and powerful groups, and have the worst reputations. Others involved in disorder have included Bordeaux, Metz, Nantes and St Etienne.

Serious violence – i.e. incidents resulting in significant injuries – would seem, however, to have been quite rare, even in skirmishes between 'sworn enemies', according to reports in the French fans' own fanzines and Internet news-pages (rare sources of detailed, up-to-date information, and probably no more biased than the academic literature). All such encounters are described in some detail and with some pride in the fanzines, so it is unlikely that the authors are 'playing down' the level of violence. In a typical round-up report on the activities and achievements of a club's supporters at, say, 12–15 away-matches, only one or two aggressive incidents will be recorded, which may not involve actual violence or injuries.

This suggests that levels of football-related violence have been generally lower in France than in Italy, the Netherlands, Belgium and Germany, although some serious incidents do occur, and further involvement of extreme-right groups may have resulted in an increase in violence.

Scandinavia

In Sweden, there were 25–30 'serious' incidents recorded during the 1995 season – an average of one incident per seven games. As usual, the term 'serious' was not defined, but this would seem to indicate levels of disorder roughly similar to those in Italy, Belgium, the Netherlands and Germany. Like many other European countries, Sweden has seen a significant increase in football-related disorder since the early 1980s. One source (Lindström and Olsson 1995) suggested a rise of 74 per cent from 1984 to 1994.

Elsewhere, Norway is known to be relatively trouble-free. Denmark has had some problems since the early 1990s – following the publication in 1991 of a research paper explaining why football hooliganism did not exist in Denmark (see Peitersen *et al.* 1991) – and some sources suggest that football-related violence at club level has still been increasing (for example, see Andersson and Radmann 1996). Yet on the international scene the Danish fans – known as the roligans – have won praise for their good behaviour, and even at club level the problems have been marginal compared with Sweden.

Austria

Although numerical evidence has again been lacking, most accounts have suggested that football-related violence in Austria has followed a pattern familiar throughout Europe, with a significant increase in violence during the 1980s, followed by a slight decline in the 1990s. The more peaceful trend has been evident amongst the majority of fans, but younger and more violent gangs of 13–15-year-old 'Wiener Hooligans' have continued to form. The 1990s also saw an increase in violent incidents involving extreme-right skinhead groups. These skinhead groups were small, but formed alliances with larger groups of soccer hooligans to inflate their numbers.

Spain

Although there have been some 'local' clashes between fans of rival teams, and some violent incidents at international matches, most football rivalries in Spain are inextricably bound up with subnationalist politics. This may help to explain the lack of data on 'football-related' violence, as clashes between, say, Real Madrid and Athletico Bilbao supporters may be seen as having very little to do with football. Members of HNT – Athletico Bilbao's largest supporters club – describe the club as 'a militant anti-fascist fan club'. Supporting a football team is clearly a political gesture: Athletico Bilbao draws support from Basques and anti-fascists living in other parts of Spain, who identify with the values represented by the club and claim that when Athletico play in a final, 50,000 fans are cheering in Madrid bars.

Switzerland

According to a 1996 fanzine of the 'Section Grenat' (a Geneva supporters' group), the word 'ultra' meant nothing to most people in Switzerland. A few groups of active supporters appeared during the 1980s, although their impact was limited. Some groups developed a reputation as 'fighters' in the late 1980s, but incidents declined and were rare during the 1990s, except between 'sworn enemies' such as Servette FC and FC Sion. No official data on levels of violence have been available, but in an Internet news-page report of fan activity at 15 matches, only one aggressive incident was mentioned. This involved only a few 'fisticuffs', and had already calmed down by the time the police arrived.

Portugal

The formation of football fan clubs, known as 'claques', in Portugal is a fairly recent phenomenon, dating only from the early 1980s. At the 1987 European Conference on Football Violence, Portuguese researchers reported that 'no violent action has been undertaken so far by the Juve Leo fan club [the largest fan club] or by any other national fan club', although they mention that 'some of the language they use in graffiti is quite aggressive and provocative' (Marques *et al.* 1987). It is interesting, and perhaps worrying, to note that the language in question is often English (e.g. 'Juve Leo Areeio Zone – Keep out red animals!'), despite the fact that few of their compatriots read or speak English. Marques *et al.* see this as evidence of 'mimetic behaviour' – direct imitation of British fans.

The major clubs appear to be similar to the French and Swiss, in that each will usually have one sworn enemy (e.g. Juve Leo and Benfica), but be on friendly or at least neutral terms with the supporters of most other teams. Their stated aims of 'joyful and festive' support for their teams, with significant emphasis on spectacular, colourful displays, also suggest that rivalry centres on these elements rather than on demonstrations of toughness. Certainly Marivoet (2002) reported that the 'claques' were unlikely to engage in organized or premediated violence, although they were known to engage in violent behaviour on occasions. Amongst smaller, local clubs, however, traditional rivalries between villages or communities can result in violent incidents at football matches.

Czech Republic

Czech football has no history of widespread or serious violence, but there have been some reports of incidents during the 1980s and early 1990s, mainly involving Sparta Prague fans. Incidents have occurred within the stadium and involved attacks on opposing players, although Sparta fans have also caused damage to trains en route to away-matches and been involved in street-fighting after derby matches (Duke 1990).

The national sports authorities have been concerned about the behaviour of what they called 'the flag carriers', and commissioned a documentary film on Sparta fans entitled *Proc?* (*Why?*). Officials admitted that this initiative did more harm than good, resulting in more widespread imitation of the Sparta fans' behaviour – which started amongst crowds leaving the cinema after watching the film!

Following a train-wrecking incident in 1985, 30 fans were arrested, and warnings were issued that the authorities would not tolerate 'the manners of English fans' in Czech football. National division clubs were then obliged to provide separate sections for away fans, and given the right to search spectators at entrances to the grounds. Further measures have included the banning of club flags and scarves and serving a weaker variety of beer at football grounds.

Greece

No general statistics or empirical data on football-related violence have been available for Greece, but isolated accounts of violent incidents suggest that hooliganism in this country has been in the 'second stage' of development, with violence moving from attacks on referees to conflicts between rival fans, but still largely within the confines of the stadium.

Albania

Very little information has been available, but a 1995 Reuters report referred to a boycott by referees in protest against increased violence in football stadiums. Although referees seem to have been the main target of violent attacks, the report also mentioned fighting in bars outside the stadium following a first-division match, where police fired shots into the air in an attempt to break up the fight. The issue of football violence was being taken seriously by the Albanian Soccer Association, who supported the referees' boycott and planned to hold meetings with the Interior and Sports Ministries to discuss the problem.

Chapter summary

Outside Britain, there has been no systematic recording of football-related violent incidents in any other European country. The lack of quantitative or reliable empirical data on football-related violence, and particularly the lack of comparable data, makes assessment of the variations and similarities between European countries very difficult. Nevertheless, it is clear that some form of disorderly behaviour has occurred in virtually every country in which football is played. Disorder of some kind appears to be a near-universal and seemingly inevitable accompaniment to the game.

Apart from Britain, the nations which have experienced the most significant problems of football-related violence are Italy, Germany, the Netherlands and Belgium. The available data indicate that levels of football-related violence in these countries have been roughly similar, with incidents occurring at around 10 per cent of matches (or with around 10 per cent of supporters classifiable as 'violent'). Austria, Sweden and Denmark have also experienced some problems with football-related violence, although these appear to have been on a smaller scale. France, Spain, Portugal and Switzerland have also experienced episodes of violence – although football hooliganism cannot be said to be a major problem in these countries. Sporadic violence has also been reported in Greece, the Czech Republic, Albania and Turkey. We may conclude with some confidence that football hooliganism is thus clearly not an exclusively 'British disease'.

5. European fan profiles and behaviour

Introduction

The previous chapter had a primary focus on the extent of football hooliganism in other European countries. We now turn to an analysis of the nature of the behaviours exhibited by fan groups in Germany, Italy, France, Holland, Austria and Scandanavia.

Germany

According to a report to the European Parliament (1996), German fans, unlike the British, tended to come from the middle strata of society, and could be divided into three broad 'types':

> the 'consumer-oriented' fan, who sits in the stand or seeks a quiet spot on the terraces and wants to see a good game; the 'football-oriented' fan decked out in his team's colours and badges, is a member of the supporters' club and stands on the terraces and supports his club through thick and thin; the 'adventure-oriented' fan who changes his spot on the terraces from game to game and wants to see something happen, whether it has anything to do with football or not.

These classifications are based on the work of the Heitmeyers (1988), who note that the 'consumer-oriented' fans pick and choose which matches they want to attend, whilst the 'football-oriented' attend every match and the 'adventure-oriented' fans seek violent experiences both inside and outside the stadium. Dwertmann and Rigauer (2002) suggest that these 'adventure' or 'experience-oriented' fans come from a variety of social backgrounds and are usually white, male and aged between 16 and 25 years.

The German police (in their annual report on football in 1993/4) used a rather more simplistic classification, based only on those aspects of fan behaviour which were of direct pragmatic interest to them. They classified fans as 'non-violent' (the peaceful fan), 'prone to violence' (the fan who will be violent given the right opportunity) and 'actually violent' (the fan who is determined to be violent). These last fans are known as 'Category C' fans, and in some cases occupy their own 'block' in the stadium (e.g. 'Block 38' at Cologne) every Saturday.

Many hard-core troublemakers have been banished from the established, official supporters' clubs, but some have formed their own gangs. The encounters between these groups are described in the magazine *Fan-Treff* as pitched battles, in which fans 'knocked each other's faces in with their belts', yet they are also reported to hold joint Christmas and anniversary parties, and hostilities are suspended for international games, when the rivals join forces. *Fan-Treff* reports that 'In the German league they crack each other's skulls. In the European championship you pitch in against the common enemy'.

Reports of increasing involvement of extreme-right, neo-Nazi organizations may have been somewhat exaggerated. Although Nazi symbols and Hitler salutes have been observed during international matches, researchers have not regarded these as evidence of significant neo-Nazi involvement in football hooliganism. An analysis of the political attitudes of German fans indicated that these symbols did have political meaning for around 20 per cent of supporters, who reported sympathy with the neo-Nazi movement, and explicit links have been noted between some fan groups and extreme-right organizations. The majority of fans, however, either supported one of the mainstream democratic parties (35 per cent) or had no politics at all (24 per cent).

Whatever the political motivations of some German fans, Thomas Schneider, a 'Fan Projects' co-ordinator (see Chapter 14), asserted in *The Times* (21 May 1996) that the Euro 96 championship would 'not be invaded by German Nazis. It is absurd and has been greatly exaggerated'. Indeed, despite the attempts by the British tabloids to revive memories of the Second World War during Euro 96, there was no evidence of any political element amongst the German supporters.

Italy

Dal Lago and De Biasi (1994) described Italian football culture as 'a form of extended municipalism'. The battle lines of the football 'ultras' were those of the ancient rivalries between regions and towns. When supporting their national team abroad, Italian fans may, like other nations, temporarily suspend traditional city and regional antagonisms.

When the World Cup Finals were held in Italy in 1990, however, the ultra groups could not overcome their parochial hostilities to join forces against international rivals. The Napoli fans abandoned the Italian national team to support their local hero Maradona, who was playing for Argentina, whilst northern 'ultras' demonstrated their hostility towards Maradona, Napoli and the southern region by supporting any team playing against Argentina. This resulted in even skinhead/racist elements amongst the northern fans cheering in passionate support of Cameroon, rather than giving any encouragement to their traditional regional enemies.

Various attempts have been made to establish demographic profiles of Italian ultras (Dal Lago 1990; Zani and Kirchler 1991; Roversi 1994). There appears to have been a wider range of social classes amongst militant football fans than in Britain, although some researchers have found that the majority of hard-core ultras are working class, with a predominance of skilled and unskilled blue-collar workers. In support of Dal Lago's claim that it is not possible to identify the ultras with a particular social class, however, some surveys have shown a fairly high proportion of students and professionals amongst the Italian ultras. There are also larger numbers of females among ultra supporters. As in France, the demographic profile of a group of football fans will tend to vary according to the social composition of the area in which the club is located, with a stronger working-class presence in Bologna, for example, and higher numbers of unemployed fans in Naples. This may account for some apparent contradictions in the findings of different surveys.

In all cases, however, the average age of the most militant and violent supporters was considerably lower than that of the more moderate supporters. In Roversi's (1994) study, 65 per cent of those involved in violent incidents were under 21 years old. Zani and Kirchler's (1991) findings showed that the average age of 'fanatic' supporters was 21, compared to an average age of 28 (in Bologna) and 36 (in Naples) amongst 'moderate' supporters. Both studies also found a higher proportion of blue-collar workers amongst the more violent or fanatic supporters. Yet, according to Dal Lago and De Biasi (1994):

> The main difference between English and Italian football cultures does not lie in the social class distribution of the supporters, but in the presence or absence of a strongly structured form of association. Italian football culture is not only local and independent of social stratification, but is also firmly organised. Football in Italy is a national fever and, above all, for millions of citizens, workers, students and professionals, a structured way of life.

In support of this view, they quote a member of one of AC Milan's ultra groups, the Brigate Rossonere:

> As an ultra I identify myself with a particular way of life. We are different from ordinary supporters because of our enthusiasm and excitement. This means, obviously, rejoicing and suffering much more acutely than everybody else. So, being an ultra means exaggerating feelings, from a lot of points of view.

The Italian ultras pioneered the highly organized, theatrical style of support that has since spread to other nations. This style has now become predominant in France, and could also be said to have influenced the Danish 'roligans', a number of Dutch supporter groups and even the Scottish 'Tartan Army'. This style is distinguished by its emphasis on spectacular displays involving co-ordinated costumes, flags, banners, coloured smoke and even laser-shows – and on choreographed singing and chanting, conducted by ultra leaders using megaphones to prompt their choruses at strategic points during the match. These spectacular and expressive aspects of the ultra phenomenon are not separate from the hooligan aspects. As dal Lago explains, 'Journalists and chairmen of clubs call ultras wonderful spectators, when everything is going well, such as celebration, but they call them hooligans when there is trouble. But, in both cases, they are talking about the same people'.

Roversi's findings would seem to confirm that a high percentage of 'ultras' are involved in violence as well as in theatrical displays: 49 per cent of his subjects had been involved in fighting at the football ground, and 25 per cent said that they fought whenever they got the chance to do so. Roversi's subsequent work (Roversi and Balestri 2000) suggested that the nature of the violence had been changing: 'On the one hand, it turns against the police; on the other it declines into pure vandalism and juvenile deviance.'

Italian ultras are often seen as a continuation of the political extremists of the 1960s and 1970s. Similarities in their behaviour are cited as evidence of this connection. On closer examination, these similarities appear to consist of the singing of songs, chanting of chants and waving of flags and banners – along with passionate allegiance to a group and the formation of shifting alliances with other groups and, of course, participation in disorder and violence amongst themselves and against the police.

It may be more helpful to regard contemporary young ultras as the spiritual descendants of the earlier youthful extremists – or rather to see both as manifestations of the same apparently innate desire amongst young Italians (and indeed the youth, particularly males, of most other nations) to shout, chant, wave flags, hold meetings and fight amongst themselves or against authority figures. The fact that many of the ultras' songs are adapted from, say, traditional communist songs is no more evidence of political sympathies than the extensive use of hymn-tunes amongst British fans is evidence of ecclesiastical affiliations.

What can be said is that all the behaviours characterizing current football hooliganism have been present in Italy, in different guises, for some time. Although the British have often been accused of exporting football hooliganism, young Italian ultras clearly also had plenty of native traditions and role models to follow, and certainly had no need to look to Britain for inspiration.

France

Football in France has never attracted the numbers of live spectators, or inspired such passionate support, as in other European countries. Despite the popularity of the sport, even major cities cannot sustain more than one team, and matches have attracted on average only a third of the spectators of their equivalents in Italy, England and Spain.

In terms of popular interest and enthusiasm for the sport, however, football enjoyed a renaissance in France during the 1980s and 1990s, following a distinct slump during the 1960s and 1970s. Various explanations have been proposed for both the slump and the renaissance, the most convincing suggesting that interest has revived largely due to the successes of French teams in international competition and the accompanying large-scale investment in the promotion of football (Mignon 1994). The revival of popular interest in football and the increase in attendance at football matches have been associated with the emergence of new types of supporters and new forms of fan behaviour – including an element of hooliganism.

The demographic profile of the French football crowd shows that all social classes (apart from the aristocracy) are well represented. Some sources have suggested that the majority of spectators are working class (Bromberger 1987), whilst others have indicated that the middle classes predominate. Patrick Mignon points out that the variation in the statistics may be due to the location of the clubs included in demographic surveys, and concludes that on a national basis 'with the exception of the upper classes, all of society is found in the stadium'. Bromberger has also noted that in France, all social groups can identify with some aspect of football.

The social background of ultra or hooligan supporters, as opposed to football spectators in general, is somewhat more difficult to determine, as no quantitative surveys have been undertaken on these groups, which emerged in the early 1980s. An analysis based on records of Paris Saint-Germain supporters detained for questioning by the police between 1988 and 1992 revealed that hooligans were young, white males, predominantly working class, employed in both skilled and unskilled jobs in more or less equal numbers. Some of the more powerful skinhead members of the Paris Saint-Germain 'kop', however, came from the upper-middle classes – sons of lawyers and senior managers. According to Mignon, a number of these supporters, who in the late 1960s and early 1970s might have expressed their dissociation from their bourgeois origins through a different form of solidarity with working people, were now involved in the 'white French', racist movement.

In line with developments in Britain, some skinhead elements amongst French football supporters no longer called themselves 'skinheads': they were now known as 'casuals' and a number shed the traditional skinhead dress and hairstyle. There has been some overlap between the original skinheads and their casual successors, and both groups have been involved in football-related racist attacks and other violent incidents associated with football matches. In addition to the skinheads and casuals, a number of less easily identifiable groups of football fans have also been suspected of having extreme-right leanings, and in some cases these links have been explicit.

Amongst the majority of supporters, however, there appears to have been a move away from the English style of dress and behaviour – which is more strongly associated with extreme-right tendencies – towards the Italian style. Originally, the 'kops' groups, found in clubs north of the Loire, adopted a predominantly English style, whilst the 'ultra' groups, located in the south, favoured the Italian style. Subsequently, the national tendency has been towards 'Italianization' and this distinction has diminished.

Mignon notes that the rather dour English style has been characterized by a lack of 'props', orchestrated displays or other visible demonstrations of group identity, relying on an established football culture to provide an innate sense of collective identity, in-group solidarity and opposition to other groups. The problem for the French fans attempting to emulate the English style is that there was no pre-existing football culture to provide the essential ideological unity and sense of belonging. The more organized and theatrical Italian model – with its badges, scarves, stickers, banners, videos, fanzines, choreographers and conductors – provided this sense of community and established a clear group identity.

Evidence from French fanzines indicates that the Italian style has been adopted with increasing enthusiasm. The stated objectives of the 'Bordeaux Devils', for example, are 'to create a good-humoured and joyous Ultra group' and 'to support our team by livening up the terraces with our displays and chants, but also to create a real group with its own identity, to promote a convivial group where people know each other and enjoy meeting each other both in the stadium and outside'. The 'Devils' Internet news pages also demonstrate an obsession with the theatrical and artistic elements of supporter activity such as 'tifos' (orchestrated displays) and 'gadgets' (brightly coloured props and paraphernalia). In fact, judging by their own fanzines, French ultras have been considerably more interested in these creative elements than they have in any form of aggression. Rivalry between clubs has seemed to centre on who staged the most spectacular 'tifos' (displays), performed the most original chants and demonstrated the greatest enthusiasm in support of their team – rather than who was the toughest.

Clubs have tended to have one main enemy, and somewhat hostile relations with the supporters of one or two other teams. The rest are regarded merely as neutral rivals, and a club will often have positively friendly relations with the supporters of at least one other team. The most frequently cited example of a friendly relationship is that between Bordeaux and St Etienne supporters. Such an alliance would be unheard of in England, and highly unlikely in Germany and Holland, where rival fans only suspend hostilities when supporting their national team in international competitions. Alliances and 'twinning' between supporter groups used to be found in Italy, but declined in the 1990s.

Thus, although the French ultras have been influenced by the Italians, there are some significant differences in their attitudes. It is no accident that the term 'tifo' in Italian means 'football fanaticism' in general, whereas in France 'un tifo' means 'a display' (specifically a choreographed display using coloured cards, banners, fireworks, etc., by fans at a football match) and nothing more. The concept seems to have lost something in translation, namely, the Italians' dominant concern with passionate loyalty, leaving only a passion for the aesthetics of loyalty. The adoption of an Italian word in itself indicates the importance of the Italian ultra influence in France, but the redefinition of the term suggests that this influence has been a matter of form rather than content: the French fans have adopted the flamboyant style of the Italians, but without the background of deep-seated traditional allegiances and rivalries.

Football rivalries may provide French fans with a sense of belonging to a group, a stage for competitive artistic display, an excuse to 'let off steam' and, occasionally, to prove masculinity in aggressive or violent encounters. The references to 'passion', 'hate' and 'enemies' in the French fanzines are, however, somehow unconvincing. They recognize that these sentiments are expected, but their expression does not appear to come from the heart, which may perhaps account for the lower levels of actual violence amongst French ultras.

The Netherlands

Although football hooliganism in the Netherlands is said to have been heavily influenced by the so-called 'English disease', the Dutch followers of the national team appear to have adopted a more Italian, theatrical style, characterized by colourful costumes and displays, and a carnival atmosphere of singing, dancing and good-natured celebration. Hostilities between rival groups are suspended as they join forces to support their national team, and no hostility is displayed towards international rivals either. At Euro 96, for example, the predicted battles between Dutch fans and their arch-enemies the Germans did not occur, nor did they take the opportunity to prove themselves against the 'market-leaders' of hooliganism in England. At home, however, hostilities continue, both between rival groups of fans and between 'hools' and the police. These encounters are described with pride and illustrated with photographs in Dutch fanzines and Internet news-pages such as the 'Daily Hooligan'.

Football hooliganism in the Netherlands has followed much the same pattern of development as other European countries, with an initial stage of sporadic violence directed mainly at referees and players, followed by a phase of increasingly aggressive encounters between rival fans, and between fans and police, inside the stadium, followed by an increase in violence occurring outside the stadium and less obviously related to the game itself. Van der Brug (1994) claims that 'Siders' (the Dutch equivalent of 'ultras') are becoming increasingly detached from their football teams and clubs, and that disorder is now a primary objective in itself:

> The numbers of people that travel to away matches are a clear indication of this tendency. In contrast to matches which promise little excitement, high-risk matches when a team with a violent Side are playing are attended by far greater numbers of young people. It often turns out that young people take to supporting another team when things at their first club become a bit dull.

In terms of socio-demographic profile, van der Brug (1994) claims that the Dutch 'Siders' are a less homogeneously working-class group than their British counterparts, although he gives no specific data on their socioeconomic backgrounds, beyond showing that their educational level is generally lower than that of their fathers, indicating a trend towards 'downward mobility' amongst football fans that has also been observed in other parts of Europe.

Van de Sande (1987) has also claimed that Dutch football fans 'can be found in all socio-economic classes', although he adds that 'the main part of the public is lower class, in so far as a lower class can be said to exist in our prosperous country!' From police data on arrests, van de Sande finds, not surprisingly, that all offenders were male, 43 per cent aged 16 to 18, 28 per cent aged 19 to 21 and almost none over the age of 30. All Dutch researchers appear to have found that hooligans have experienced a problematic school career and lack of effective parental control (for example, see van de Sande 1987; van der Brug and Meijs, 1988, 1989). These factors are frequently cited as causes of football hooliganism, rather than as characteristics of football hooligans.

Austria

Horak *et al.* (1987) found that members of Austrian fan clubs were generally young (average age 18.6 years, younger in the 'more active' fan clubs) and belonged mainly to the working and lower-middle classes – although a high percentage (23 per cent) were unemployed. An element of 'downward mobility' was also noted, with fans achieving lower standards of education and social status than their parents. Whatever their 'official' social class, active fans followed 'masculine-proletarian norms of behaviour' in which 'physical violence is a standard means of solving conflicts, and … an important factor in the process of self-identification among the young'. Half their interviewees had been in trouble with the police, mainly for vandalism but some for incidents involving physical violence – although the researchers pointed out that violence in this subculture was 'more expressive-affective in nature than instrumentive' and that serious injuries were very rare.

When incidents did occur, according to Horak and his colleagues, they differed from the international norm in that clashes were not between rival groups of fans but between juvenile fans and other spectators. Hostilities were not based on rivalries between different clubs but on 'antagonism between the inhabitants of small cities and a specific urban sub-culture'. Austrian fans were none the less highly loyal to their teams, and both 'tough' and 'moderate' fans indicated willingness to engage in violence on behalf of their club. In line with other European nations, fans tended to cause more trouble at away-matches than at home games.

During the 1990s, observers noted an increasing involvement of neo-Nazi skinheads in Austrian football hooliganism. Although understandable fears tend to lead to exaggeration of this factor, and the numbers of skinheads in Austria is small, reports of alliances between skinheads and 'hools' have contributed to concern about the threat to public order posed by this 'combined force'.

Scandinavia

At conferences and in research papers on football fans, the Scandinavian countries have tended to be lumped together under one heading. We have followed this tradition for convenience and because there is a degree of cultural unity between the Nordic nations, but must emphasize that there are considerable differences in fan profiles and behaviour between Sweden, Denmark and Norway, which are outlined separately below. In a paper presented to the 1996 'Fanatics' conference in Manchester, Andersson and Radmann reported that both Sweden and Denmark had problems with football hooliganism, whilst Norway did not. During the 1990s, both Sweden and Denmark have seen outbreaks of football-related violence. Norway has not experienced similar problems, with the exception of some incidents provoked by a group nicknamed 'Ape Mountain', supporters of the Oslo club Vålerenga.

Sweden

Most of the problems in Sweden have involved supporters of the three Stockholm clubs AIK (Black Army), Djurgarden (Blue Saints) and Hammarby (Bajen Fans). A public investigation into hooliganism, by the National Council for Crime Prevention in 1985, concluded that those responsible for violence and hooliganism were 'troublemakers' rather than 'ordinary lads', on the grounds that 60 per cent of those arrested had criminal records. This research has since been criticized, however, for flawed methodology, particularly in terms of sample selection, sample size and questioning methods.

Subsequent projects have focused on finding solutions to the problem of hooliganism, rather than finding out what it consists of, such that demographic data on fans have been limited. As in other European countries, however, a significant current concern is that the fans involved in violence have been getting younger. In the mid-1980s, 18–20-year-olds were most frequently involved in assaults and acts of violence, whereas by the mid-1990s the statistics indicated an increase in the number of 15–17-year-olds involved in violent incidents.

Andersson and Radmann (1996) reported that around 25–30 'serious' incidents occurred during the 1995 season – i.e. approximately one 'serious' incident per seven matches. Unlike most other writers on this subject, Andersson and Radmann took the trouble to specify what they mean by the term 'serious'. Their definition is worth quoting in full, not merely out of gratitude but because it provides some insight into the behaviour patterns of Swedish supporters. They defined 'serious' as:

> any one of the following situations: groups of supporters in direct conflict with each other or the police or guards; attempts by supporter groups to carry out any of the above acts but which have been prevented by the police; and attacks or attempted attacks by the spectators on players or officials.

Although the proportion of trouble accounted for by these different behaviours was not stated, it is interesting to note that attacks on officials and players were still frequent enough to warrant inclusion in the Swedish hooligan repertoire, whilst in many other European countries violence is now almost exclusively directed at opposing fans or at the police. It is also worth noting that in this report, and therefore perhaps in many others where the terms are not defined, 'serious' does not necessarily always mean 'violent'.

Hooliganism in Sweden, as in the other Scandinavian countries (and indeed other countries throughout Europe), has been a club-level problem, and has not occurred at international matches. Even at club level, however, it is important to get the scale of the problem into perspective. An investigation of the 3,000 members of one of the main fan clubs – Djurgarden's 'Blue Saints' – reported that just 30 (1 per cent) of these fans would 'be prepared to start a fight', with a further 20 (0.6 per cent) willing to 'join in a fight'. The remaining 2,950 declared themselves to be mainly interested in football. Even if the fans questioned were 'down playing' their violent tendencies, these figures suggest at least that the majority of Swedish supporters do not see themselves as violent. These data may not be reliable, but the comments of a police officer lend support to the view that the problem of hooliganism in Sweden has been exaggerated. 'I'm fed up with all this talk of hooligans,' he said. 'I don't like the word. If you were to count the real troublemakers, those whom one can really call hooligans, then you would find three all told in Gothenburg.'

These uncertainties and disagreements about the scale, or even the existence, of a football hooligan problem in Sweden have not prevented the authorities from taking action to tackle the problem. Measures adopted in 1996 included registration and investigation of fans and a '22-point programme' to prevent football-related violence, clarifying the responsibilities of clubs for the behaviour of all spectators the grounds, and for their members' behaviour at away matches. Racist and other prejudiced slogans are banned, as are slogans insulting the opposing team or even 'booing' of the opposing team or players! Any aggressive or violent incidents incur serious fines and result in all of a club's matches being graded as 'high-risk'. Some clubs also brought in private security firms to keep order. Despite these measures, the start of the 1996 season was marred by several violent incidents – although the evidence suggests that only a very small minority of supporters engage in such behaviour.

Denmark

The successful rise of the Danish national football team since 1980 has been championed by its enthusiastic but peaceful supporters. These are the 'roligans' (from 'rolig' meaning 'peaceful'), who are seen as the antithesis of the typical English hooligan. The majority of roligans (42 per cent) are in skilled or civil service jobs. The average age is 31 – considerably older than football fans in other European countries. Overall, around 15 per cent of fans are women, but the organised Danish Roligan Association reports a 45 per cent female membership.

The leading, fully professional Danish football clubs, Bröndby and Copenhagen FC, attract the largest supporter groups. The Bröndby supporter club boasts 10,000 registered members, making it the largest in Scandinavia. Football is a family activity in Denmark. Not only are there large numbers of women in the stands, but many families come with young children and even infants.

Of all the Scandinavian fans, the roligans appear to have the closest ties to both the game itself and the clubs. Surveys have indicated that between 80 and 85 per cent of roligans have themselves played club football. According to Eichberg (1992), the secret of the roligans good nature is that they have not forgotten that 'Football is to do with laughter'. The serious patriotic associations of the game are caricatured in the roligan displays: faces are painted with the country's red and white colours, which match the bright scarves and T-shirts and 'the whole is topped with the Klaphat, a grotesque red and white hat with movable cloth hands attached for applause'. Even the influence of excessive alcohol consumption, another trademark of the roligan, seems only to further the festive cheerfulness and peaceful sociability of the fans. The carnival atmosphere often spills out into the streets where large groups of dressed-up liquored roligans have been known to lead conga dances through towns.

Eichberg regards this behaviour as more than simply a manifestation of the 'culture of laughter' but also as a form of social control. When individuals attempt right-wing outbursts such as shouting 'Sieg Heil' and other such provocative remarks, they are 'immediately calmed down by other Danes'. This control may also have a lot to do with the fact that right-wing political adherents are a weak minority amongst roligans (12 per cent). Some 47 per cent define themselves as socialist, with women reporting an even higher percentage – 65 per cent. Only 5 per cent of the women claimed to support the right-wing populist Progress Party.

Like most other European countries, Denmark has experienced more problems internally, at club level, than at international matches. (In fact, hooliganism in the Scandinavian countries is confined almost exclusively to club-level games, behaviour at international matches being generally exemplary.) Despite the saintly reputation of the roligans, Denmark has experienced a few outbreaks of violence at club matches during the 1990s, particularly at local derbies in Copenhagen. Presumably not all Danish football supporters subscribe to the dominant roligan culture. It must be said, however, that even problems at club level have been described as 'marginal'.

Norway

Norway has, for the most part, been free of football-related violence. The only exceptions to the 'model fan' image are the supporters of the Oslo club Vålerenga – the so-called 'Ape Mountain' – whose deviant exploits have included robbing a hot-dog stand (somehow 41 people managed to get arrested following this incident in 1993); roughing up, but not injuring, a linesman (1995); one violent attack on a rival female supporter (1995); and one assault on a policeman during a local derby. The most highly publicized incident involved the antics of just one fan who scaled the roof of a beer tent during the 1992 European Championships in Målmo and was accused of starting a 'riot'.

Apart from these incidents, which can hardly be said to constitute a serious problem, the behaviour of Norwegian supporters, at club level as well as internationally, has been characterized by vociferous, but peaceful, enthusiasm. Even between arch-rivals such as the provincial clubs Rosenberg and Brand, there has been little or no overt hostility. In a non-violent atmosphere, they compete fiercely with each other for the best songs, costumes and beer-drinking parties. Andersson and Radmann (1996) suggest that the conduct of Norwegian police may help to explain the largely peaceful behaviour of the fans. Whilst the police have absolute responsibility for football crowds, 'they never appear in large groups, or go armed with helmets and weapons when on duty at club matches'. This is in direct contrast to the approach of the Swedish police, who have attended most matches equipped with the full regalia of shields, helmets, visors and weapons.

Stages of development

Despite the fact that national characteristics reflecting different historical, social, political and cultural traditions have affected the nature and scale of football-related violence in different European countries, there are significant cross-national similarities in the 'stages of development' of the problem. In most countries, there appears to have been an initial stage of sporadic violence inside the stadium, directed at officials such as referees or at players themselves. This is followed by a second stage involving an increase in aggression between opposing groups of fans and between fans and police/security officers, still within the confines of the stadium, involving violent encounters during pitch invasions and the creation of 'territories' which rival fans attempt to 'capture'. The third stage involves a significant increase in violence outside the stadium, including pitched battles between rival groups of fans in the streets; 'ambushes' at railway stations, in car parks and bus-terminals; acts of petty theft and vandalism;

and frequent clashes with the police. In this third stage, observers almost invariably notice an increasing detachment of hooliganism from the game of football, whereby participation in violence – or at least some form of ritual warfare – outside the stadium appears to be an end (excuse the pun) in itself.

This is, of course, an oversimplification: there are overlaps between these stages and also some exceptions to this pattern. Yet most of the European countries experiencing problems with football fans have seen a pattern of development incorporating at least some elements of this 'three-stage' process, whatever other socio-historical-political-cultural influences may have been involved. Whilst recognizing the limitations of such a broad-brush, generic picture of the development of football hooliganism, we must also be aware of the dangers of becoming so bogged down in the details of cross-cultural differences that we fail to see the international patterns.

In summary, the evidence indicates a more or less universal pattern of development, which is none the less 'contoured and fuelled' by different socio-cultural-historical factors in different European countries, resulting in both recognizable similarities and important variations in the nature and scale of football-related disorder.

Further study – Europe and beyond

Since 2000, two edited collections have been produced of contributions on football fan behaviours from Europe and indeed the wider world. As well as Britain and Europe, *Fear and Loathing in World Football* (Armstrong and Giulianotti 2001) includes essays on Croatians in Australia, Mauritius, Calcutta, Yemen, Mexico, Cameroon, and Argentina. *Fighting Fans* (Dunning *et al.* 2002), on the other hand, covers Argentina, Australia, West Africa, Peru, South Africa, Japan and North America as well as the usual British and European suspects.

Chapter summary

In most European countries, football-related violence is largely an 'internal' problem, with the majority of incidents occurring at club-level matches, whilst supporters of the national team abroad are generally well behaved. The English are an obvious exception to this rule, and rivalries between some other nations, such as the Dutch and German supporters, have led to occasional violent conflicts. But the pattern of violence between club-level enemies contrasting with relatively peaceful support of the national team seems fairly well established in many European countries. This pattern is partly responsible for the prevalent assumption that only England has a serious problem of football violence – because the violence of English fans is highly visible on the international stage, whilst other nations' hooligans confine themselves mainly to parochial warfare.

Whilst football hooliganism is clearly not an exclusively 'British disease', the British are, however, frequently blamed for 'spreading' it to Europe. The Leuven University study (see Walgrave et al. 1987) concluded that 'all the lines lead back to British hooligans. They are seen as the professionals. They are the great example to hooligans from all over the rest of Europe'.

The Leuven conclusions are somewhat of an oversimplification. The historical evidence, and the research findings on cross-national variations summarized in this chapter, suggest that although some football supporters in some European countries may regard the English hooligans as role models, others have quite deliberately adopted a very different – indeed opposite – style of behaviour. Those who have consciously rejected the English model include the Scottish 'Tartan Army', so the 'disease' can certainly no longer be called 'British'. Throughout Europe, we find that whilst some countries may exhibit some of the symptoms of the so-called 'English disease' (the Danish roligans drink a lot, for example, and the Italian ultras fight), the manifestation of these symptoms is not sufficiently uniform to justify a confident diagnosis (the roligans do not fight, for example, and the toughest of the Italian fighters tend to avoid alcohol). So have the English hooligans somehow selectively infected the Italians with their bellicosity and the Danes with their drinking habits? Do the Norwegians, but not the Swedes, have some natural immunity to this disease? Has the Scottish Tartan Army experienced a miracle cure?

Clearly, the picture is rather more complex than the Leuven conclusions would suggest. The evidence indicates that different forms of football culture, including 'hooligan' elements, have developed in different European countries. This development has certainly involved some cross-cultural influence, but the fact that British hooliganism had a ten-year head start on the rest of Europe does not imply that all subsequent 'hooliganisms' are mere imitations. The Leuven researchers are right, however, to point out that the British, or more accurately the English, are widely regarded as the 'market-leaders' in this field. English hooligans provide the benchmark against which the violent elements amongst other nations' supporters judge their performance. It is no accident that these groups – and indeed any groups striving for a 'fierce' and powerful image, whether they are in fact violent or not – tend to give themselves English names and use English football jargon in their slogans, chants and graffiti.

There are some indications that the international influence of the belligerent English style may be on the wane, as self-proclaimed non-violent, fun-loving groups such as the Danish roligans and Scotland's Tartan Army succeed in grabbing the headlines. As we suggest later in Chapter 9, a concerted pan-European media conspiracy to give blanket coverage to the 'carnival' groups, whilst ruthlessly cutting off the oxygen of publicity supply to the 'hooligan' groups, might help to encourage this new fashion.

Part III

Explaining football hooliganism

Having dealt with the nature and extent of football hooliganism, both in the UK and Europe, we turn now to an examination of the various theoretical explanations that have been offered both by academics and by others. Chapter 6 takes a first pass at the various theoretical explanations and shows that British football hooliganism has been over-researched, with some of the academic debate marked by acrimony and silly writing. The chapter reviews some fallacious populist explanations, including blaming the violence on alcohol or sophisticated organized gangs, and then examines the principal British academic theories. These included protest, skinhead-style, 'aggro' (the illusion of violence), male identity rituals, the social exclusion of the 'uncivilized', media amplification and the search for peak experiences. Chapter 6 also shows that the hooligans have been mostly male, young and working class.

Chapter 7 presents a more detailed second pass at the British theoretical explanations. The major research and perspectives on football hooliganism derive mainly from British work conducted since the late 1960s. There are deep divisions within social science circles concerning explanations of football hooliganism, with often vitriolic debate between Marxist sociologists, so-called 'figurationalists', social psychologists and more empirically oriented researchers. This atmosphere has hindered the emergence of truly multidisciplinary perspectives. It is generally agreed that British football hooliganism has probably been over-researched. Despite a general decline in violence at British football matches, the phenomenon still attracts a disproportionate amount of research activity.

The principal sociological, psychological and anthropological approaches are critically reviewed – including those of Ian Taylor, John Clarke, Stuart Hall, Peter Marsh, John Williams and his colleagues, Gary Armstrong and others. In 1971, Professor Ian Taylor took a Marxist sociological perspective, suggesting that violence was the only means open for the 'lumpenproletariat' to express its concern at the hijacking of football by big business. In 1978, John Clarke's subcultural perspective concluded that football-related violence was associated with the skinhead style. Also in 1978, co-author Peter Marsh and his social-psychological colleagues constructed the idea of 'aggro'. They observed Oxford United fans and concluded that what was misconstrued as hooliganism was actually an illusion of violence involving rituals and displays of aggression between young men. Marsh has revised some of his conclusions in the light of more lethal football violence which occurred in the 1980s.

During the 1990s, the social anthropologist Gary Armstrong followed Sheffield United and concluded that what was going on was a disorganized acting-out of working-class male identity rituals. Armstrong is particularly keen to debunk the theory that the violence is organized by structured groups, which he claims is a police and media justification for increased powers to deal with people whose behaviour doesn't fit within increasingly restrictive social norms.

The most prolific English academics were Eric Dunning, Patrick Murphy and John Williams from the University of Leicester. Writing in the 1980s and early 1990s, their social historical perspective focused on social exclusion and the cultural traditions of the 'uncivilized', rough, working-class: maleness, solidarity and aggression. The road to eradicating hooliganism was one that addressed the wider issues of social justice.

In 1991, the journalist Bill Buford took a more populist 'biological' perspective, describing the adrenalin rush brought on when it 'goes off'. More academically, the psychologist John Kerr in 1994 sought to provide an understanding of the motivation behind the hooligans' search for 'peak' and 'flow' experiences. Other theorists reviewed include Richard Giulianotti, who has examined the carnivalesque culture of Scottish football fan support, and Garry Robson, who has undertaken a detailed sociological analysis of the myth and reality of Millwall fandom.

Research in other European countries has grown in scale since the early 1980s. The work of German, Dutch and Italian social scientists is reviewed in Chapter 8. Much of this research has taken British theoretical perspectives as a starting point, although more 'local' approaches are evident in some countries. The increase in work in these countries has led to a more Europe-wide approach to the problems of football violence, with a number of collaborative programmes undertaken. The level of cross-cultural variation in the patterns of behaviour of football fans, however, presents a number of problems for this kind of research.

Chapter 9 shows how football hooliganism is a highly visible phenomenon, as journalists and TV cameras are present at virtually every match. Since the 1960s, journalists have been sent to football matches to report on crowd behaviour as much as on the game itself. As a result, media coverage of football-related disorder and violence is extensive, and the British tabloid press in particular devote apparently unlimited column inches to any incident that occurs, complete with sensationalist headlines. Many researchers, and many non-academic observers, have argued that this sensationalism, together with a 'predictive' approach whereby violence at certain matches is anticipated by the media, has actually contributed to the problem. The British press have also been criticized for their xenophobic approach to the coverage of international matches and tournaments.

Although there is no direct equivalent of the British tabloid extremes in other European nations, most researchers have identified problems relating to media coverage of football hooliganism. In all the countries with significant levels of football-related disorder, researchers have found that hooligans relish the media coverage they receive, and often positively seek it with rival groups actively competing for column inches and mentions in sensational headlines.

The publicity-seeking tendencies of football fans can, however, be turned to beneficial effect. The extensive and highly positive coverage of the new, non-violent, 'carnival' groups such as Scotland's 'Tartan Army' and the Danish 'roligans' has clearly been seen by them as a 'victory' over their badly behaved rivals, and has helped to reinforce and perpetuate their exemplary behaviour.

Football violence in Britain is often reported in the media as resulting from excessive alcohol consumption. In Chapter 10, we see that the large majority of social scientists who have conducted research on hooliganism do not share this view. Neither is it the view popularly held in many other European countries. Little research has focused specifically on the role of alcohol in football hooliganism. This is because it has been considered, at best, a peripheral issue in most studies. Some investigators, however, have recently claimed that drinking can 'aggravate' football violence and have supported calls for further restrictions at football grounds. Little evidence has been provided to support their claims.

There is wide cross-national variations in the consumption of alcohol by football fans and in its apparent effects. The case of Scottish fans, whose behaviour has changed markedly for the better since the mid-1980s, despite continuing patterns of 'heavy' drinking, is considered. It is clear that alcohol-related behaviours are not immutable and can change in relatively short periods of time. The example of the Danish roligans is also considered. These have drinking patterns very similar to those of English fans, put present few problems to the authorities. Drunkenness amongst the Danish fans is typically accompanied by good humour and positive sociability. Other groups of fans, such as the Italian ultras, rarely drink to excess when attending football matches and the role of alcohol in football violence in that country is thought to be completely insignificant.

In Chapter 11, we find that the true extent of racism amongst football supporters is almost impossible to quantify. Extensive speculation and debate on the subject are not supported by much reliable empirical data.

For the media and public opinion, however, racism among football fans is a serious problem, and often blamed for outbreaks of violence, particularly at international matches. Amongst academics and professionals involved with football, the role of racism and far-right groups in football violence is a hotly debated issue. Some agencies, such as the British National Criminal Intelligence Service, regard their influence as minimal, whilst others have directly blamed them for violent incidents.

In Britain, racist chanting at matches still occasionally occurs, but at nowhere near the levels it reached in the 1970s and 1980s, when black players were often greeted with monkey-noises and bananas. The decline may be due in part to campaigns designed to combat racism, such as the 'Let's Kick Racism out of Football'. Elsewhere in Europe there are some indications that the problem may be more persistent. In one survey, 20 per cent of German fans reported sympathies with the neo-Nazi movement. In many cases, however, Nazi symbols and slogans may be used purely to shock and provoke, without any underlying political conviction.

The problem is certainly being taken seriously across Europe, and a number of initiatives have been launched, including the 'When Racism Wins, the Sport Loses' campaign in the Netherlands, 'No al Razzismo' in Italy and Europe-wide initiatives such as 'All Different, All Equal' and 'Fans against Racism in Europe'. The success of these initiatives is difficult to measure, but the UK has certainly seen a recent decrease in racist behaviour at football grounds.

6. An overview of British theories of football hooliganism

Introduction

Social scientists have been offering explanations of football hooliganism since the late 1960s, ranging from a concern with macro sociopolitical changes to the role of lead pollution and zinc deficiencies. This field was monopolized by the British, with most universities having a least one post-graduate student writing a thesis in this area. Leicester University devoted an entire centre to research on football fans, with De Montfort and Manchester quickly following their lead. Academics in other European countries joined the debate at a theoretical level in the late 1970s – particularly the Italians and the Dutch. With the gradual spread of football sub culture style, and its sometimes aggressive patterns of behaviour, throughout most of Europe in the late 1970s, their interest became more focused on the behaviour of fans in their own countries than with purely theoretical perspectives.

Contemporary research on football violence is now largely European in scope, as reflected in a number of conferences in the UK and Italy and in major publications since the early 1990s. Despite the continuing popularity of the subject, however, a genuine consensus concerning the origins of the problem, in whatever country, and the most effective means of tackling the phenomenon, have yet to emerge. In some instances one has a distinct sense of déjà vu, with perspectives once applied to English football matches in the 1960s now being reworked to serve as explanations for events in, say, Genoa in the 1990s. The manifest failure of some theoretical approaches has also led some researchers to return to more simplistic explanations – some suggesting further bans on alcohol as a way of stemming the problems, particularly in the UK, even though their earlier research had failed to find that drinking was a significant factor.

To some extent, of course, football violence itself has declined in frequency in most European countries since 1990, most noticeably in the UK. The return of English clubs to European competition was marked by some outbursts of fighting between English fans and their opponents, but there has been little to match the ugly scenes of the 1980s. Major championships, despite the apocalyptic predictions in the media prior to the games, have passed off with relatively little incident.

This decline in the phenomenon, however, has done little to dent the amount of research focusing upon it. *The Sunday Times* (8 August 1993) showed how, between 1986 and 1993, the Football Trust had donated £900,000 to fund research centres at Oxford and Leicester Universities. Eight other academic institutions were also named as having funded their own research. Thus the study of football hooliganism had become an academic growth industry. And judging by the number of articles, books and conference proceedings, the subject is as popular as ever. The academics have given the subject a thoroughly 'good kicking', even though many old-timers in the field may think that there is little more to discover or say about football hooliganism. Moorhouse for example has argued that 'By any estimation of its social significance violence around football has been overstudied, as well as being poorly studied ... The debate on hooliganism has lost all power to generate any new social insights' (2000: 1464).

Criticisms such as this might appear to work against new work in this area. However Moorhouse's remarks would seem to be directed at the debate on rival theories of causation about who the hooligans are and why they behave as they do. We would observe that previous academic research has far less to say on other salient questions: for example, on the definition of the phenomenon; on questions about its nature or extent; or on issues of social control. We refer to questions such as, what is football hooliganism? How much of it is there? What kinds of behaviours are we talking about? What strategies and tactics are used by the police, the authorities and others to tackle football hooliganism?

Despite all this continued research activity, there is, as we have seen, no single, universally adopted definition of football hooliganism. Neither has there been, prior to this volume, a definitive overview of the field – no comprehensive textbook providing a balanced analysis of the competing approaches and the evidence purporting to support them. The reason for this becomes apparent when one delves into the published literature. Here more time is devoted to demolishing the views of other 'experts' than to developing alternative explanations and, as we shall see, the atmosphere is often more reminiscent of a rowdy conflict between rival football fans themselves than it is of calm, rational, academic debate. Rather mirroring the object of their study, academics have focused as much on 'putting the boot in' to each other's theories and methods, sometimes using obtuse sociological jargon, as they have on providing intelligible explanations. For example, in response to an academic journal article, T. Smith (2000) writes:

> In his analysis of football hooliganism, Anthony King claims to reveal the historical, conceptual scheme young, male supporters draw upon … In this response I examine King's critique of his fellow theorists; challenge his 'Freikorps-Fans' analogy; demonstrate the problem he has in establishing the sex–violence link and question the relevance of his concept of postmodernity.

In some cases the writing is not just incomprehensible but also pretentiously silly. Take this abstract from a paper on Scottish football fans:

> This short paper seeks to explain the activities of Scottish fans in Genoa and Turin during the 1990 World Cup, by drawing on some key concepts offered by contemporary writers in the field of post-modernism and post-structuralism. These writers include Foucault, Derrida, Barthes and Baudrillard. All emphasize a re-empowerment of agency, evading more conventional forms of domination: Foucault within the domain of enabling discourse, Derrida on the open interpretation of the sign's apparent meaning, Barthes on the 'nature' of jouissance and the body principle, and Baudrillard on the public toying with their media representation. It is argued that Scottish fan behaviour in Italy was structured by two opposing forms of 'self-knowledge', relating to either expressions of violent machismo or instrumentally ambassadorial conduct. The eventual triumph of the latter is most clearly shown through an application of Goffman's conception of 'impression management', as the social interaction of Scottish fans with other 'teams' in Italy is detailed chronologically. The paper concludes with some recommendations aimed at the relevant authorities, with a view to maximizing the internationalism of Scottish fans at future competitions (Giulianotti 1991).

Explanations as to who the hooligans are and why they do it are manifold. There are simplistic populist explanations and there are more complex academic theories. It is however clear that, despite academic denials, there are commonalities in all this theoretical work. At the risk of over-simplification, we might find by the end of the next two chapters that we can broadly conclude that violent English fans are male; largely young and working class; that they are acting out something to do with post-modern masculine identity; and that they do it because it's fun.

Populist explanations

One populist view is that 'all fans are animals' (and we have omitted the f-word adjective which often accompanies this explanation). They behave like beasts and so should be treated as such. The suggestion here is that football fans are feral young men, yet research has consistently shown that up to 17 per cent of fans are women (see Williams *et al.* 1989: 9) and that all ages and social classes attend sporting events (for example, see Dunning 1989: 16.)

Another populist theory blames alcohol for the violence. Alcohol is often banned from stadiums even though this flies in the face of the research evidence (see Frosdick 1998a). Alcohol may be a contributing factor at football in some Anglo-Saxon cultures, but the Danes, Dutch and Irish manage to drink vast amounts without particular problems of violence. And sports such as rugby have strong links with alcohol but with very few problems of violence. We shall say something more about football hooliganism and alcohol in Chapter 10.

A populist police explanation claims that sophisticated organized gangs orchestrate the violence. Consider this quotation from the NCIS: 'While football hooliganism is rather different from other organised criminal activities where profit is the main motive, we noted in our annual Threat Assessment that as well as being violent it is also highly organised and attracts other serious criminal activity such as drugs dealing and counterfeiting' (2001b). Well the police would say that, wouldn't they, since it justifies the whole industry they've created to deal with soccer hooligans (see also Armstrong 1998). But, as we have seen, the nature and extent of the phenomenon are rather more complex, with organized violence forming only a small part of a picture which also includes disorganized, spontaneous and contagious actions and even words. The police may sometimes also be guilty of over-egging the pudding. Anecdotal evidence from Football Safety Officers' Association members suggests that there are good examples of intelligence between club safety officers being rather at odds with the police intelligence for particular matches.

'Hooligan porn'

The main theoretical output on football hooliganism dates from the 1980s and 1990s, with only a few worthwhile recent contributions. An Internet search for something like 'football violence' will reveal a whole clutch of more recent publications by reformed hooligans turned 'hooliologists'. These purport to describe and explain the phenomenon of football hooliganism but may be criticized as representing little more than cashing in on public appetite for the subject. These types of books, together with the various pseudo-documentaries which have appeared on video, DVD and television over recent years, represent what Luke Chapman (2002), writing in *When Saturday Comes* magazine, has labelled as 'hooligan porn'. Referring to one particular television series, Chapman describes it as 'Masquerading as serious analysis and comment from the "men who were there", it was instead more of a glorified wallow in nostalgia, imbued with a whiff of Guy Ritchie-like fascination for all things proletarian and geezerish'.

One example is provided by the cover for the DVD of the film, *The Football Factory*, which is based on the novel by John King (1997). This is described as: 'a study of middle England, football violence and male culture. The story centres around Tommy Johnson, a bored twenty-something who lives for the weekend, casual sex, watered down lager, heavily cut drugs ... And occasionally kicking the f*ck [*sic*] out of someone.' Also writing in *When Saturday Comes*, Rob Chapman (2004) succinctly summarizes this type of output:

> There's usually a bit about the casuals (rarely developed beyond and arbitrary list of bands and brands), a smidgen of cod-sociology about alienated yoof and sink estates, and tons about rucking. It's hoolie-porn and the publishers want the money shot every few pages. And that's exactly what you get. One long tedious litany of 'aving it and mixing it and calling cards and gaining prestige by running the opposition off New Street station ...

We consider that the label 'hooligan porn' might justifiably be applied to much of the recent output and so we shall not dignify it with further discussion.

British academic explanations

Chapter 7 will present a detailed discussion of the various British academic theories. Our purpose in this section is to take a 'first pass' at these theories and their critics and so provide the reader with a brief overview of the field.

In 1971, Professor Ian Taylor took a left-realist or Marxist sociological perspective, suggesting that violence was the only means open for the 'lumpenproletariat' to express its concern at the hijacking of football by big business (Taylor 1971a). In 1978, John Clarke's subcultural perspective concluded that football-related violence was associated with the skinhead style (Clarke 1978). Both these explanations were criticized as politically motivated theories lacking any supporting evidence and indeed as 'a deliberate eschewing of analysis of empirical data of any kind' (Hobbs and Robins 1991: 554).

Also in 1978, co-author Peter Marsh and his social-psychological Oxford colleagues constructed the idea of 'aggro'. Marsh *et al.* observed Oxford United fans and concluded that what was misconstrued as hooliganism was actually an illusion of violence involving ritual displays of aggression between young men (Marsh 1978a; Marsh *et al.* 1978). This theory was criticized for overlooking the injuries that can and do occur when opposing groups rush at each other (see Canter *et al.* 1989: 113).

During the 1990s, the social anthropologist Gary Armstrong followed Sheffield United and concluded that what was going on was a disorganized acting out of working-class male identity rituals (Armstrong and Harris 1991; Armstrong 1998). Armstrong is particularly keen to debunk the theory that the violence is organized by structured groups, which he claims is a police and media justification for increased powers to deal with people whose behaviour doesn't fit within increasingly restrictive social norms – as echoed by Brick (2000). Both Marsh and Armstrong have been criticized for overgeneralizing about hooligan styles from empirical work at just one club (see Redhead: 199/a481). Moorhouse is also quite scathing of Armstrong's assertion that 'football hooliganism cannot really be "explained". It can only be described and evaluated' (Armstrong 1998: 21). Moorhouse notes the length of this description – more than 370 pages – and argues that, 'all the, seemingly endless, detail is deployed to very little analytical effect' (2000: 1463).

A more recent single-club study comes from Robson (2000), who examines the myth and reality of Millwall fandom. Millwall fans have somewhat of a violent media stereotype, but Robson paints a very detailed picture of the historical background, social roots, rituals and culture of 'Millwallism', arguing that the rough traditions of Millwall fandom can be firmly located in its urban working-class context and the history of southeast London.

The most prolific English academics have been Eric Dunning, Patrick Murphy and John Williams from the University of Leicester. Writing in the 1980s and early 1990s, their social historical perspective focused on social exclusion and the cultural traditions of the 'uncivilized' rough working class: maleness, solidarity and aggression. The road to eradicating hooliganism was one that addressed the wider issues of social justice (Williams *et al.* 1984; Dunning *et al.* 1988; Murphy *et al.* 1990). Armstrong and Harris (1991) accused the Leicester researchers of failing to scrutinize carefully enough the data upon which their conclusions were based. Providing a further illustration of the acrimony of the debate, Dunning *et al.* (1991) responded to Armstrong's temerity by attacking his work and robustly defending their own.

In 1991, the journalist Bill Buford took a more populist 'biological' perspective, describing the adrenalin rush brought on when it 'goes off' (Buford 1991). More academically, the psychologist John Kerr (1994) sought to provide an understanding of the motivation behind the hooligans' search for 'peak' and 'flow' experiences. He argues that football hooliganism is a 'paraletic' result of 'reversal' from a 'metamotivational state', i.e. the lads kick off because they are bored. However his work is full of obtuse psychological terminology and his reasoning has been criticized as a priori, i.e. there is no evidence for his theory except itself (see Spracklen 1997).

Giulianotti (1991) has analysed the changes in Scottish football supporting whereby previously violent fans have reinvented themselves as the 'Tartan Army', whose 'carnivalesque' style of supporting mirrors that of the Danish roligans. As with Kerr, the main problem with Giulianotti's work is that, as we have already shown, his arguments are hidden behind almost impenetrable (this time) sociological jargon.

Anthony King (1995) has offered an adaptation of Waddington's 'flashpoints' model (see Waddington *et al.* 1989) to show how, in the case of a Manchester United match in Turkey in 1993, violence arose not as a result of any particular intention of the fans, but because a mutual position of antagonism arose through a complex set of social interactions involving history, media reporting, the national and masculine culture of the English fans and the political situation in Turkey.

Building on Marsh's argument that the misconstruction of 'aggro' can result in inappropriate interventions which can escalate ritual displays into real violence, Clifford Stott and his colleagues have argued that certain police tactics can result in an otherwise peaceful crowd becoming violent (see, for example, Stott and Reicher 1998; Stott *et al.* 2001). In their analysis of policing at the 1990 World Cup in Italy, Stott and Reicher (1998) show how 'the assumption, on the part of the police, that all fans were potentially dangerous and their treatment of fans as such led, over time, to a situation where fans who initially eschewed violence, came into conflict with the police'. Thus 'the assumption that fans are inherently dangerous may become a self-fulfilling prophecy'.

As well as inappropriate policing, there is also convincing evidence of media amplification leading to moral panic and the self-fulfilling prophesy of violence (see Hall 1978). We shall examine this aspect in more detail in Chapter 9. In addition to media and perhaps police amplification, one of the present authors has suggested the possibility of 'academic amplification', arguing that:

> This focusing of social science enquiry on rival theoretical explanations of football hooliganism, whilst important in helping to generate understanding of the causes of the phenomenon itself, nevertheless

does little to assist in the development of public policy. It may also unwittingly have contributed to moral panic and amplification of the real extent of the problem (Frosdick 1999: 7).

Who are the hooligans?

In 1980, Trivizas noted the lack of criminological data on football hooligans and undertook a study of Metropolitan Police arrest records. He found that mature adults were comparatively rare in his sample and that 'more than two-thirds (68.1 per cent) of those charged with football-related offences were manual workers, the majority being apprentices; 12 per cent of football offences were committed by unemployed persons and 10 per cent by schoolboys' (1980a: 281). Subsequently, Dunning *et al.* (1988) also investigated the identity of persons arrested for football-related violence. They began their analysis by noting that 'The available data on football hooligans, however, contrast markedly with survey data on crowd composition. They show a far higher concentration towards the bottom of the social scale' (p. 186). Their own research then supports this view by showing that 'the overwhelming majority – 475 or 91.5 per cent of the employed football hooligans on whom we have information work, or worked, in manual occupations' (p. 189).

Although, as we have just seen, Dunning *et al.*'s conclusions were criticized by Armstrong and Harris (1991) – in a suitably vitriolic fashion – they have stood the test of time. Citing Dunning *et al.* (1988), a University of Leicester fact-sheet concludes that:

> Most of the evidence on hooligan offenders suggests they are generally in their late teens or early 20s (though some leaders are older), that they are mainly in manual or lower clerical occupations or, to a lesser extent, are unemployed or working in the 'grey' economy, and that they come from mainly working class backgrounds (SNCCFR 2001: 5).

Note that they are also almost exclusively male, and that their social background does not mean they do not have the disposable income necessary to follow their chosen interest.

One of co-author Steve Frosdick's dissertation students (Kelly Faulkner) decided to analyse the work of six of the theorists referred to above – Taylor, Clarke, Marsh, Kerr, Dunning *et al.* and Giulianotti – to find out what explanations were offered as to the gender, race, age and social class of football hooligans. Faulkner (2004) found that, as the Marsh report (Carnibella *et al.*) had suggested in 1996, it was indeed possible to locate the various theories within a common framework. In short, the theorists were in broad agreement that football hooligans were male, white, working-class young adults.

Chapter summary

Research into football hooliganism has seen exponential growth to the point where some commentators have argued that there is little new to discover. Whilst this may be true of theoretical explanations of the causes football hooliganism, it is not the case in respect of other aspects, for example examining the nature and extent of the phenomenon or questions of social control. The academic debate has been marked by acrimony with rival theorists more concerned to score points off each other than to advance understanding. The debate has not been helped by a tendency by some writers to hide their arguments inside obtuse psychological or sociological jargon and in some cases the writing has been pretentiously silly.

Populist theories that 'all football fans are animals', that the violence is caused by alcohol and that the bulk of hooliganism is organized were debunked and the offerings of reformed hooligans – the so-called 'hooliologists' – dismissed as 'hooligan porn' not worthy of serious academic scrutiny. The principal British theorists were then reviewed in brief, taking a 'first pass' at the range of competing causal explanations on offer. Finally, the chapter looked at theories about who the hooligans were, concluding that they were exclusively male and largely young, white and from working-class backgrounds.

7. British theoretical perspectives in detail

Introduction

Research on football violence has been a growth industry since the late 1960s in Britain, and academics in other European countries have steadily been catching up since the mid-1980s. To many observers, the subject is now probably over-researched and, with the exception of Robson (2000), little in the way of new, original insights have been forthcoming since the early 1990s. This 'overpopulation' of social scientists in a relatively small research niche is undoubtedly responsible for the distinctly unfriendly nature of much of the continuing debate. The various schools of thought often divide into openly hostile factions and the level of vitriolic discussion in the literature and at conferences is reminiscent of the ritual aggression which once characterized the earliest forms of football itself. Even some of the groups, such as the 'Leicester School', fell out amongst themselves and those who were once co-authors of major studies were later openly critical of each other.

Amid all this bad-tempered discourse, however, are a number of quite clearly delineated theoretical perspectives which, in reality, can easily be accommodated in a broader framework for understanding the causes and patterns of contemporary football hooliganism in Europe. Whilst some of the perspectives may be lacking in specific applicability, or even in basic evidence, most are loosely compatible with each other, despite strenuous attempts by their authors to deny the salience of rival explanations.

The easiest way of charting a path through the literature is to take a historical route, beginning in the late 1960s when football hooliganism became, quite suddenly, a cause for major concern in Britain. It should be noted, however, that many of the early studies in this area saw hooliganism not as a novel phenomenon at all but simply a continuation of patterns of youth behaviour which had previously been the preserve of such visible groups as teddy boys, mods and rockers, and skinheads. For others, football hooliganism was largely a fiction generated by hysterical journalists – it was the agenda of the media, rather than the behaviour of football fans, which required an explanation.

The Harrington Report

Amongst the earliest publications concerning 'modern' football violence was the report by the British psychiatrist, John Harrington (1968), which is generally recognized as the first serious attempt to probe what was then a new social phenomenon. His report was based on questionnaire data and from direct observation at football matches, with additional evidence being obtained from interested groups including the police, the St John Ambulance Brigade and transport operators. In addition, a sample of public opinion was obtained through the unlikely medium of the *Sun* newspaper – a poll that indicated that 90 per cent of respondents thought that football hooliganism was increasing and constituted a 'serious' problem. This stood in distinct contrast to the views of the police authorities. Almost 50 per cent of these reported no increase in football-related violence and two indicated a decrease.

The emphasis in the Harrington Report was principally on individual pathology and reactions to the immediate stimuli provided by the setting in which fans were placed. Terms such as 'immaturity' and 'loss of control' were frequently used, with little attention paid to wider social forces or group dynamics. Harrington justified his position by saying, 'Whilst the significance of these deeper and more remote influences on hooliganism should not be ignored, we feel the importance of immediate "here and now" factors both individual, social and connected with the game must be considered'.

It was, of course, expedient – as somewhat cynical sociologists were quick to point out – to put the blame on a small number of individuals rather than on social or political forces, since Harrington's report was commissioned by the then Minister of Sport, Denis Howell. Ian Taylor was quick to highlight the report's shortcomings:

> the content of the report, while interesting, is not as important as the social function it performed. Simply to employ a psychiatrist for a national government report is to legitimate the idea in the popular mind that 'hooliganism' is explicable in terms of the existence of essentially unstable and abnormal temperament, individuals who happen, for some inexplicable reason to have taken soccer as the arena in which to act out their instabilities. The psychological label adds credibility and strength to the idea that the hooligans are not really true supporters, that they may legitimately be segregated

from the true supporter (who does not intervene), and that they can be dealt with by the full force of the law and (on occasions) by psychiatrists (Taylor 1971a).

Further rejection of Harrington's report was made in a joint report by the Sports Council and the government-funded Social Science Research Council. This criticized both the lack of explanatory theory and the *ad hoc* sampling procedures used in the main study. The failings of the Harrington Report were such that it is now rarely mentioned in the textbooks and the British government quickly commissioned a further, more wide-ranging report in the following year.

The Lang Report

This working party was chaired by Sir John Lang, Vice Chairman of the Sports Council, and their report was published by the Ministry of Housing and Local Government (1969). The working party consisted of representatives of the Football Associations and Leagues, Home Office, police forces, Scottish Office and representatives of football players and managers – no psychiatrists, sociologists or academics at all. The group was left to define its own terms of reference and, not surprisingly given its composition, was solely concerned with actual events at football matches. Wider social issues were not considered and even journeys to and from football grounds were excluded from the terms of reference.

The working party made a total of 23 recommendations, of which three were given special emphasis. First, that there should be maximum co-operation between a football club and the police. Secondly, that there should be absolute acceptance by everybody of the decisions of the referee. And, thirdly, that seats should be provided in place of standing accommodation. In dealing with offenders at football matches it was recommended that 'a form of punishment for spectators who misbehave themselves, involving the necessity of such offenders having to report on subsequent match days at a place and time away from the ground, should be strongly supported'. It was also felt that 'it is desirable that the punishment of convicted offenders should match the seriousness of the offence'.

These same, somewhat anodyne, conclusions presaged the conclusions of numerous other reports which have stemmed from quasi-governmental investigations in the intervening years. What was remarkable about the Lang Report was that it was the first to seek solutions to a problem which, at that time, had not been clearly defined – even less understood. There were no data to indicate the scale of the problem and even basic statistics concerning arrests and injuries were absent from the report.

No distinction was made between criminal behaviour and simple misbehaviour and many people commented on examples of received opinion being reworked to give the appearance of hard facts. We find, for example, the statement 'There can be no doubt that the consumption of alcohol is an important factor in crowd misbehaviour' without any evidence being presented concerning the frequency or extent of drinking behaviour amongst football fans.

Ian Taylor

The critics of both the Harrington and Lang Reports were themselves developing alternative theoretical perspectives on football hooliganism, with Ian Taylor being amongst the first to publish sociological analyses (see Taylor 1971a, 1971b, etc.). From a Marxist standpoint he argued that the emergence of football hooliganism reflected the changing nature of the sport itself and, in particular, the changing role of the local club as a working-class, neighbourhood institution. As professional football became increasingly organized after the Second World War, the role of the local club became less part of the community and more a commercial sports arena aimed at paying spectators.

This process of embourgeoisement of football, Taylor argued, was part of a more general 'collapse' of the traditional working-class weekend, which previously incorporated traditional leisure pursuits developed in the latter part of the nineteenth century. These included not only football but brass bands, whippet racing and even archery. The violence on the terraces, therefore, could be seen as an attempt by disaffected working-class adolescents to re-establish the traditional weekend, with its distinctly manly, tribal features.

Throughout Taylor's writings in the early 1970s there is great emphasis on the erosion of democracy in football clubs. Not only were clubs now increasingly run by wealthy businessmen, the increase in players' wages and their promotion to the status of superstars made them remote from the local communities which supported their teams. This sense of alienation experienced by fans was further exacerbated, according to Taylor, by a more general alienation of fractions of the working-class which resulted from changes in the labour market and the decomposition of many working-class communities. Violence erupted at football matches, therefore, partly because of the decline of working-class traditional values and, specifically, as an attempt to retrieve control over the game from a nouveau-riche elite.

Taylor's analysis of the phenomenon was, and still remains, rather speculative. There is certainly evidence from 1980 onwards to show that a number of those involved in violence at football matches do not come from stereotyped working-class backgrounds but from the recently expanding middle-class sectors. The implied underlying motivation of football hooliganism has also been absent from the accounts of football fans themselves, few seeing themselves as part of a proletarian vanguard seeking to erase the inequalities so evident in their national sport. But Taylor's historical perspective, and his emphasis on the need to consider the impact of dramatic changes in the ordinary lives of working-class adolescents, provides a reasonable context for the more narrowly focused approaches which were to follow. His concern with the 'democratization' of football also continues to be relevant in discussions about how the problems of football violence can be reduced and, in particular, the role that clubs themselves can play in fostering a more responsible and orderly following. Taylor himself, however, is pessimistic about the impact that such arguments may have:

> Calls for the 'democratization' of football clubs ... have not met with an active response from professional football clubs as a whole, despite token schemes for participation of youngsters in club training and related activities. Professional football is part of the local economy and, perhaps more importantly, local civic power: and is no easier a target for real democratisation than the political economy and structure of power at the level of the state itself (1982b: 169).

Subculture theories

Approaches to understanding football fan behaviour in terms of subcultural styles were promoted principally by sociologists at the Centre for Contemporary Cultural Studies at Birmingham University. John Clarke and Stuart Hall, in particular, argued that specific subcultural styles enabled young working-class people, and males in particular, to resolve essential conflicts in their lives – specifically those of subordination to adults and the subordination implicit in being a member of the working-class itself (see Clarke 1973, 1978; Hall *et al.* 1978). Postwar subcultures, such as those of the teddy boys, mods and rockers, skinheads and, in later years, glamrock, punk, house, etc., have all been examples of these symbolic attempts to resolve structural and material problems.

For Clarke and his colleagues, the style of the skinheads – amongst the earliest exponents of football hooliganism in Britain – reflected almost a parody of working-class traditions, with its emphasis on workmen's jeans and boots and on self-reliance, toughness and racism. It was, according to Clarke, an attempt at the 'magical recovery of community' through adherence to a highly symbolic style and pattern of behaviour – which included violence. Other subcultures, such as the mods, adopted a very different style as a means of resolving their collective social identity – the carefully manicured and smart appearance associated with upward mobility and escape from the working-class values so explicitly championed by the Skinheads.

There is little in Clarke's work at this level, however, to enable us to understand why some individuals choose one particular 'solution' rather than another. To account for the skinheads, and subsequently for football hooligans, he was forced to include a sociopolitical analysis not dissimilar to that presented by Ian Taylor, with emphasis on working-class alienation from an increasingly commercial game. For Clarke, however, whilst new generations of working-class youth had inherited the traditional ties to football, and the pattern of 'supportership' characteristic of a previous generation, they had failed to inherit the tacit social controls which went with that behaviour. Violence became their way of doing what their fathers had done – demonstrating loyalty and commitment to their local team and all it stood for. The problems arose from inter-generational changes reflecting much wider shifts in the class structure of British and, in particular, English society.

As football increasingly became a focus for subculture style and activity, the patterns of behaviour on the terraces came to mirror, in many ways, aspects of the game itself:

> Their own collective organisation and activities have created a form of analogy with the match itself. But in their case, it becomes a contest which takes place not on the fields but on the terraces. They have created a parallel between the physical challenge and combat on the field in their own forms of challenge and combat between the opposing ends. Thus, while the points are being won or lost on the field, territory is won or lost on the terraces. The 'ends' away record (how good it is at taking territory where the home supporters usually stand) is as important, if not more, than their team's away record. Similarly the chants, slogans and songs demonstrate support for the team and involve an effort to intervene in the game itself, by lifting and encouraging their team, and putting off the opposition … The violence between the sets of fans is part of this participation in the game – part of the extension of the game on the field to include the terraces too (Clarke 1978: 54).

This emphasis by Clarke on the close relationship between football fans and their teams was important. There were many commentators at the time who claimed that violence at football games was caused principally by 'infiltrators' – by young men who were not true supporters at all but who were simply using the football grounds as a convenient arena for their aggressive lifestyles. Clarke's attention to some of the details of football fan behaviour and talk also represented a significant step forward from the more speculative theorizing of Ian Taylor. In this sense he provided a stepping stone between broad sociological perspectives, more fine-grained analyses, conducted by, amongst others, one of the present authors (Peter Marsh) and what became know as the 'Oxford School' or 'Ethogenic approach' (see below).

Media amplification

The treatment of football hooliganism in the media became a subject of inquiry in mid-1970s, following the work by Stan Cohen (1971) and others on the 'distortion' of the behaviour of the mods and rockers and other youth groups. Stuart Hall and his colleagues noted that despite all the press coverage given to football hooliganism, relatively few people in Britain had any direct experience of the phenomenon. The media, therefore, rather than factual evidence, directly guided public concern about football hooliganism. It constructed impressions of 'thuggery', 'riots' and 'chaos', provided definitions of why such acts constituted a major social problem and provided 'quasi-explanations' of the patterns of behaviour. Much of the public debate about hooliganism was conducted in the absence of any other perspective or source of evidence.

Hall was at pains to stress that he did not see the press as causing football hooliganism in any direct sense: However:

> I do think that there is a major problem about the way the press has selected, presented and defined football hooliganism over the years … I don't think that the problem of hooliganism would all go away if only the press would keep its collective mouth shut or look the other way. I do however … believe that the phenomenon know as 'football hooliganism' is not the simple 'SAVAGES! ANIMALS!' story that has substantially been presented by the press (Hall 1978).

Hall went on to argue that not only was the press reporting of this kind a problem in its own right, it also had the effect of increasing the problem it set out to remedy, principally by suppressing the true nature of the problem. In line with deviancy amplification theory, he argued that distortions of this kind, in generating inappropriate societal reactions to, initially, quite minor forms of deviance, effectively increase the scale of the problem. Reactions by fans to the increased controls upon their behaviour, such as caging and segregation, often produced scenes far worse than those prior to such attempts at control. Fans also started to act out some of the things that the press had accused them of doing. Manchester United fans, for example, used the chant 'We are the famous hooligans, read all about us!' on entry into towns where away-games were to be played. Other fans complained that since they had been treated as animals they may as well act like them, and bloody violence was often the result.

The 'moral panics' generated by the media are discussed more fully in Chapter 9. We should note here, however, that almost all research and theoretical approaches to football hooliganism have been obliged to take note of the very significant impact of media reporting and its clear effect on patterns of behaviour on the terraces.

Ethogenic approach

In contrast to sociological theories, with their heavy emphasis on class and macro-political changes, co-author Peter Marsh's work focused much more directly on observed behaviour and on the accounts provided by fans themselves. The theoretical background to the work stemmed from Harré and Secord (1972) and the rather grandly labelled 'ethogenic approach' or 'new paradigm' in social psychology. This approach, for all its philosophical 'window dressing' was, in essence, very simple. Instead of conducting laboratory experiments and treating people as 'subjects' of empirical inquiry, to understand their behaviour, one should simply ask them. Thus, for three years, Marsh spent his time at football matches, on trains and buses full of football fans travelling to away-games and in the pubs and other arenas where supporters spent the remainder of their leisure time. Whilst there were some concessions to empirical methodology in the research, the principal aim was, first, to obtain an 'insider's' view of football hooliganism and, secondly, to use this to establish an explanatory model.

On the basis of this work, Marsh concluded that much of what passed for violent mayhem was, in fact, highly ritualized behaviour which was far less injurious, in physical terms, than it might seem. He suggested that the apparent disorder was, in fact, highly orderly, and social action on the terraces was guided and constrained by tacit social rules. These enabled the display of 'manly' virtues but, through ritualizing aggression, enabled the 'game' to be played in relative safety. Being a 'football hooligan' enabled young males, with little prospects of success in school or work, to achieve a sense of personal worth and identity through recognition from their peers. The football terraces provided, in his terms, for an alternative career structure – one in which success and promotion were attainable. Whilst violence, in the sense of causing physical injury, was part of the route to success, it was an infrequent activity. There was far more talk about violence than actual fighting (see Marsh 1978a, 1978b; Marsh and Harré 1978; Marsh *et al.* 1978, etc.).

Marsh was accused of saying that football hooliganism was harmless and of 'whitewashing' the unacceptable behaviour of football fans. This, in turn, provoked widespread outrage in the media and even in some academic circles. The empirical evidence, however, clearly indicated that the scale of football violence in the 1970s had been seriously over-estimated. Relying on statistics from police forces, health workers and official government reports, together with direct observation at football grounds, Marsh claimed that there was about as much violence at football games as one would expect, given the characteristics of the population who attended matches. If there was no violence, he argued, that would be truly remarkable – so much so that it would motivate dozens of research projects to explain this oasis of passivity in an otherwise moderately violent society.

The methodology employed in Marsh's study has been, with some justification, criticized by more traditional social psychologists. The lack of overt concern with such issues as social class has also been the subject of negative review by many sociologists, especially Williams *et al.* from the 'Leicester School' (see below). Marsh was also obliged to revise some of his conclusions in the light of more lethal football violence which occurred in the 1980s. He continues to argue, however, that football hooliganism shifted, in part, from a ritual to a more dangerous pattern of behaviour principally because of the inappropriate measures which were introduced to combat the problem and because of the extensive media distortion of true events at football matches.

The Leicester School

The work of Taylor, Clarke, Hall, Marsh, etc., constituted in the late 1970s what John Williams and his colleagues at Leicester University have called an 'orthodoxy' of approaches to football hooliganism. Whilst these perspectives differed considerably from each other, they were the ones which were most frequently referred to in debates on fan behaviour. The 'Leicester School' sought to change this state of affairs by introducing what they claimed was a more powerful explanation of hooliganism based on the sociology of Norbert Elias and his emphasis on the 'civilization process' (see Williams *et al.* 1984; Dunning *et al.* 1988; Murphy *et al.* 1990, etc.).

This approach, most usually referred to as 'figurational' sociology, is difficult to summarize briefly. One of its major assumptions, however, is that throughout recent history public expectations of a more 'civilized' world, and more civilized behaviour, have gradually 'percolated' through the social classes in Europe. Such values, however, have not fully penetrated areas of the lower working-class – what Dunning and his colleagues refer to as the 'rough' working-class. Social behaviour in this section of society is largely mediated by subcultural values of masculinity and aggression. In order to account for contemporary football violence, therefore, we need to pay attention to the structural aspects of this section of society and the traditional relationship between members of this strata and the game itself:

> A useful way of expressing it would be to say that such sections of lower-working-class communities are characterised by a 'positive feedback cycle' which tends to encourage the resort to aggression in many areas of social life, especially on the part of males ... In fact, along with gambling, street 'smartness', an exploitative form of sex and heavy drinking – the capacity to consume alcohol in large quantities is another highly valued attribute among males from the 'rougher' sections of the working-class – fighting is one of the few sources of excitement, meaning and status available to males from this section of society and accorded a degree of social toleration. That is because they are typically denied status, meaning and gratification in the educational and occupational spheres, the major sources of identity, meaning and status available to men from the middle classes (Williams *et al.* 1984).

The approach of the Leicester School, with its emphasis on the dynamics of the lower working-class, has much in common with the perspectives taken by Taylor and Clarke. The issue of sources of meaning and identity amongst working-class youth had also been treated explicitly by Marsh. In the work of Dunning *et al.* there were, however, some subtle differences. On the issue of class the focus was not on the relative deprivations of the lower working-class, with violence being a consequence of alienation and embitterment, but on specific subcultural properties which provide a legitimation of violent behaviour.

The extent to which such differences of emphasis constituted a radically new approach, however, is the subject of some doubt. Perhaps, for this reason, and in order more fully to assert its own identity, the Leicester School has been renowned for the amount of time and effort that it has devoted to criticizing the work of other social scientists in the field. It is difficult to find a single author outside this group who has escaped their wrath at one time or another.

Setting aside the internecine squabble in this area of academia, the Leicester group, with substantial funding from the Football Trust, has conducted the bulk of field research on British football fans in recent years, both in the UK and abroad, and is largely responsible for bringing together research workers in other European countries. This voluminous output has resulted in more being known about the behaviour of British football hooligans than any other 'deviant' group in history.

The implications and utility of all of this research, however, are unclear. The applicability of the work to problems in other European countries, which lack the highly specific social class structures found in England, is also limited. There is further doubt about some of the research methods employed, particularly in the early years of the Leicester Centre. Much of the evidence provided by Williams and his colleagues comes from participant observation studies. The book *Hooligans Abroad* (Williams *et al.* 1984), for example, was based on three such studies and much of it is impressionistic and anecdotal.

In the book's Preface we are assured that John Williams 'is young enough and sufficiently "street-wise" and interested in football to pass himself off as an "ordinary" English football fan'. Such assertions, however, vouch little for scientific rigour and credibility. Whilst Williams is quick to challenge the results of other field studies on the basis that the authors had been talking to the 'wrong people', the justification of his own 'sampling' is weak and based, inevitably, on the practicalities of conducting this kind of research – you spend time with 'subjects' to whom you have access.

Williams' concern with drinking behaviour amongst working-class football fans, whilst implicit in the theoretical background, has become more prominent in recent years. He clearly sees alcohol as being an 'aggravating' factor in much of football violence, even though he stops short of suggesting causal connections (see Chapter 10). It is also the case that Williams later parted company from his colleagues Dunning and Murphy over the relevance of the 'figurational' approach, particularly in the light of growing research on football violence in other European countries. In 1991, he argued, for example:

> the high level of generality at which the theory operates, its apparently universalistic applicability, and the sometimes fractious and defensive relationships between 'Eliasians' and their critics, also give the theory an aura of 'irrefutability' and arguably leads, in the case of violence at football, to the underplaying of important national and cultural differences in patterns and forms of hooliganism (Williams 1991b: 177).

In reply to this philosophical 'desertion' by Williams, Eric Dunning – perhaps the most senior member of the Leicester School – comments testily: 'I shall try to show in detail why John Williams' arguments, along with those of authors who have argued along similar lines, are wrong' (1994, p. 128).

In subsequent years, Williams, together with other members of the Sir Norman Chester (Leicester) Centre for Football Research, turned his attention to developing and evaluating various attempts to control the behaviour of football fans, whilst not losing sight of the need to tackle the more fundamental roots of football violence. The group also became increasingly involved in Europe-wide initiatives. Dunning meanwhile formed his own more general 'Centre for Research into Sport and Society'. From 2004, however, Williams and Dunning were reunited when their centres were merged back into a new 'Centre for the Sociology of Sport'.

Ethnographic approaches

Detailed ethnographic work has been conducted by Gary Armstrong, focusing principally on groups of Sheffield United supporters (see Armstrong and Harris 1991; Armstrong 1998). As we have come to expect from writers in this field, Armstrong is highly critical of both the 'structural-Marxist' approaches of Taylor, Hall, etc., and the 'figurational' school of Dunning, Williams, etc. His view was, first, that violence was not a central activity for football fans:

> it is asserted here that the hooligans among Sheffield United fans were not particularly violent people; that there was amongst them no core of men from a violent, deprived sub-culture; that much of the hostility to football hooliganism in Sheffield was based on exaggerated fears led by the media and the police ... we shall argue that the evidence provided by participant observation shows clearly that the basic data regarding football hooliganism is significantly different from that previously assumed and, therefore, much theorizing on the subject has been misapplied effort (Armstrong and Harris 1991).

This rather grand assertion might have had more credibility had the study not been concerned solely with a relatively small group of fans (40–50) in one town in northern England. There are also some striking inconsistencies in their reporting of the evidence. In contrast to the assertion that Sheffield fans were not particularly violent, Armstrong and Harris (1991) go on to say that:

> The menace of Sheffield football hooligans is not a fiction concocted by the police ... The violence, when it occurs, is real and cannot be explained away, as Marsh tried to do, as mere ritualized aggression which would seldom be really violent if only the group's control of events was not thwarted by the intervention of the authorities.

Despite the inherent weaknesses in this study, Armstrong did at least demonstrate that not all football hooligans were from what Dunning and Williams refer to as the 'rough' working-class. But this is a fairly obvious point made by many other field researchers and even Dunning himself. Rather naively, Armstrong comments that many of the fans in his study were 'intelligent, amusing and often good company' – something which he appears to view implicitly as being inconsistent with a 'tough' working-class background. Whilst he offers little in the way of empirical data himself, he criticizes the reliability of statistics offered by other researchers, including Dunning. He notes that in one survey by the Leicester School of the social class composition of West Ham's 'Inter City Firm', the occupations of two of the members were listed as being 'bank manager' and 'insurance underwriter' – occupations about which he is, quite reasonably, sceptical. An objection to such 'facts' masquerading as empirical data is well founded. What is less acceptable, however, is the rejection of large-scale empirical methodologies in favour of only semi-structured qualitative and ethnographic methods. The data yielded by small-scale ethnographies are localized and, by necessity, selective. Whilst Armstrong accepts this point he argues that, given sufficient detail, such data provide the basis for objective testing. There is little in his published work, however, which is sufficiently detailed or clear, apart from the fact that many of his informants were middle-class types, to provide any basis for such testing.

Armstrong has also turned his attention to examination of police surveillance of football fans and official information-gathering procedures (Armstrong and Hobbs 1994). Here he notes that one by-product of football hooliganism has been the legitimation of covert tactics by the British police and the introduction of surveillance tactics which previously might have aroused concerns about infringement of civil liberties. This issue is dealt with in Part IV.

In contrast to the work of Armstrong, Richard Giulianotti's studies on Scottish fans (1991, 1995a, etc.) are far more theory based and substantially more detailed. His research with Scottish football fans, at home and in other countries such as Sweden, has highlighted the inapplicability of much of the research conducted in England, and the theoretical perspectives associated with it. Rather than football violence stemming from social structural factors, Giulianotti argues that Scottish football fan behaviour derives from specific cultural and historical forces. This, in turn, distinguishes the 'friendly' Scottish fans quite sharply from their English 'hooligan' peers. In one paper he notes the fact that 5,000 fans, known as the Tartan Army, won the UEFA 'Fair Play' award in 1992 for their friendly and sporting conduct (Giulianotti 1995a). This appeared to represent a distinct cultural change in the activities of Scottish fans since their pitch invasion after a match against England at Wembley in 1977 and the removal of the goalposts.

Whilst much of Giulianotti's work is in the form of traditional ethnography, much emphasis is placed on a conceptual framework provided by Foucault and concern for the treatment of 'discourse'. The work of the sociologist Erving Goffman, with its emphasis on astute observation and understanding, also provides a methodological framework for Giulianotti. Armed with this sometimes obfuscating intellectual kit, and having conducted fieldwork studies with Scottish fans in Italy and Sweden, he provides an analysis of the changes in Scottish fan temperament over the past two decades.

Prior to 1980 Scottish fans were seen as exemplars of the heavy-drinking, macho style of hooligans whose pitched battles were amongst the bloodiest in Britain. Alcohol, rather than divisive social issues, was generally viewed by the authorities and some social scientists as being the primary ingredient for transforming relatively ordinary supporters into mindless thugs. Many of these fans also relied for part of their identity on being 'harder' than the English fans, and clashes between the two groups were common. This image of Scottish fans – or 'sub-discourse' in Giulianotti's terms – detracted from more meaningful examination of the roots of hooligan behaviour, to be found partly in religious sectarianism.

After 1980 a distinct change occurred – a new sub-discourse. Increasingly, Scottish fans sought to distance themselves from the 'British hooligan' label and particularly from the unruly behaviour of English fans abroad. Having been prevented from playing their biennial matches against England at Wembley, following the small problem with the demolition of the goalposts, they constructed a quite novel way of maintaining a sense of dominance over them:

> Spurred on by the popular stereotypification of the antithetical English fan as instrumental soccer hooligan, and the international debate on subsequently penalizing English soccer which tended to conflate English and British fans, Scottish fans coated themselves, with the brush of the authorities and the media, in a friendly and internationalist patina ... (Giulianotti 1995a).

We have already criticized Giulianotti for his style of writing, but what he is saying here, in essence, is that the Scottish fans sought to beat their historical English foes by being nice! In this they certainly succeeded, partly aided by a distinctly anti-English tone in many Scottish newspapers and the now positive line adopted with respect to their own fans. Finding considerable satisfaction in this new image, the role of heavy drinking amongst Scottish fans now took on a new twist. Alcohol consumption did not decline with the rise of the 'friendly' image. Rather, the meaning of drinking was radically transformed. Instead of it being a precursor of violence it was held to predispose friendly interaction and sociability, particularly towards strangers abroad, but possibly with the exception of the English.

We deal with this issue in more detail in Chapter 10. We should note here, however, that Giulianotti's insightful work has provided evidence for the mutability of football hooligan behaviour over a relatively short period of time. The overt, antagonistic reporting of English fans in the Scottish press, which sponsored much of the change in the conduct of the Tartan Army, remains a problem which will, eventually, need to be resolved, and there have been signs that the press have turned their attention to other, local moral panics, such as the use of ecstasy, etc.

Ethnographic work on the behaviour of Scottish fans has also been conducted by Moorhouse, who questions the applicability of 'English' theoretical perspectives to problems in Scotland (for example, see Moorhouse 1991a, 1991b). His review of such perspectives, however, was limited to the approaches of Ian Taylor and Eric Dunning, with reference to John Clarke. Moorhouse highlights the differences between England and Scotland in terms of the relationship between fans and their clubs. The large supporters clubs and associations in Scotland, particularly in the case of Glasgow Celtic and Rangers, enable a much stronger sense of involvement and, in some ways, are more akin to the situation in prewar Britain. The relevance of Taylor's concern with the disenfranchisement of fans is, therefore, very limited in Scotland.

Moorhouse also questions media reporting of Scottish fan behaviour, claiming that many of the events in which these supporters were involved had been distorted and sensationalized. Rather than seeing a dramatic change in the activities of these fans after 1980 he suggests that 'the behaviour of Scottish fans crossing the border does not appear to have altered that much over, say, ninety years'. He goes further to assert that the previous patterns of behaviour which gave rise to so much concern largely consisted of minor rowdyism and 'bad manners'. It was the 'moral panic' about their conduct which gave rise to distorted perceptions and fears.

Further study

Apart from our own analysis in this and the preceding chapter, the various discourses on football hooliganism have been extensively reviewed and variously criticized by a good number of academic commentators. You may therefore wish to read alternative reviews of the literature, which you will find in Canter *et al.* (1989), Hobbs and Robins (1991), Williams (1991a) and Giulianotti (1994a).

Chapter summary

The major research and theoretical perspectives on football hooliganism derive mainly from British work conducted since the late 1960s. The principal sociological, psychological and anthropological approaches have been critically reviewed – including those of Ian Taylor, John Clarke and Stuart Hall; Peter Marsh; John Williams and his Leicester colleagues, Eric Dunning and Patrick Murphy; Gary Armstrong, Richard Giulianotti, etc.

There are deep divisions within social science circles concerning explanations of football hooliganism, with often vitriolic debate beween Marxist sociologists, so-called 'figurationalists', social psychologists and more empirically oriented researchers. This atmosphere has hindered the emergence of truly multidisciplinary perspectives.

It is generally agreed that British football hooliganism has probably been over-researched. Despite a general decline in violence at British football matches, the phenomenon has attracted a disproportionate amount of research activity.

8. Theoretical approaches from Europe and beyond

Introduction

We have been concerned so far in Part III with British theoretical and research perspectives. This is not due to simple chauvinism on our part but to the fact that the vast bulk of the literature has been generated by British authors. Even research elsewhere in Europe has tended to draw on work in this country for its theoretical and, in some cases, methodological direction. Increasingly, however, nationally distinctive approaches to the subject have developed, particularly in Italy, Holland and Germany.

The cross-national differences in patterns of football hooliganism were dealt with in Chapters 4 and 5. In this chapter we review some of the major approaches which have been taken in continental Europe to understanding the origins of these collective behaviours. We also look at the emergence of the 'fault-line' hypothesis proposed by Eric Dunning and which suggests a way of moving towards an understanding of football hooliganism as a global phenomenon.

Italy

Work by Italian social scientists on the 'tifosi' of Italian 'calcio' has developed since the early 1990s, led by the sociologists Alessandro dal Lago of Milan University and Antonio Roversi of Modena University and by the social psychologist Alessandro Salvini from Padova. Their approaches to the phenomenon, however, are quite different and stem from quite different theoretical backgrounds.

Dal Lago (1990) views football fan behaviour as essentially ritualistic and much of his approach stems directly from the work of Peter Marsh and his colleagues in England. He hypothesizes three main factors which underlie the expressive behaviour of football fan groups. First, football allows for identification by fans with a specific set of symbols and linguistic terms. These enable and encourage the division of the social world, and other supporters or 'tifosi' in particular, into 'friends' and 'enemies'.

Dal Lago's second, rather unremarkable, point is that the football match in Italy is not simply a meeting between the two teams. For the fans it is an opportunity for an 'amico/nemico' ritual confrontation. Such rituals can, in specific and foreseeable circumstances, be transformed into physical clashes. Here, like Marsh (1978a), he recognizes historical parallels with the role played by the hippodromes in Ancient Rome and Byzantium, which were hosts to the tightly knit groups of Circus Factions – the supporters of the chariot racing teams (see Cameron 1976). Such comparisons, however, dal Lago sees as irrelevant and possibly misleading. He advises against presuming a continuity in reality on the basis of superficial similarities with historical groups and patterns of behaviour.

Finally, dal Lago sees the stadium in which football is played as being much more than a physical environment. For fans it is the symbolic stage on which the ritual of friend/enemy is enacted. From about 1980, since when the ultras have occupied specific territories within the stadiums, there have been two types of performance at football matches, with the ultras' ritual constituting a play within a play.

Whilst dal Lago emphasizes that much of the social behaviour of the ultras within the stadiums is ritualized to the extent that symbolic gestures, insults and chants substitute for physical aggression, there are circumstances in which 'real' fights can occur. This depends on two factors: first, a 'storico', or tradition of rivalry between the two groups; and, secondly, on situational factors, such as the development of the other 'play', the football game itself. Contrasting football fans with medieval knights, he argues that the 'wars' in which they engage cannot be too violent or too bloody. Like the knights, the fans share a common code of 'chivalry'. They use the same medium of chants and songs to express their hostilities, rather than weapons or fists, simply changing the words to proclaim their own identity, and the culture of 'fighting' which they share concerns essentially symbolic behaviour. Dal Lago admits, however, that when 'fighting' takes place outside the stadiums it can more readily result in 'real' violence:

> In order to defeat the enemies [outside the ground] ultra groups try to adopt urban guerilla tactics (particularly setting ambushes near to stations and involving the police). But the violence is restricted to the throwing of stones and to sudden attacks. Usually every group is satisfied by the escape of the enemies from the sacred territory and by a short resistance against the police (dal Lago and de Biasi 1994: 86).

Antonio Roversi sees the violence of the ultras as being much less ritualized (and therefore relatively non-injurious) than does dal Lago. He argues that hooligan violence is related to, and is a direct continuation of, fighting between older supporters. He refers, for example, to the rivalry between Bologna and Fiorentina and quotes an old Bologna fan as saying, 'The Tuscans are terrible. It is in their blood. We used to turn up in a friendly mood, not wanting to say anything. But we always had to fight' (1991).

For Roversi, contemporary ultras simply take as their adversaries the previous rivals of their fathers and continue long-standing traditions of feuding and, on occasions, violent encounter. The Bolognesi continue to hate the Toscani in just the same way as their predecessors, and football provides an arena for the expression of these historical enmities. The new ultras now use a more 'colourful' and 'lively' style of expression – not only of rivalry but of passion for the game itself.

A second aspect stressed by Roversi is the 'Bedouin syndrome'. New alliances, new 'twinnings' and new hostilities started to develop between ultras of a number of cities. These alliances and enmities overlapped with political ideologies. Extreme right- and left-wing political stances were an important element of in-group cohesion and out-group hostility: 'it is certainly the case that political extremism was definitely a glamorous example for the young hooligans, not only because its symbolism coincided with the hard line image they wanted to create for themselves, but also because the organizational and behavioural model fitted their aims like a glove' (Roversi 1991). Groups which Roversi sees as adopting such political extremism include the left-wing Bologna, Milano, Torino and Roma ultras, with Lazio, Inter, Verona and Ascoli adopting neo-Nazi right-wing styles.

Finally, Roversi concludes that although ultras may exaggerate their active participation in violence at football matches for the purposes of presenting a hard, tough image; the violence in which they participate is not just rhetorical. Experience of fights and clashes with rival fans forms, in his terms, a common heritage of many young ultras and is a more general part of an experience of violence expressed outside the football grounds as well.

The principal difference between Roversi and dal Lago seems to be not so much about whether the social activities of Italian fans in and around football stadiums forms a ritual, in the sense that it relies on symbols and implicit social rules, but the extent to which such a framework minimizes physical injury. Roversi has the gloomier view in this context:

The work of Alessandro Salvini is very wide in terms of theoretical and empirical approaches. His starting point for work on football fans in Italy draws extensively from the work of Marsh *et al.* but is placed in a more strictly psychological context:

After taking into consideration the aggressive behaviour of the violent supporters ... the model suggested by Marsh and Harré is considered appropriate. It considers the deviating fanaticism like a particular ritual manifestation of symbolic aggressiveness. The observation and empirical research carried out by the authors [in Italy] arrive at similar conclusions, though giving particular importance to the lowering of the responsibility level and the self-achievement process to be found in this type of fanatic (Salvino *et al.* 1988).

In other work Salvini (1988) examines the limitations of the ritual model and, in particular, the circumstances under which 'de-ritualization' can occur – i.e. the change from largely symbolic to more seriously injurious violence. Salvini's theoretical model to explain more general aspects of football fan aggression is based on cognitive social learning theory, which he uses to explain the phenomena of 'dominance and aggression', 'self-identity and group affiliation' and acceptance of group norms with the ultras. He also examines the role of situational variables and the impact these have on transforming ritual behaviours.

His interview and questionnaire studies in Italy have focused on the beliefs and attitudes of 'moderate' 'tifosi' and the fans most likely to be classed as ultras. The results of these are complex but, in brief, it is clear that ultras reject some of the common assumptions made in Italy about the origins of hooliganism. They fail, for example, to see the problems in the stadiums as being the result of a new kind of 'terrorism' or infiltration by gangs of delinquents. Equally, they dismiss simplistic theories about the decline in family and educational values. They do agree, however, that violence at football matches is reflective of increased violence throughout Italian society and that the roots of the problem do not lie with the game or even its supporters.

Less substantial psychological research in Italy has been conducted by Bruna Zani (see Zani and Kirchler 1991), who rejects sociological analyses in favour of empirical study of the immediate precipitating factors in football violence. On the basis of interview and questionnaire data she concludes that participation in violence depends on a high level of identification with the football club, low educational attainment, the level of similarity with other supporters, etc: ' these results suggest a rather "classic" picture of the violent fans in the stadium: those who participate in disturbances are, in general, young, unemployed, poorly educated people who are members of a fanatic club and attribute responsibility for their behaviour to external rather than internal factors.'

Zani and Kirchler, unlike some sociologists, see violence at football matches as quite independent of what happens on the pitch. In this sense they side with dal Lago:

> There may actually be two matches going on in the football stadium:
> the first match concerns the football teams on the pitch, the second
> involves fanatic fans who are not interested in football as such, but
> in the opportunities that football offers to meet with club-mates and
> to give vent to the emotions and energies in battles with others.
> (Zani and Kirchler 1991).

The psychologist Christine Fontana, using the same data as those of
Zani and Kirchler above, outlines additional explanations of the violence
in football stadiums offered by fans themselves. Most fans see football
violence as being closely linked to violence in society and a third of all
fans attribute hooliganism to lack of parental education. Fontana also
notes the fans' view that, contrary to the view of Zani, there are direct
links between violence at matches and the game itself. Bad decisions by
referees, for example, can increase tension amongst fans which can lead
to aggression.

Germany

Work in Germany has, in the main, been more solution oriented than
theoretical. Since the 1980s, for example, the major effort has been invested
in the development of special 'fan projects' and other interventions aimed
at reducing the problems (see Chapter 14). Hahn (1987), however, uses
a combination of subcultural and identity-seeking approaches to explain
the emergence and persistence of football violence in Germany. He argues
that it has become increasingly difficult for young Germans to realize
their personal identity. The development of subcultures – many of them
with extreme right-wing overtones – allows them to 'find solidarity and
to test strategies helping them to cope with life'.

In many of these of these subcultures the aim is to shock through
provocative actions – a protest against conventions, norms, regulations
and even aesthetic standards. In this context football offers a convenient,
visible platform for such intentional behaviour, specifically because it
enables confrontations with perceived rivals – not only opposing fans but
also the police. Thus, according to Hahn (1987), attempts by the police
to control the behaviour of fans are often counter-productive since they
increase the significance of the 'game' for the fans: 'The stadium and its
environment become more and more interesting for the youth, who feel
incited to enlarge their elbowroom and to defend it in an aggressive way.
Violent non-regulated behaviour increases, which is more and more often
aimed at stewards, opposing fans and objects'.

Work by Gunter Pilz (1996) takes a similar line but uses a rather different
theoretical framework. On the basis of interview data he concludes that

football violence is a 'cry for help' by many young people who have failed to find meaning in mainstream society and have little hope for the future. What he sees as the 'bizarre' violence of football fans is an indication of the underlying forms of inequalities, forms of coercion and 'exaggerated' discipline in German society. Like Hahn, Pilz argues against football hooliganism being treated as purely a 'law and order' problem. His view is that repressive as well as socio-pedagogical measures do not solve the problem of the hooligans unless they are embedded in structural measures which effectively improve the everyday lives of young people:

> hooligan behaviour can be interpreted as 'normal' and hooligans as the 'avant-garde' of a new type of identity. As long as there are no real changes at the structural level, the possibilities for reducing violence are limited. Hooliganism seems to be the risk of modernisation, commercialisation and professionalisation of sport and society (Pilz 1996).

Pilz's line of argument is strongly reminiscent of that of Ian Taylor, although more 'liberal' than explicitly Marxist in its elaboration and conclusions.

Most other commentary from social scientists in Germany has focused on the neo-Nazi image of many hooligan groups and on outbreaks of racist activity at football matches. Many claim that this image, fostered very much by the German media, does not accurately reflect the reality of most groups of football fans. In a 1996 interview with the *Guardian* newspaper, for example, Volker Rittner, argues that 'Nazi symbols have a provocative role; they break down taboos. But the point is not political – it is to get noticed and mentioned in Monday's newspapers'.

Neither do many German 'hools' fit the 'disenfranchised, oppressed lumpenproletariat' image of Hahn and Pilz. The Heitmeyers (1988), for example, suggest that there are three types of German football fan: the consumer-oriented fan who picks and chooses which matches to watch; the football-oriented fan who attends every match; and the 'experience-oriented' fans who seeks violent 'adventures' inside and outside the stadiums. Such categories do not divide along social class or political lines.

Whilst the issue of right-wing extremism amongst German fans may have been exaggerated in media reporting, there have been some quite notable groups, such as the now banned Dortmund Borussenfront, whose Nazi symbols and racist chants were more than just 'provocative'. As we saw in Chapter 5, surveys of football fans in Germany have also shown that over 20 per cent sympathize with neo-Nazis and share similar political views.

The Netherlands

Empirical work in the Netherlands has been limited, primarily, to that of van der Brug (1989, 1994), although van de Sande (1987) has provided rather more speculative analyses based on van der Brug's data. Much of van der Brug's research has been on the social composition and demographic features of various groups of Dutch fans. He does, however, offer some insights into the cause of hooliganism in Holland.

First he challenges Veugelers (1981) for assuming that the rise of Dutch hooliganism was predicated on similar social and class factors that Ian Taylor saw as the root of the English problem. According to van der Brug (1994), both the style of play and the roots of fan behaviour are quite different in the two countries:

> Veugelers overlooks the differences between the two national football cultures. English soccer still has … a number of characteristics that … are closely linked to male working-class values: rather uncomplicated, attacking football on the pitch. Proportionally, there is a lot of standing room off the pitch. Unlike continental football, English football is characterised by 'man-to-man combat' and physical struggle. Moreover, in Holland the gap between working-class and middle-class culture is much smaller.

Van der Brug takes a fairly orthodox psychological approach to explaining both the rise of football hooliganism and the increase in certain types of crime, such as vandalism, in Holland. The two key factors, which he claims account for 60 per cent of the variation in hooliganism, are absence of effective parental control and a 'problematic' school career. The social background of Dutch 'siders', as measured in terms of fathers' occupation, is in line with the normal distribution for that country, unlike the case in England where there is a greater dominance of fans from working-class backgrounds. Van der Brug, however, identifies a clear 'downward mobility' among fans engaged in hooliganism and criminal acts. These tend to have lower educational and occupational levels than their fathers: 'It seems that in Holland there is a relationship between individual downward mobility and participation in football hooliganism, a situation which is quite different from the pattern in Britain, where the explanatory factors are much more collectivistic and highly related to social class' (van der Brug 1994: 180).

A study conducted by Russell and Goldstein (1995) in Holland is one of the few to compare so-called hooligans with 'non-fans' – the aim being to identify the specific psychological features which distinguish between the two. With rather limited sampling (60 fans and 43 non-fans) they found that Utrecht supporters were higher than non-fans in terms of 'psychopathic and anti-social tendencies'. On the basis of this the authors concluded:

> In addition to being impulsive and exhibiting weak behavioural controls, [Dutch football fans] also seek excitement. Action is sought out as a means of avoiding dull, repetitive activities that they generally find boring ... It may be just this element in the syndrome that makes the potential for fan violence at football matches an attractive prospect (Russell and Goldstein 1995: 201).

Russell and Goldstein concede that their study contained major methodological weaknesses, not least the sampling procedures employed. The differences in levels of 'psycopathy' between the two groups, whilst significant, are also relatively small (a mean difference of 1.29). It would be unwise, therefore, to rely too heavily on their conclusions.

Other European research

Research in other European countries has tended to be descriptive and rather atheoretical. The work of Horak in Austria, for example, traces the emergence of football hooliganism in that country without offering too much in the way of explanation for shifts in fan behaviour (see, for example, Horak 1991, 1994). The research by Eichberg (1992) in Denmark is similarly descriptive, but with a rather confusing 'gloss' which includes reference to psychoanalytic concepts and to the issue of matriarchy in Danish society. Material from both these authors is included in the chapters on cross-national differences in football violence (see Part II).

Other *ad hoc* European work has included a Belgian conclusion that the highest risk of disorder is at a match between two teams supported by hard-core hooligans (Vreese 2000); a Spanish study linking skinheads with football hooliganism in Barcelona (Costa *et al.* 1996); and a history of early nineteenth-century football hooliganism in Sweden (Andersson 2001).

Conclusions on European theoretical approaches

We have seen that the bulk of theory and research on football violence has developed within British academic circles. It is clear that whilst many of the perspectives provided by social scientists in the UK are largely compatible with each other, there are major ideological rifts between the various research groups. This 'in-fighting' has delayed the development of a more productive, multidisciplinary approach to the phenomenon. It is also the case that many of the more sociologically oriented approaches to explaining football hooliganism have little utility outside Britain, or even England, because of major differences in national class and social structures.

Some perspectives which are relatively free of class-based analyses (e.g. Marsh, Armstrong, etc.) provide for easier 'translation' to fan groups in other countries. Thus, the ethogenic approach of Marsh and his colleagues has been used as a basis for analysing the behaviour of fans in Italy and for the development of theoretical perspectives in that country by Salvini and dal Lago. It is clear, however, that no Europe-wide explanatory framework has yet been developed. It may be the case, given the distinctive nature of ultras, hools, roligans, etc., that such a framework may be unachievable or inappropriate. The sociological and psychological factors which lie at the root of football violence in, say, Italy may be quite different from those which obtain in Germany or Holland. The football stadium provides a very convenient arena for all kinds of collective behaviour. There is no reason to suppose, therefore, that the young men who use such arenas in different countries are all playing the same game.

Increasingly, research of a purely 'domestic' kind is emerging in Italy, Germany, Holland and elsewhere which does not rely so heavily on British theoretical models. Increasing contact between research groups will enable more genuine cross-cultural perspectives to emerge and for the salience of alleged causal factors to be identified more clearly. The role of alcohol, for example, which is discussed in more detail in Chapter 10, has already been shown to be ambiguous when comparing the behaviour of English and Scottish fans. Its role was also seen as even more culturally dependent when examining the activity of Danish fans.

The degree to which individual personality variables are predictive of football violence in different countries is relatively unexplored. It is unlikely, however, that specific factors common to fan groups throughout Europe will emerge. Again, there is no reason to suppose that the individual motivations and psychological profiles of an Italian 'tifoso' will necessarily be in line with that of the English football hooligan. The variations between the two are likely to be more significant than any revealed commonalities.

Finally, it may well be that relative demise of football hooliganism in the UK, certainly inside the stadium, will be followed by similar changes in continental Europe. There has, after all, been a degree of imitative behaviour on the part of other European fans who themselves acknowledge the English as being the leaders in this particular pattern of behaviour. It could be that despite increased pan-European research on football violence, social scientists will soon discover that there are more serious social issues with which to be concerned in their home countries. Rising levels of youth crime, delinquency, alienation and the spread of right-wing extremism in many European countries may come to be seen as a more significant threat to European social stability than the anti-social behaviour of a relatively small number of highly visible football hooligans.

Towards a world understanding of football hooliganism?

It is clear that some form of disorderly behaviour has occurred in virtually every country in which football is played. Disorder of some kind would appear to be a near-universal and seemingly inevitable accompaniment to the game of football, and is unlikely to be completely eradicated. But we cannot conclude from this that all disorder or violence associated with football is of the same nature, or influenced by the same causal factors, regardless of the form it takes or the culture in which it occurs. Nor can we assume that the same remedies will be equally effective in preventing or reducing football-related disorder in different cultures.

Amongst the academics engaged in the football debate, even the most vociferous and belligerent defenders of a particular explanatory theory have come to admit that universal explanations cannot accommodate all cross-cultural variations. In a moment of modesty, Eric Dunning suggests that, with hindsight, his seminal work *The Roots of Football Hooliganism* (Dunning *et al.* 1988) should have been entitled *The Roots of English Football Hooliganism*. In a significant recent contribution to the debate Dunning argues that:

> It is important to stress that it is unlikely that the phenomenon of football hooliganism will be found always and everywhere to stem from identical social roots. As a basis for further, cross-national research, it is reasonable to hypothesise that that problem is fuelled and contoured by, among other things, what one might call the major 'fault lines' of particular countries (2000: 141).

Dunning illustrates this 'fault-lines' hypothesis with reference to social class and regional inequalities in England and to religious sectarianism in Scotland. Elsewhere in Europe he mentions linguistic subnationalisms in Spain and the Italian rivalries between cities and between the North and the South (see Dunning 2000; Dunning *et al.* 2002). One might disagree with Dunning about the precise nature of the relevant 'fault-lines' in these countries, or perhaps argue that these examples are oversimplified, but the evidence suggests that his central point should be accepted.

Similar tensions are evident between the former East and West in Germany and between the political left and right. Extending this thinking, we might consider race relations and the resurgence of the far right as a major 'fault-line' in France, recalling that perhaps the most serious recent incident there was the abandonment of the France v. Algeria match at the Stade de France in 2001. Further afield, religious communalism is the major flaw in Mauritian society, where terrace violence involving supporters of communal teams – Hindu, Moslem and Creole – increased during the 1990s in parallel with increased communal identities (see Edensor and Augustin 2001).

It is interesting to reflect on the extent to which Dunning's 'fault-line' hypothesis may be applied to England. Thinking back to our discussion of the wider social context in Chapter 3, we may remind ourselves of Lord Bassam's view that:

> English football disorder cannot be removed from its wider social context. In many ways it is a manifestation of a wider social problem of alienated young males demonstrating their frustration in an anti-social and violent way. It occurs in high streets up and down the country every weekend. Mediterranean holiday resorts are equally at risk (Home Office 2001: 15).

If it is right that the current 'fault-line' in English society is anti-social behaviour by alienated young males, then it would seem that Dunning's hypothesis also has merit in the English football hooliganism context.

Chapter summary

Research in other European countries has grown in scale since the early 1980s. The work of German, Dutch and Italian social scientists has been reviewed. Much of this research has taken British theoretical perspectives as a starting point, although more 'local' approaches are now evident in some countries. The increase in work in these countries has led to a more Europe-wide approach to the problems of football violence, with a number of collaborative programmes undertaken. The level of cross-cultural variation in the patterns of behaviour of football fans, however, presents a number of problems for this kind of research. It is suggested that the focus purely on behaviour at football games in Europe may be too limiting. The subject might be better considered in the context of the more general rise in juvenile crime and delinquency in many countries and the emergence of new deviant subcultures.

Looking wider than Europe, Dunning's 'fault-line' hypothesis is reviewed and it is concluded that his central point that football hooliganism is a manifestation of a country's social 'fault-lines' should be accepted.

9. The media and football hooliganism

Introduction

We have looked at some of the issues around media coverage of football hooliganism in several of the previous chapters. But since, in Britain, at least one academic 'school' regards 'media amplification' as one of the principal causal factors in explaining football hooliganism, the topic merits more detailed discussion – hence this chapter.

Football hooliganism can be seen as something of an 'easy target' for the media. With journalists present at every match across the country, the chances of a story being missed are slim. Television cameras also mean that disturbances within stadiums are caught on video. Since the 1960s, in fact, journalists have been sent to football matches to report on crowd behaviour, rather than just on the game (see Murphy *et al.* 1988).

The British tabloid press in particular have an 'enthusiastic' approach to the reporting of soccer violence, with sensationalist headlines such as 'Smash these thugs!', 'Murder on a soccer train!', 'Mindless morons' and 'Savages! Animals!' (see Melnick 1986). Whilst open condemnation of hooligans is the norm across the media, it has been argued that this sensationalist style of reporting presents football violence as far more of a concern than it actually is, elevating it to a major 'social problem'. The problem of press sensationalism was recognized in the *Report on Public Disorder and Sporting Events*, carried out by the Social Science Research Council and the Sports Council (1978). It observed that:

> It must be considered remarkable, given the problems of contemporary Britain, that football hooliganism has received so much attention from the Press. The events are certainly dramatic, and frightening for the bystander, but the outcome in terms of people arrested and convicted, people hurt, or property destroyed is negligible compared with the number of people potentially involved.

Furthermore, some critics argue that media coverage of hooliganism has actually contributed to the problem.

History

Press boxes were first installed at football matches in the 1890s, although the reporting of football matches goes back considerably further than this. The study by Murphy *et al.* (1988) shows that disorder was a regular occurrence at football matches before the First World War, and newspaper reports of trouble were common. However, the style of reporting was a long way away from the coverage which hooliganism receives today. Most reports before the First World War were made in a restrained fashion. Little social comment was made and the articles were small and factual, often placed under a heading such as 'Football Association Notes':

> Loughborough had much the best of matters and the Gainsborough goal survived several attacks in a remarkable manner, the end coming with the score: Loughborough, none Gainsborough, none. The referee's decisions had caused considerable dissatisfaction, especially that disallowing a goal to Loughborough in the first half, and at the close of the game he met with a very unfavourable reception, a section of the crowd hustling him and it was stated that he was struck (*Leicester Daily Mercury*, 3 April 1899).

It is hard to imagine a present-day report of an incident such as this being written with such impartiality and lack of concern.

During the interwar years, the style of reporting began to change. As newspapers gave more space to advertising, stories had to be considered more for their 'newsworthiness' than before. What is interesting to note about Murphy *et al.*'s study here is that they argue that the press facilitated (consciously or not) the view that football crowds were becoming more orderly and well behaved by underplaying, or just not reporting, incidents which did occur. At the same time, however, a small amount of concern and condemnation began to creep in to reports. This trend continued for a decade or so after the Second World War and it is this period which is often referred to as football's hey-day: a time of large, enthusiastic, but well behaved crowds. Murphy *et al.* argue that this was not necessarily the case and that although incidents of disorder were on the decrease, those that did occur often went unreported.

The roots of today's style of reporting of football violence can be traced back to the mid-1950s. At a time when there was widespread public fear over rising juvenile crime and about youth violence in general, the press began to carry more and more stories of this nature and football matches were an obvious place to find them. Although many reports still attempted to downplay the problem, the groundwork was laid as articles began frequently to refer to a hooligan minority of fans. By the mid-1960s, with the World Cup to be held in England drawing closer, the press expressed dire warnings of how the hooligans could ruin the tournament. The World Cup passed without incident but the moral panic concerning hooliganism continued to increase.

By the 1970s calls for tougher action on trouble-makers became common place in the tabloid's headlines: 'Smash these thugs' (*Sun* 4 October 1976), 'Thump and be thumped' (*Daily Express* 25 November 1976), 'Cage the animals' (*Daily Mirror* 21 April 1976) and 'Birch 'em!' (*Daily Mirror* 30 August 1976). During the 1980s, many of these demands were actually met by the British authorities, in the wake of tragedies such as the Heysel deaths in 1985, 'Cage the animals' turning out to be particularly prophetic. As these measures were largely short-sighted, they did not do much to quell the hooliganism, and may have in fact made efforts worse. As such, football hooliganism continued to feature heavily in the newspapers and mass media in general and still does today.

Theory

The main bodies of work we will consider here are that of Stuart Hall in the late 1970s and that of Patrick Murphy and his colleagues at Leicester in the late 1980s. Stuart Hall (1978) suggests four good reasons for examining the media coverage of football hooliganism. First, he considers that the nature and pattern of the media coverage make it worthy of examination in its own right. Secondly, since only a very small proportion of the population have any direct experience of football hooliganism, it is worth examining the principal source of information which they do have, namely, the media reports of hooliganism. Thirdly, since public concern about football hooliganism is based on impressions rather than hard facts, so the source of those impressions merits closer study. Fourthly, Hall notes that, as well as making reports about an issue, the press also has a unique role in determining public opinion about that issue.

Hall identifies what he calls the 'amplification spiral' whereby exaggerated coverage of a problem can have the effect of worsening it:

> If the official culture or society at large comes to believe that a phenomenon is threatening, and growing, it can be led to panic about it. This often precipitates the call for tough measures of control. This increased control creates a situation of confrontation, where more people than were originally involved in the deviant behaviour are drawn into it ... Next week's 'confrontation' will then be bigger,

more staged, so will the coverage, so will the public outcry, the pressure for yet more control ... (Hall 1978).

This spiral effect, Hall argues, has been particularly apparent in the coverage of football hooliganism since the mid-1960s. The press technique of 'editing for impact' is central to Hall's theory. The use of 'graphic headlines, bold type-faces, warlike imagery and epithets ...' serves to sensationalize and exaggerate the story.

This approach is supported by the later study by Murphy *et al.* (1988). They argue that the particular shape which football hooliganism has taken since the 1960s, i.e. 'regular confrontations between named rival groups', has arisen partly out of press coverage of incidents, in particular, the predictive style of reporting which often appeared in the tabloids such as 'Scandal of soccer's savages – warming up for the new season' (*Daily Mirror* 20 August 1973) and 'Off – to a riot' (*People* 2 August 1970). In 1967, a Chelsea fan appearing in court charged with carrying a razor said in his defence that he had 'read in a local newspaper that the West Ham lot were going to cause trouble' (Murphy *et al.* 1988).

This predictive style of reporting is most apparent when the English national side is involved in international tournaments. During the build-up to the 1990 World Cup in Italy, the English press gave out grave warnings of violence. The *Sun* quoted anonymous English fans as saying there was going to be 'a bloodbath – someone is going to get killed' (31 May 1990), whilst the *Daily Mirror* claimed Sardinians were arming themselves with knives for the visit of the English who were 'ready to cause havoc' on the island (27 May 1990). This anticipation of trouble meant that media presence at the tournament was very substantial, and competition for a 'story' fierce, resulting in journalists picking up the smallest of incidents. John Williams (1992b) also claims that journalists may have paid English fans to pose for photographs.

Murphy *et al.* (1988) argue that 'By defining matchdays and football grounds as times and places in which fighting could be engaged in and aggressive forms of masculinity displayed, the media, especially the national tabloid press, played a part of some moment in stimulating and shaping the development of football hooliganism'. Furthermore, Murphy *et al.* argue that the press have played a role in decisions over policy-making to deal with football hooliganism, resulting in largely short-sighted measures which have in the main shifted violence from the terraces on to the streets and towns outside the football grounds.

Evidently, social explanations of football violence do not make great headlines and it is rare that a report of football violence in the popular press will include such an insight – if it does, it tends to be a short remark, buried away at the end of the article. Thus, as Hall (1978) points out, 'If you lift social violence out of it's social context, the only thing you are left with is – bloody heads'. In fact, the explanations offered to us by the popular press usually aim to dismiss the violence as irrational, stupid and ultimately animalistic – 'RIOT! United's fans are animals' (*Sunday People* 29 August 1975) and 'SAVAGES! ANIMALS!' (*Daily Mirror* 21 April 1975).

This has serious consequences, creating one of the populist explanations we discussed in Chapter 6. As Melnick (1986) points out, 'The mass media in general and the national press in particular can take major credit for the public's view of the soccer hooligan as a cross between the Neanderthal Man and Conan the Barbarian.' By labelling the actions of football hooligans like this, it is easy for the tabloid press to make calls for tougher action from the authorities. If the violence has no rationale or reason then what can be done but use force against it?

> Another idea might be to put these people in 'hooligan compounds' every Saturday afternoon … They should be herded together preferably in a public place. That way they could be held up to ridicule and exposed for what they are – mindless morons with no respect for other people's property or wellbeing. We should make sure we treat them like animals – for their behaviour proves that's what they are (*Daily Mirror* 4 April 1977).

Contrasted with these calls for harsh punishments have been more blatant forms of glorification of hooliganism, most obviously in the publishing of 'league tables of hooligan notoriety':

> Today the *Mirror* reveals the end-of-term 'arrest' record of First Division Clubs' supporters covering every league match played by 22 teams. The unique report compiled with the help of 17 police forces reflects the behaviour of both 'home' and 'away' fans at each ground. The record speaks for itself; Manchester United were bottom of the League of Shame by more than 100 arrests (*Daily Mirror* 6 April 1974).

League tables were published in several other newspapers, including the *Daily Mail*, during the mid-1970s. However, when a report by a working group in the government's Department of the Environment (1984), entitled *Football Spectator Violence*, recommended that the police should compile a league table of the country's most notorious hooligan groups to help combat the problem, many newspapers replied with disgust and outrage that this should be published (which it wasn't going to be), arguing that doing so could incite hooligan competition. Importantly, as Murphy *et al.* assert, this shows that the press recognize that publicity can influence football hooliganism.

This interest in 'league tables' is neither historical, nor indeed is it confined to the tabloids. For example on 16 August 2001 The *Guardian* reported the release of the annual figures by the National Criminal Intelligence Service under the headline, 'Hooligan disease that clings to football', noting that 'North-east giants Sunderland and Newcastle top the league of the most unruly fans'. The following year, under the headline 'Hooliganism on increase in First Division football', The *Guardian* (9 August 2002) set out four actual league tables with the clubs listed from most arrests to least – as though arrests somehow equalled points – and reported that 'the club with the worst arrest record, though, was Stoke City'. We saw earlier in Chapter 3 how such claims cannot withstand even the most cursory analysis of the meaning behind the statistics, yet the media – even the broadsheets – persist in squeezing out the most sensationalist headlines they can.

Criticism has also been aimed at the tabloid press for the attitude it takes in its build-up to major international matches. Two days before England's semi-final match against Germany in the 1996 European Championships, the *Mirror* carried the front-page headline 'Achtung! Surrender. For you Fritz ze Euro 96 Championship is over', whilst the editorial, also on the front page, consisted of a parody of Neville Chamberlain's 1939 announcement of the outbreak of war with Hitler: 'Mirror declares football war on Germany.' Elsewhere, the war metaphors continued: 'Let's Blitz Fritz' (*Sun*) and 'Herr we go' (*Daily Star*). Condemnation of the tabloids was widespread, but in fact they had done it before. Before England played the Federal Republic of Germany in the semi-final of the 1990 World Cup, the *Sun* printed the headline 'We beat them in 45 … Now the battle of 90'.

Following the disturbances across Britain after the match, in which a battle between English fans and police broke out in London's Trafalgar Square and a Russian student was stabbed in Brighton, mistakenly being identified as a German, some critics were keen to point the finger at the xenophobia of the tabloid press in encouraging racist and violent action. A report produced by the National Heritage Select Committee (1996), led by Labour MP Gerald Kaufman, concluded that the tabloid press coverage 'may well have had its effect in stimulating the deplorable riots'.

Even without considering whether the disturbances that night constituted 'deplorable riots' or not, this claim is highly debatable. What is clear, however, is that certain double standards exist within the tabloid press. On the one hand they are keen to label the actions of hooligans as 'moronic' and 'evil' whilst at the same time they encourage the jingoistic and xenophobic views so prevalent within the national hooligan scene. A study by Blain and O'Donnell (1990), involving 3,000 newspaper reports from ten countries covering the 1990 World Cup, claimed that 'There is nothing elsewhere in Europe like the aggressiveness towards foreigners of the British popular press'.

It is not just in the international context that one finds this aggressive style of reporting but also in general football journalism. Headlines such as 'C-R-U-N-C-H', 'FOREST'S BLITZ', 'POWELL BLAST SHOCKS STOKE' and 'Doyle's karate gets him chopped' were found in the sports pages of just one edition of the *Sunday People* (3 April 1977). Stuart Hall claims that if football reporting is shrouded in violent, war metaphors and graphic imagery then one should not be surprised that this spills over on to the terraces: 'the line between the sports reporter glorying in the battles on the pitch, and expressing his righteous moral indignation at the battle on the terraces is a very fine and wavery one indeed' (1978: 27).

Further study

For an excellent discussion of media reporting of England football fans, see the book chapter 'Tears, tantrums and tattoos' by Emma Poulton in Mark Perryman's *Hooligans Wars: Causes and Effects of Football Violence* (see Poulton 2001).

The role of the media in other European countries

Studies of media reporting of football hooliganism elsewhere in Europe have been rather limited. This may be due to the more 'benign' reporting of fans in other countries or to the relative novelty of the football violence phenomenon in some cases. The most significant studies have been conducted in Italy and the Netherlands, with less substantial work in Denmark and Austria. Work on Scottish fans by Giulianotti, however, is also relevant in this section.

Italy

Alessandro dal Lago (1990) analyses the coverage of football hooliganism in the Italian media. He identifies two phases in reporting football matches by the press. Before the 1970s each match was covered at most by two articles. The attention of the reporters was more focused on the players than on the terraces, and when violence occurred it was reported as a secondary event in the context of the article. The second phase comes from the mid-1970s. Now attention was focused on the 'ends' (the terraces behind the goals favoured by the Italian ultras) and outside the stadium. Football incidents were given the 'honour' of separate articles independent from the reports of football matches.

Dal Lago recognizes the amplifying role which the media plays and claims that the ultras are aware of it to the extent that banners displayed in the 'ends' frequently include messages to journalists. For example in June 1989, a week after a Roma supporter had died and three Milan fans arrested, a banner displayed by the Milan ultras was directed at Biscardi, a presenter of a popular sports programme *Il Processo del Lunedi* (*The Monday Trial*). It read 'Biscardi sei figlio di bastardi' ('Biscardi you are a son of bastards'). Dal Lago states that widespread hatred exists on the part of both groups, with expressions such as 'beasts' and 'stupid' used by the ultras to describe the media and by the media to describe the ultras.

The Netherlands

A study by van der Brug and Meijs (1988) set out to see what the influence of the Dutch media coverage of hooliganism is on the hooligans themselves. A survey was conducted in which there were 53 respondents from different 'siders' (groups of fans so called after the section of the ground in which they are usually located) in Holland. Put to them were a series of statements to see whether they agreed, disagreed, etc. Statements which featured the strongest levels of agreement amongst the respondents were 'It is fun when the side is mentioned in the newspaper or on television', 'Siders supporters think it is important that newspapers write about their side' and 'When I read in the newspaper that there will be extra police, it makes the coming match more interesting'. The authors conclude that 'There is no doubt whatsoever that the media have some effect on football hooliganism'.

Scotland

We have seen earlier that the media have played a large part in the shaping of the present-day view of football hooligans in England. It is interesting, therefore, to consider the example of Scottish fans and their transformation, in the public's eyes, from British 'hooligans' to Scottish 'fans'. Since 1981 the Scottish 'Tartan Army' has consciously sought to acquire an international reputation for boisterous friendliness to the host nation and opposing fans through 'carnivalesque' behaviour (for example, see Finn and Giulianotti 1996). The media have played a very important role in this. By organizing themselves into very large groups at matches abroad, the Scottish fans attract a great deal of media attention, but by displaying themselves as nothing more than friendly, albeit drunken, fans their press coverage is predominantly positive. The Scottish media have been behind this transformation, namely by representing English fans as hooligans and by underplaying any trouble which has occurred involving Scottish fans.

Denmark

A similar story exists in Denmark where the 'roligans' (see Chapter 5) have an impeccable reputation as the antithesis of the 'English hooligan'. Peitersen and Skov (1990) identified the role that the media played in forming this reputation:

> The Danish popular press were an active force in support of the Danish roligans and the fantastic reputation that they have achieved in the international press … the Danish popular press came to have a similar role to that played by the English popular press for the hooligans, but with reversed polarity. While the Danish press supported recognisable positive trends encompassing companionship, fantasy, humour and pride, the English press helped to intensify and refine violence among English spectators by consciously focusing on and exaggerating the violence and the shame.

Austria

Roman Horak (1990) also claims that a spate of de-amplification of football violence in the Austrian press occurred in the mid to late 1980s. As a result, hooligans lost the coverage which they had previously thrived upon, and the number of incidents decreased.

Conclusion

It is evident that the media play a very significant role in the public's view of football hooliganism. By far the biggest problem lies in the sensationalist reporting of the British tabloid press. We have seen how the press has helped form the modern phenomenon of football hooliganism, how it has shaped public opinion of the problem and how it may directly influence the actions of fans themselves.

There is considerable evidence to support the claim that football hooligans enjoy press coverage and positively attempt to obtain coverage of themselves and their group. In fact, a hooligan group's notoriety and reputation stems largely from reports in the media. The following conversation between two Millwall supporters talking to each other in 1982, is somewhat revealing:

> C – keeps a scrapbook of press cuttings and everything, you should see it, got this great picture from when Millwall went to Chelsea. Great, this Chelsea fan photographed being led away from the shed, with blood pouring out of his white tee shirt. He's clutching his guts like this (illustrates), got stabbed real bad. You see that thing in

the *Sun* on 'Violent Britain'? No? Well I was in it. Well not directly like. I had this Tottenham geezer see. Sliced up his face with my blade – right mess (Pratt and Salter 1984).

In *Football Hooliganism: The Wider Context*, Roger Ingham (1978) recommended that the media should reduce their tendencies to, 'sensationalise, inflate, exaggerate and amplify their stories', advocating 'more accurate reporting of events, more careful choice of descriptive terminology, greater efforts to place the events themselves in appropriate contexts'. Ingham also called for the press to think before printing anticipations of disturbances, going so far as to recommend that the Press Council 'play a more active role in attempting to ensure accurate and responsible reporting'.

However, over 25 years on from Ingham's writings we are still faced with the same situation and it is one which looks unlikely to go away. As Melnick (1986) pointed out 'in the newspaper business, "bad news is good news"'. A glimmer of hope perhaps stems from the Scottish example talked about earlier, demonstrating that football fans can produce 'good' stories in the press, although it may be fair to say that many of the stories have only been deemed 'newsworthy' because of the emphasis on the contrast with English fans.

Horak's claim is also encouraging, indicating that media de-amplification (i.e. playing down stories of football hooliganism) can lead to reductions in levels of violence. In this sense, therefore, Euro '96 might be seen as a turning point in press coverage of football. Apart from the disturbances in London following the England v. Germany match, the Euro '96 provided almost nothing in the way of hooliganism stories for the press and, as such, stories concentrated on the English team, rather than the fans. Of course there are other explanatory factors for the media de-amplification subsequent to Euro '96. First was the fact that England were bidding against Germany to host the 2006 World Cup and so the media were encouraged not to report incidents of football hooliganism for fear of the adverse publicity this would create for the bid. On one memorable occasion, the pundit Jimmy Hill was speaking to camera during the half-time interval of a live television broadcast when he commented that the BBC were not permitted to show the scenes taking place at that moment just outside the window of his studio. A further factor arose from the changing commercial nature of the football business during the late 1990s. Some football clubs began to give up their position as community institutions and instead become public limited companies listed on the stock market. Now the pressure came from the City for the media to avoid doing anything – for example reporting hooliganism – which might upset the share price and so lose value for the shareholders. Similarly, since the 'revenue mix' for football began to rely less on gate money and more on commercial sponsorship, so again the pressure was on the media to avoid stories which might damage the value of the brand.

The role of the media was raised in a report to the European Parliament (1996) on football hooliganism by the Committee on Civil Liberties and Internal Affairs (see also Chapter 12). In this the committee recognizes that:

> The media act as magnifiers – they magnify acts of violence and provoke further acts of violence. The media show social problems – the violence in and around football, xenophobia and the racism which is its expression – as if under a magnifying glass. What is nasty becomes nastier because it seems to appear anonymously.

It then goes on to recommend that the media 'participate in the promotion of respect for fair play in sport, to help promote positive sporting values, to combat aggressive and chauvinistic behaviour and to avoid any sensationalism in treating information on violence at sporting events'. Short of outright censorship, however, it is hard to imagine how legislation can reduce sensationalism and exaggeration in the media.

Chapter summary

Football hooliganism is a highly visible phenomenon, as journalists and TV cameras are present at virtually every match. Since the 1960s, journalists have been sent to football matches to report on crowd behaviour as much as on the game itself. As a result, media coverage of football-related disorder and violence is extensive, and the British tabloid press in particular devote apparently unlimited column inches to any incident that occurs, complete with sensationalist headlines.

Many researchers, and many non-academic observers, have argued that this sensationalism, together with a 'predictive' approach whereby violence at certain matches is anticipated by the media, has actually contributed to the problem. The British press have also been criticized for their xenophobic approach to the coverage of international matches and tournaments. (It may be no coincidence that English fans tend to be the most belligerent in these contexts.) This tendency was particularly apparent during the Euro '96 championships, when at least one tabloid newspaper represented the England v. Germany match as a resumption of the Second World War.

Although there is no direct equivalent of the British tabloid extremes in other European nations, most researchers have identified problems relating to media coverage of football hooliganism. In all the countries with significant levels of football-related disorder, researchers have found that hooligans relish the media coverage they receive, and often positively seek it with rival groups actively competing for column inches and mentions in sensational headlines.

The publicity-seeking tendencies of football fans can, however, be turned to beneficial effect. The extensive and highly positive coverage of the non-violent, 'carnival' groups such as Scotland's 'Tartan Army' and the Danish 'roligans' has clearly been seen by them as a 'victory' over their badly behaved rivals, and has helped to reinforce and perpetuate their exemplary behaviour.

The influence of the media was highlighted in a European Parliament report on football hooliganism, which recommended that the media avoid sensationalism and promote fair-play and sporting values. We would go further, and recommend a systematic, pan-European media campaign to promote the non-violent 'carnival' groups whilst ruthlessly cutting off the oxygen of publicity supply to the 'hooligan' groups.

10. Football violence and alcohol

Introduction

One of the populist explanations for football hooliganism which we mentioned in Chapter 6 was the notion that football hooliganism is somehow caused by excessive alcohol consumption. Certainly this is the view held by many policy-makers, and has resulted in a range of British legislative controls over alcohol which we will consider in more detail in Chapter 13. At the European level, this view has resulted in a complete ban on alcohol sales at matches played under the jurisdiction of the Union of European Football Associations (UEFA), such as the 'Champions League'. At football matches played under the jurisdiction of the International Federation of Football Associations (FIFA), such as the 1998 World Cup in France, the sale and possession of alcohol in the stadium are also prohibited by the rules of competition. In this chapter, we therefore want to examine the evidence base for the implementation of these kinds of controls.

Little research on football hooliganism has included a specific focus on the role of alcohol. Work by John Williams *et al.* (1984) and Richard Giulianotti (1994b) includes discussion of the possible 'aggravating' effects in the case of English and Scottish fans, but few empirical data are presented concerning consumption rates or specific effects of alcohol. For most researchers and theorists, the issue of alcohol is, at best, peripheral and in Italian work it is, as we might expect, not considered at all.

The 'alcohol–violence connection'

This peripheral consideration by researchers is in stark contrast to the media coverage of football fan behaviour, particularly in the UK. Here 'drunkenness' is by far the most often reported cause of violent disorder, even in circumstances where there is no evidence of excessive drinking. In line with this populist view, most official inquiries into football hooliganism have dwelt on the 'problem' of alcohol and urged its restriction at football matches. Even government-sponsored publications concerning crime prevention initiatives include sweeping conclusions about the 'dangers' of alcohol consumption by football fans: 'Some offences are alcohol-related by definition – drink-driving for example. But these are by no means the only ones where alcohol plays a large part. Public disorder, including football hooliganism and vandalism is particularly associated with it' (see for example CJS Online 2002).

It is quite instructive to go back through the various UK Government reports into safety and security at sports grounds (see also Chapter 13) to see what they have to say about alcohol, what recommendations they make for its control and what the evidence base for those recommendation is. This was a dissertation topic selected by one of Steve Frosdick's students (Paul Williamson).

Going chronologically through the reports, Williamson found that the first four (Home Office 1924; Home Office 1946; Department of Education and Science 1968; Harrington 1968) say nothing whatsoever about alcohol. The first mention comes in the Lang Report (Ministry of Housing and Local Government 1969), which noted that, 'there can be no doubt that alcohol is an important factor is crowd misbehaviour, both because it stimulates quarrelsomeness and because empty bottles are dangerous missiles' (para. 49). The report therefore recommended that 'all liquor supplied at grounds should be sold in plastic containers and not in bottles or cans' (para. 50). The report noted that 'There would be no advantage in refusing licence facilities to football club grounds – this would merely stimulate spectators to bring in their own supplies from outside' (para. 50). It therefore recommended that liquor be sold in grounds in 'modern refreshment rooms'.

The next report followed the Ibrox stadium disaster in 1971 (Home Office 1972). The report noted the differences in drinking habits in England and Scotland and that the sale of alcohol in grounds in Scotland was rejected by both the football authorities and the police. The following report was also from Scotland (Scottish Education Department 1977) and supported the view that 'a strong relationship exists between alcohol and violence and that a good deal of the disturbances associated with football is due to the amount of alcohol consumed before, during and after matches' (para. 20). The report concluded that 'every effort should be made to discourage over-indulgence in alcohol' and therefore recommended restrictions on the carriage of alcohol into grounds – also noting the potential use of bottles and cans as missiles. The report ended with the optimistic hope that alcohol sales at grounds could in future be allowed under controlled conditions. However various alcohol-related controls and offences were subsequently introduced through the Criminal Justice (Scotland) Act 1980, which in effect imposed an absolute ban on alcohol in stadiums.

Back in England, the Department of the Environment Working Group (1984) came to the conclusion that the restrictions introduced in Scotland would not be appropriate in England, noting that 'The majority of football clubs are untroubled by violence and would unnecessarily be penalised financially and the vast majority of non-violent spectators would suffer as a result' (para. 5.34). Nevertheless, in the face of the recommendations, the (Thatcher) government went ahead and introduced in England and Wales similar legislation to Scotland by way of the Sporting Events (Control of Alcohol) Act 1985. There was a ban, but the legislation allowed licensing magistrates to grant an exemption and thus allow sales under certain conditions. It also created a number of criminal offences, for example to be drunk inside the ground or to possess alcohol in any part of the ground that offers sight of the pitch.

This was policy-making driven by populism and moral panic rather than the facts. As Ryan (2003: 117) puts it, 'In the 1980s other senior Conservative politicians were happy to concede that in penal matters the popular press counted for more than informed opinion'. Thus controls on the availability of alcohol at football matches have existed since the 1980s in Britain, yet the rationale for these seems to have been as much to prevent the use of bottles as missiles as to inhibit quarrelsome behaviour.

Lord Justice Popplewell's reports (Home Office 1985, 1986) into the 1985 Bradford stadium fire and the 1985 Heysel stadium disaster in Belgium also made comments that 'Alcohol plays a part in some of the outbreaks of violence which occur at sports grounds. Even if it does not give rise to violence, it gives rise to disorderly behaviour' (Home Office 1986, para. 4.77). He supported the controls in the 1985 legislation; however, he made no recommendations that alcohol should be banned. Following the Hillsborough stadium disaster in 1989, Lord Justice Taylor's reports (Home Office 1989, 1990) also noted that 'There can be no doubt that an excited and volatile crowd is more difficult to control and more prone to disorder if it includes numbers who have been drinking' (Home Office 1990, para. 49). There is some evidence to support this view. For example, in a case study analysis of the two Southampton v. Portsmouth derby matches in 2004, one of the present authors noted that the first match – a Tuesday evening kick-off in the League Cup – featured considerable drunken disorder in the city prior to the match, whilst the second – a Sunday lunchtime kick-off – involved no trouble at all (Frosdick 2004).

At the European level, the Council of Europe (1985) *European Convention on Spectator Violence and Misbehaviour at Sports Events, and in Particular at Football Matches* included recommendations to prevent drunken persons entering the stadium and to restrict and preferably prohibit alcohol in grounds. The European Parliament (1996) included a Europe-wide ban on alcohol in its own recommendations. Much of the debate, however, was driven by British and German MEPs and it is clear that alcohol was seen as a significant factor in this context only by northern Europeans. Nevertheless, the UEFA regulations for safety and security in the stadium provide that, throughout Europe, 'No public sale or distribution of alcohol is permitted within the stadium or its private environs' (UEFA 2004: 10) for matches played under UEFA jurisdiction. Thus restricting or even prohibiting the possession and consumption of alcohol in stadiums has become one of the management controls intended to counter the risks associated with crowd violence and misbehaviour across Europe.

Consideration of the association between drinking and football hooliganism lies within a much broader debate concerning the role of alcohol in the generation of violent and criminal behaviour. This issue has been reviewed at length in other publications and we will not dwell here on the complexities of the issue (for example, see Marsh and Fox 1992; Sumner and Parker 1995). It is clear, however, that the perceived alcohol–violence connection is primarily restricted to northern European and Anglo-Saxon cultures. Even then, alcohol is seen as an aggravating factor rather than a primary cause of football hooliganism. Elsewhere in the world quite contrary perceptions exist. Where alcohol can be shown to have a direct impact on levels of aggression and anti-social behaviour, the effect is largely mediated by immediate social factors and more general, pervasive cultural expectations.

Anomalies in alcohol controls

The various alcohol controls throw up a variety of anomalies. The situation seems to be that there are different approaches across different countries, between different sports in the same country and even within the same sport or indeed within the same stadium, depending on the type of match being played. Whilst some countries have a complete ban, others have different laws in different places and for different sports. In the USA, for example, laws restricting alcohol vary from state to state and from sport to sport. There are even major differences within the same state. In Texas, for example, the local ordinances vary dramatically, even between political precincts within the same town. In Dallas, some parts of the city are completely 'dry', others allow only the sales of wine and beer and yet others have no restrictions at all. At the Texas Stadium, home of the Dallas Cowboys, alcohol was banned until about 1995. Now beer can be sold, but not 'hard liquor'. So some stadiums have no alcohol at all, whilst in others you can even order beer to be served to you in your seat!

The old Wembley Stadium provides a useful case study. When staging a FIFA or UEFA match, no alcohol was allowed. Yet at the FA Cup Final, alcohol was sold at the concourse bars, although the law does not allow spectators to take their beer back to their seats, since they would then be within sight of the pitch. However, when rugby matches were played at Wembley, this restriction did not apply and so rugby fans could in theory drink their beer whilst watching the game. The same anomaly has been found at several English stadiums where both rugby and football are played.

The effectiveness of the controls?

Referring to the complete ban in Scotland, Lord Justice Taylor (Home Office 1989, 1990) said that there was no doubt that 'this measure has greatly reduced the problem of misbehaviour at Scottish football grounds'. However, as we shall see below, this explanation overlooks the impact of the parallel transformation of Scottish fans from violence into the carnivalesque.

We would argue that such blanket bans are too simplistic. In an article in 1998, one of the present authors reported that:

> At the Olympia Park in Munich, the stadium management and police used to sit down before each game and assess the risk of disorder before determining whether alcohol sales would be allowed. So Bayern Munich v FC Kaiserslautern would be fine for alcohol sales, but Bayern Munich v 1860 Munich would not. This seems to me to have been an entirely sensible risk-based approach. However, 18 months ago, a new police chief arrived and directed that no alcohol at all be sold either in the stadium or in the surrounding Olympia Park for any football match. Fans are free, however, to congregate in the bars just beyond the park where they can and do drink themselves silly (Frosdick 1998a).

Stoke City football club also provide an interesting case. At their old ground in the town centre, all the catering outlets had at least a small view over the pitch and so it was not possible for the club to get permission to sell any alcohol in the ground. According to the stadium manager, many of the fans remained in the local pubs until 2.55 pm, arriving very late and causing long queues at the turnstiles. The police often asked for the kick-off to be delayed because large numbers of fans were still queuing to get in. On one occasion, a public address announcement was made at 2.55 pm that the kick-off would be delayed until 3.15 pm. The fans waiting outside promptly turned round and went back to the pubs until

3.10 pm! The new Britannia Stadium is built on the site of an old coal mine about 20 minutes walk from the town. Parking is difficult and the only public transport is a bus service. Having a new ground meant the club were now able to get a liquor licence. Alcohol is sold up until kick-off, from 15 minutes before until 15 minutes after half-time and then again after the match. The fans now tend to arrive early to enjoy a drink before the game, at half-time and even after the match, although this tends to be only when their team have won. There have been few arrests for drunkenness and no matches when the sale of alcohol is prohibited. Sales were even permitted for the last game of the 1997/8 season, against Manchester City, when very serious disorder was anticipated and indeed did break out. In fact more than 20 people were hurt, 300 ejected from the ground and 15 arrested. But the stadium management felt that a ban on alcohol at the ground would have caused very serious problems in the town. It was better to get the fans in and control them at the stadium (see Frosdick 1998a).

Culture and alcohol

The cultural nature of the relationship between alcohol and football is evident from a rare 'natural experiment' involving Aston Villa fans attending a European Cup Final against Bayern Munich in the Feyenoord Stadium in Rotterdam. This took place in 1982 at a time when concern about the drinking behaviour of English fans was at a peak. The bar at the back of the terraces occupied by Villa fans served lager which, unknown to them, was alcohol-free (Bayern fans had access to 'normal' lager). John Williams comments on this 'trick' in *Hooligans Abroad*:

> Villa supporters who made the endless trek back and forth to the bars, carrying six cartons with the aid of a specially designed cardboard tray, believed themselves to be en route to getting well and truly 'steaming' … To get drunk in the Villa end that night, one would need to drink more than the 'lager' on sale to English fans. What officials later described as the 'big con' was in full swing. While fans in other sections of the ground were sinking the real thing, Villa fans were the subject of a non-alcoholic delusion (Williams *et al.* 1984).

While most observers of this 'con' noted with interest the apparently 'drunken' behaviour of Villa fans, Williams is more ambivalent about the extent to which the effects of alcohol are psychologically mediated. He suggests, for example, that the drunkenness in some cases might have been 'real' and due to drinking prior to the game – a suggestion for which he offers no evidence. Elsewhere in Williams's writing the ambivalence concerning alcohol is replaced with self-contradictory stances. Take, for example, his view expressed at a conference in 1989:

> We are regularly told that it is drink which releases the full force of this natural wickedness, and that curbs on drinking will bottle it up. Someone should inform the Danes and the Irish of these findings. Supporters from these countries were among the most drunken and the most friendly fans in West Germany. The message might also reach UEFA who sanctioned a major brewer as the Championships' sponsor!

This dismissal of the relevance of alcohol by Williams is followed, three years later, by a *non sequitor* call for restrictions on the availability of alcohol to British fans abroad, 'We recommend that for the foreseeable future, and with the support of the continental authorities concerned, an alcohol ban should operate for all England matches on the continent' (Williams 1992b). Other inconsistencies are evident in Williams's work and it is, perhaps, ironic that he should make such recommendations given his insistence that football violence derives from deeply entrenched social factors within British society rather than from immediate situational or psychological processes (see Chapters 6 and 7).

The roligans

The Danish fans, about whose 'drunken but friendly' behaviour Williams makes favourable comment, are an interesting example. The Danish 'roligans' are fanatical football supporters who are renowned for their levels of beer consumption. They are also northern European and might be expected, therefore, to be amongst those for whom group drinking sessions often end in belligerence and fighting. Their conduct, however, is quite different from that associated with English fans and, to a lesser extent, with their German and Dutch contemporaries. The analysis provided by Eichberg of the Danish Sport Research Institute sums up their distinctiveness succinctly:

> The roligan displays a feature which links him with his counterpart, the hooligan: excessive alcohol consumption. English, Irish and Danish fans compete for the position of being the most drunk – yet fundamentally different behaviour patterns arise. Where the heavy drinking of English hooligans impels aggression and violence, the roligan is characterised by the absence of violence and companiable cheerfulness (Eichberg 1992: 124).

The behaviour of Danish fans has also been the subject of much favourable comment by the media and the police. In a magazine article commenting on the amusing and good-natured antics of the Danes in Sheffield during Euro '96, Cassell and Rea (1996) noted:

> Such characteristics endeared Sheffielders towards them. No matter how much lager they consumed, and how badly the team performed, the atmosphere wherever they congregated was nothing short of a party. The city did well out of it ... Numerous pubs ran dry. The police and council officials expressed their amazement that such amounts of beer could be consumed by so many football supporters with no trouble at all.

The police view

The 'surprise' expressed by the police about the good-natured drunkenness of Danish fans is understandable given their assumptions about alcohol and hooliganism in the UK. We should note, however, that the police are less ready to blame drink than some newspaper reports have suggested. A study was conducted of the views of police commanders who were responsible for crowd control at all 92 English League clubs. They were asked 'How serious an influence is heavy drinking in contributing to football-related disorder in your town?' Concerning 'home' fans, only 11 per cent saw it as being the 'single most serious influence', whilst a further 20 per cent rated it as 'serious'. Almost half the commanders felt that alcohol was an influence, but not a serious one, whilst the remainder felt that it was not an influence at all. Their views regarding visiting 'away' fans, however, were a little different. Here 18 per cent felt that alcohol was the most significant influence whilst 35 per cent rated it as serious.

These are, of course, views rather than empirical facts and based upon, we presume, observations that many fans in the UK, and 'away' fans in particular, tend to consume alcohol prior to engaging in acts of hooliganism. Despite the implicit assumptions, however, this does not mean that acts of hooliganism would necessarily be less frequent if alcohol were less readily available, or likely to increase in frequency when drinking levels were higher.

Unexpected consequences of alcohol bans

Increasing restrictions on the availability of alcohol at football matches may not only be inappropriate but perhaps also have negative side-effects. Fans may take drugs instead. There may be unnecessary losses of revenue or safety risks created from a rush to get a drink during a restricted period of sales.

There has been evidence that such restrictions have prompted some fans to substitute a variety of drugs for lager. John Williams has noted an increase in the use of cannabis as a direct consequence of the potential penalties for being in possession of alcohol in a British football stadium. Others note the increased use of MDMA (ecstasy) in such contexts.

Stadium managers faced with an event where the risk of spectator misbehaviour is high have a whole basket of management controls to choose from. These cover such areas as ticketing, signage, access control, deployment of police and stewards, spectator segregation and protection of the playing area, as well as alcohol controls. We would argue that the control mix should be considered on a match-by-match basis, with stadium managers and the police selecting the control measures which best suit what is known about the location and layout of the stadium, the nature of the crowd attending and the event itself.

Alcohol controls which the police and stadium management feel are not needed for that event may create unacceptable risks elsewhere. For the commercial manager, a ban on alcohol sales creates a risk to revenue. The fans will not buy cola instead. They will drink outside and come in late, reducing what is known in the trade as 'ancillary spend per head'. For many spectators, a ban on alcohol quite simply reduces their enjoyment of the event, and where it has been needlessly imposed from outside, may create feelings of resentment. And local residents and businesses have to put up with more noise and disorder around the ground than might otherwise be the case. From a safety point of view, there are compelling arguments that a total ban results in late arrivals and a last-minute rush to get in at the turnstiles.

But even restrictions on when alcohol can be sold and on where it can be consumed can themselves cause safety risks. According to John Beattie, the stadium manager at Arsenal FC, the rush to buy and consume alcohol at half-time causes large crowds and near crushing on the concourse, which is often blocked by people drinking alcohol. This also causes difficulties for other people wishing to purchase food or use the toilets (see Frosdick 1998a).

Evidence of a more concrete kind concerning unanticipated effects of restrictions comes from a study in the USA, the implications of which are generalizable to other countries and settings. Boyes and Faith (1993) conducted a detailed study of the impact of a ban on alcohol at (American) football games at Arizona State University. They hypothesized that such a ban would lead to 'intertemporal' substitution of the consumption of alcohol – i.e. fans would increase their consumption immediately prior to, and after leaving the football games. Such substitution, they argued, could be more damaging than the effects which might arise from intoxication within the stadium and such negative consequences could be measured in, for example, increased numbers of fans driving before and after the match whilst over the legal blood alcohol limit. The authors argued that there were three reasons to expect such a consequence:

> First, alcohol in the body does not dissipate quickly ... Thus the effects of increased drinking in the period prior to the regulated period may carry over into the regulated period. Second, the level of intoxication, during any period depends on the rate of consumption as well as the volume. Thus, even if there is not a one-for-one substitution of consumption from the restricted period to the adjacent unregulated periods, average intoxication taken over the adjacent and unregulated periods can increase. Third, studies indicate that the probability of having a traffic accident increases at an increasing level of intoxication. Thus, the social costs of drinking and driving in the unregulated periods may increase (Boyes and Faith 1993: 596).

Boyes and Faith examined police data concerning alcohol-related driving accidents, detected driving whilst intoxicated cases and other measures for the periods before and after the restrictions on alcohol in the stadium. They found significant increases of up to 40 per cent in blood alcohol concentrations in drivers stopped by the police. This was despite an increase in the penalties for driving whilst intoxicated and an increase in the legal driving age in the post ban period.

The implications of this study are very relevant to restrictions on alcohol at British football stadiums. They also suggest that the UEFA Europe-wide ban on alcohol at football matches may be misguided. If alcohol is a significant determinant of anti-social behaviour, directly or indirectly, the effects of intertemporal substitution of drinking, which alcohol bans are likely to generate, will tend to increase the likelihood of aggression both prior to and shortly after the games. Such behaviour, of course, is also likely to occur outside the stadiums where it is more difficult to police and control.

The case of the Scots

If total bans on alcohol at football games are inappropriate, for the reasons discussed above, alternative means need to be explored for modifying alcohol-related behaviour amongst football fans, and English fans in particular. This may seem an impossible prospect. The change in the behaviour of Scottish fans, however, is of interest in this context.

We have seen in other chapters that, although Scottish fans are often 'heavy' consumers of alcohol, the belligerent behaviour which used to be associated with their drinking has changed quite substantially since the mid-1980s. As Giulianotti (1995a) has noted, the Criminal Justice (Scotland) Act 1980, which prohibits the possession of alcohol at, or in transit to, a football match, has done little to dent the degree to which alcohol is very much part of the football experience. None the less, it is generally agreed that the 'drunkenness' of Scottish fans now presents far less of a threat to law and order than it might once have done.

This transformation of Scottish fan behaviour, according to Giulianotti, has come about through their desire to distance themselves from their English rivals and to present an image of themselves throughout Europe as the 'friendly' supporters. In pursuit of this aim the meaning of alcohol has been substantially altered and now, instead of being a precursor to aggression and fights, is the 'liquid' facilitation of positive social affect and good humour. Although some 'traditional' drunken fighting remains amongst Scottish fan groups, the majority seem to have moved away from the English 'hooligan' model to one which is more characteristic of the Danish roligans. If this radical change of behaviour can occur amongst the Scots, without any apparent decline in their consumption levels, then we must assume that similar shifts are possible in English fan culture. Whilst drinking among Dutch and German fans generally presents less of a problem, we might also anticipate the possibility of further change in these groups as well.

Conclusion

In this context, we consider that restrictions on alcohol at football matches throughout Europe may be inappropriate and, in line with Boyes and Faith, counterproductive. Alcohol may be an aggravating feature of football hooliganism in some cultures, but it cannot be held to be a primary cause. We feel that it is more appropriate to direct attention towards the ways in which alcohol-related behaviours, rather than consumption levels, may be moderated amongst football fan groups. It is in this area, we believe, that research activity and policy development might be most profitably be directed.

For example, Nottingham Forest Football club have for some years had specially trained 'alcohol stewards' deployed in the concourse areas. The safety officers at Nottingham Forest have developed a particular expertise in helping other clubs to gain permission to sell alcohol in their stadiums. They have a ten-point plan of licensing conditions. Namely, that:

• Alcohol bars should be separate from fast-food outlets.

- Notices should be displayed showing the serving times and the maximum number of purchases by one person.
- Only beer, lager and miniature plastic bottles of spirits should be sold.
- Each person should be allowed to buy no more than four drinks at a time.
- Beer and lager should be served in disposable plastic glasses (and it is impossible to carry more than four of these at a time).
- All bars should close five minutes after the start of the second half, with twenty minutes then allowed for customers to finish their drinks.
- Alcohol consumption should be strictly confined to the permitted consumption area.
- There should be adequate signage to define the consumption area.
- There should be an adequate number of clearly defined stewards to supervise each area.
- Each bar should be monitored by CCTV cameras.

Whilst not a universal panacea, these ten points do offer a helpful framework within which stadium managers can consider the (re)introduction of alcohol sales.

Chapter summary

Football violence in Britain is often reported in the media as resulting from excessive alcohol consumption. This populist view, however, is not shared by the large majority of social scientists who have conducted research on hooliganism. Neither is it the view popularly held in many other European countries. Little research has focused specifically on the role of alcohol in football hooliganism. This is because it has been considered, at best, a peripheral issue in most studies. Some investigators and a variety of government reports, however, have claimed that drinking can 'aggravate' football violence and have supported calls for further restrictions at football grounds. Little evidence has been provided to support their claims. Europe-wide restrictions on the availability of alcohol at football games ignore the wide cross-national variations in the consumption of alcohol by football fans and its apparent effects.

We considered the case of Scottish fans, whose behaviour has changed markedly for the better since the mid-1980s, despite continuing patterns of 'heavy' drinking. It is clear that alcohol-related behaviours are not immutable and can change in relatively short periods of time. The example of the Danish roligans was also considered. These have drinking patterns very similar to those of English fans, put present few problems to the authorities. Drunkenness amongst the Danish fans is typically accompanied by good humour and positive sociability. Other groups of fans, such as the Italian ultras, rarely drink to excess when attending football matches and the role of alcohol in football violence in that country is thought to be completely insignificant.

Attention was given to a study in the USA which suggested that restrictions on the availability of alcohol at certain times may lead to increased problems due to 'compensatory' drinking at higher levels in the periods immediately before and after the restricted period.

It is concluded that restrictions on fans' drinking have little impact on levels of hooliganism and, in some cases, may be counterproductive. Future research should be directed towards the modification of alcohol-related behaviours.

11. Racism and football fans

Introduction

Racism is a problem for football across Europe and has become an important factor in the problem of football hooliganism itself. The actual extent of racism is virtually impossible to measure as detailed statistics in this context have been almost non-existent. Home Office figures (2003b, 2004) show that there were 47 arrests for racist chanting in 2001/2, 78 in 2002/3 and 63 in 2003/4. At face value, this hardly represents a serious problem, although the very substantial issues with the statistics have been thoroughly explored in Chapter 3 – thus we know that they do not actually tell us very much.

Nevertheless, acts of football disorder, especially on the international scene, have frequently been referred to as 'racist', or perpetrated by racist groups, and some clubs have been viewed as having an inherently racist support. In this chapter the various forms of racism will be considered, with emphasis on the role of extreme right-wing groups, as these have frequently been reported to be involved in football-related violence. The various campaigns and schemes designed to combat racism will also be considered.

The first professional black player in Britain is believed to have been Arthur Wharton, who signed for Darlington FC in 1889. Nowadays, a black player is by no means unusual. In fact, some 15 per cent of professional players are black. However, in the 2001 survey of Premier League supporters, only 0.8 per cent of the sample comprised black British or black Asian fans (SNCCFR 2001). It is argued that this is due to a prevalence of racism amongst traditional soccer fans. In an attempt to redress the problem, the Commission for Racial Equality (CRE), the Football Supporters Association (FSA) – latterly the Football Supporters Federation (FSF) – and the Professional Footballers Association (PFA) have all launched initiatives to try to rid football grounds of racism and encourage more people from ethnic minorities to attend matches, the most notable campaign being 'Let's kick racism out of football'. Their various techniques and levels of success will be discussed later, but let us start by examining the actual types of racism that exist in football stadiums.

Forms of racism

Racist chanting

Racist chanting represents the kind of 'hate speech' referred to by Brick (2000) and thus we saw in Chapter 3 how such behaviour has become included within the general spectrum of football hooliganism. Racist chanting and abuse from the terraces were arguably at its worst in the 1970s and 1980s, when football players from around the world began to join the English league. However Dixie Dean, a black player for Everton in the 1930s, has talked about suffering racist abuse back then, and one can hardly describe racism as a particularly new phenomenon.

Racist chanting in the 1970s and 1980s often took the form of members of the crowd making monkey noises at black players on the pitch. One of the most infamous examples was at John Barnes' debut for Liverpool in the 1986/7 season when the team played Everton and bananas were thrown from the terraces, the implication being that there was a monkey on the pitch (see Hill 1989). Other abuse has been more specific. For example, after the Deptford fire in 1981 when 13 black youths were burnt to death, a chant that could be heard at Millwall was 'We all agree, niggers burn better than petrol'. Anti-semitic chants and hissing (gas) noises have also been heard, aimed particularly at Tottenham Hotspur supporters. Other chants are more closely linked to patriotism and the national team, for example, 'There ain't no black in the Union Jack'.

Moran (2000) has described his own dreadful experiences as a black professional footballer and highlighted the continued racist incidents in football during the 1990s. The *Daily Telegraph*, for example, reported how, following the murder of a Leeds fan in Turkey, a Leicester player 'was taunted with abuse and cut-throat gestures by a section of the visiting supporters for the crime of being the only player of Turkish descent in English football' (10 April 2000).

The Football (Offences) Act 1991 made racist chanting at football matches unlawful. The UK law states that it is 'An offence to engage or take part in chanting of an (indecent or) racialist nature at a designated football match'. Unfortunately, the 1991 law was largely inadequate as chanting was defined as the 'repeated uttering of any words or sounds in concert with one or more others'. As a result an individual shouting racist abuse on his or her own could only be charged under the 1986 Public

Order Act for using 'foul and abusive language' at the football ground. This loophole allowed several offenders to escape conviction for racism at football matches. The law has since been amended to state that the offence is committed 'whether alone or in concert with one or more others'. The London Metropolitan Police have achieved a successful prosecution on the basis of two different comments by one individual. The law also defines what is meant by 'racialist nature': namely, 'Anything that is threatening or abusive or insulting to a person by reason of colour, race, nationality or ethnic or national origins'. So individuals and groups who repeatedly utter racist abuse are clearly committing a criminal offence.

Far-right groups

The level of influence that far-right groups have amongst football fans is a highly debatable issue but over the years they have been present in many football grounds across Britain. Garland and Rowe (1996, 2001) suggest that far-right groups have targeted football fans since at least the 1930s, when the British Union of Fascists tried to attract the young working-class male supporters into their brigade of uniformed 'stewards'. In the 1950s the White Defence League sold their newspaper *Black and White News* at football grounds in London. It was the 1970s, however, that saw far-right groups rise to prominence as the problem of football hooliganism grew in the national conscience. The National Front was the most active group in the 1970s, giving regular coverage in its magazine *Bulldog* to football and encouraging hooligan groups to compete for the title of 'most racist ground in Britain'. Copies of *Bulldog* were openly sold at many clubs and, at West Ham, club memorabilia was sold doctored with NF slogans. Chelsea, Leeds United, Millwall, Newcastle United and Arsenal, as well as West Ham United, were all seen as having strong fascist elements in the 1970s and 1980s. After the Heysel stadium tragedy when a wall collapsed killing 39 people fleeing from Liverpool fans, British National Party leaflets were found on the terraces.

It seems, however, that the problem of far-right groups waned in the 1990s. It has for years now been uncommon to see the open selling of far-right literature or memorabilia at football matches and an incident such as the John Barnes one would be very unlikely to happen now. But this does not mean to say that the problem has gone away, especially amongst the support for the English national side. During the 1980s, far-right groups were often in attendance at England's matches abroad. Williams *et al.* (1984) identified a presence of National Front members in the English support, especially amongst the Chelsea contingent, at the 1982 World Cup in Spain.

In another infamous incident in 1995, far-right groups were involved in disturbances abroad, namely, at the England v. Republic of Ireland 'friendly' match at Lansdowne Road, Dublin when fights between rival fans caused the game to be abandoned after half an hour. Supporters of the British National Party and a militant group called Combat 18 were said to have been involved after racist literature was found at the scene. Anti-Republican chanting could clearly be heard at the match and some claim that the violence was actually orchestrated by an umbrella group called the National Socialist Alliance.

The attractions of football matches to far-right groups are obvious. Football grounds provide a useful platform for the groups to make their voices heard. From them their views can be directed into millions of homes. It also seems as if football grounds can be a means to recruit young support. As Dave Robins (1984) points out, 'The hard-man, though, lives in a more dangerous and unchanging world. Permanently sensitised to "trouble" in his environment, his paranoid fantasies about defending his "patch" against outsiders make him ripe for manipulation by the politics of the extreme right'.

The actual influence of far-right groups amongst club support, however, is believed by many to be minimal. Garland and Rowe (1996) cited a national police source as saying that:

> We are aware that certain right-wing parties have been looking at football hooligans because they see them as an organised group and try to recruit them for this purpose with, I have to say, fairly limited success … It has been seen as an opportunity by many, but I don't think it has been a dramatic success, there is no evidence for that.

Some debate also exists as to whether right-wing groups deliberately targeted soccer fans as recruits or whether soccer fans were drawn into the groups because of the opportunities they offered for violence. Robins was drawn towards the former argument, citing the leafleting campaigns of the 1980s, whilst David Canter *et al.* (1989) argued that the right wing groups merely cashed in on soccer violence, rather than instigated it. In an excellent discussion of racism and the far right, Nick Lowles concludes that: 'Despite the activity of fascist groups at football grounds around the country, there is little evidence to show that many people were recruited into political activity. This is particularly so with the hooligans, who, generally, proved too ill-disciplined and independent for groups such as the [National Front]' (2001: 112–3).

Is football hooliganism motivated by racism?

Whilst concerns about racist chanting and about the possible influence of far-right groups have brought racism within the hooligan debate, the links between racism and football hooliganism are not apparent from the literature. A number of writers have pointed out that is convenient to see racists in football as hooligan 'others' who are members of far-right groups rather than as ordinary supporters and members of the football industry itself – the so-called 'racist/hooligan couplet' (see Back *et al.* 1999; Garland and Rowe 2001). One of Steve Frosdick's dissertation students – Robert Broomhead – chose to investigate the extent to which English football hooliganism was motivated by racism and xenophobia (Broomhead 2004). He first examined the work of the principal theorists on racism in Britain, particularly those who also write about racism in football, for example Solomos (1989, 2003) and Back *et al.* (1999). He then examined the principal football hooligan theorists whose work we have reviewed in Chapters 6 and 7. Broomhead (2004) concluded that:

> ... it is evident that theorists of racism in British society do not to any extent see 'football hooliganism' as motivated by racism and xenophobia. The literature analysed does not refer to 'football hooliganism' to any great extent. Theorists of 'football hooliganism' do not refer to racism as a primary causal factor of 'football hooliganism' however it is referred to in some cases as a contributory factor. This is most common amongst contemporary theorists especially those focussing on England fans abroad.

Anti-racism initiatives

Dating from the 1990s we have seen a number of attempts by various groups and organizations to combat racism (as opposed to hooliganism) in football. These have come from the club level, supporter level and from organizational bodies such as the Commission for Racial Equality (CRE), the Professional Footballers Association (PFA) and the Football Supporters Association (FSA) – latterly the Football Supporters Federation (FSF) following its merger with the National Federation of Football Supporters Clubs.

In 1993 the CRE and PFA launched the 'Let's kick racism out of football' campaign, 'with the aim of highlighting anti-racist and equal opportunities messages within the context of football' (Garland and Rowe 1996). It aimed to encourage clubs and supporters groups to launch their own campaigns to combat racism at their clubs. A ten-point action plan was laid out for clubs, as follows:

1. Issue a statement saying that the club will not tolerate racism, and will take action against supporters who engage in racist abuse, racist chanting or intimidation.

2. Make public announcements condemning any racist chanting at matches, and warning supporters that the club will not hesitate to take action.
3. Make it a condition for season ticket holders that they do not take part in racist abuse, racist chanting or any other offensive behaviour.
4. Prevent the sale or distribution of racist literature in and around the ground on match-days.
5. Take disciplinary action against players who make racially abusive remarks at players, officials or supporters before, during or after matches.
6. Contact other clubs to make sure they understand the club's policy on racism.
7. Make sure stewards and the police understand the problem and the club's policy, and have a common strategy for removing or dealing with supporters who are abusive and breaking the law on football offences.
8. Remove all racist graffiti from the ground as a matter of urgency.
9. Adopt an equal opportunities policy to cover employment and service provision.
10. Work with other groups and agencies – such as the police, the local authority, the PFA, the supporters, schools, etc. – to develop initiatives to raise awareness of the campaign and eliminate racist abuse and discrimination.

The campaign stated that 'If football is to be played and enjoyed equally by everyone, whatever the colour of their skin, and wherever they come from, it is up to us all, each and every one of us, to refuse to tolerate racist attitudes, and to demand nothing less than the highest standards in every area of the game'. A magazine, *Kick It!*, was produced with funding from the Football Trust and 110,000 copies of a fanzine, *United Colours of Football*, were given out free at grounds across the country on the opening day of the 1994/5 season.

Initial reaction to the scheme was not entirely positive. Some thought that it might only serve to bring negative publicity to the game, by highlighting the problem of racism in football. Others claimed that racism was not a problem at their ground and therefore they had no need for such a campaign. Despite this, the first season of the campaign had the support of all but one of the professional clubs and all professional authorities.

In a survey conducted by Garland and Rowe in December 1994, 49 fanzine editors from a wide range of clubs were asked to comment on levels of racism at their club. Many were sceptical about the success of 'Let's kick racism out of football', with only 32 per cent citing the campaign as a factor in the perceived decrease in racism at football matches since

1990. Garland and Rowe suggested that this lack of support might stem from mistaken expectations of the campaign.

Nevertheless, the year 2004 marked ten years of the campaign, which has evolved from 'Let's kick racism out of football', through the 'Advisory group against racism and intimidation' (AGARI), through the slogans 'Let's kick racism' and 'Respect all fans', to its more recent abbreviated name, 'Kick it out'. These are all the same campaign, which has continued and thrives to the present day. The campaign is still supported and funded by the PFA, the football authorities and the Football Foundation (formerly the Football Trust). On the international stage, the campaign plays a leading role in the Football Against Racism in Europe (FARE) network and is supported by UEFA, FIFA, the Council of Europe, the European Commission, European parliamentarians and the British Council. 'Kick it out's core priorities are as folows:

- Working with the professional game by offering advice and guidance on all aspects of race equality within professional football.
- Using the appeal of the game to address young people within schools, colleges and youth organizations, through the development and delivery of resources and educational materials.
- Working at grassroots and amateur levels to tackle racial abuse and harassment in parks football.
- Raising the issue of the exclusion of south Asians as professional footballers from the game.
- Capacity-building local ethnic minority communities to engage with professional clubs and the structures of the game.
- Developing partnerships to raise the debate and tackle racism in European football.

As mentioned earlier, the original aim of the CRE and PFA was to encourage clubs to launch their own initiatives, rather than control the whole campaign themselves. In this sense it has been largely successful, as it prompted many clubs to launch their own campaigns.

The most ambitious of these have included Derby County's scheme 'Rams against racism' and Charlton Athletic's 'Red, white and black at the Valley'. Millwall have also been particularly active. Within these campaigns we find all the stakeholders – including supporters' organizations, the police, safety officers, the football authorities, local authorities, race equality organisations and football clubs – working together to eliminate racist chanting from football. Derby County dedicated a home-match day in 1994 to the cause of combating racism after liaisons between club officials, the club's Football and Community Development Officer and the Racial Equality Council. Anti-racist banners were displayed, campaign messages printed in the match-day programme and players were involved.

Some 250 free tickets were also given out to local children. A long-term aim of the scheme was to encourage the local Asian community to attend more games as well as encouraging local Asian footballing talent.

Red, White and Black at the Valley was a leaflet launched by Charlton Athletic in conjunction with the police, the local Racial Equality Council, Greenwich Council and the supporters' club. The aim was to present Charlton Athletic as being a club that people from all minorities could come and watch without fear of harassment from other supporters. After the leaflet had been distributed the club continued by producing posters and issuing statements in the programmes. Players also visited local schools and colleges. Garland and Rowe point out that it is difficult to calculate how effective these schemes have been, although a drive by the police (acting on a tip-off from the club) was successful in removing racist fans from one end of the Valley ground.

The first fan-based group set up specifically to fight racism was Leeds Fans United Against Racism And Fascism (LFUARAF). This was formed in 1987 to combat the influence of far-right groups at Elland Road, especially the most visible displays of paper selling, etc. The first step was to distribute anti-racist leaflets outside the ground, then in 1988 it contributed to *Terror On Our Terraces*, a report on the involvement of the far-right amongst the Leeds crowd. This prompted the club to recognize the problem and they issued an anti-racist statement signed by both management and players. Within a few months the number of far-right paper sellers decreased significantly.

In Scotland, supporters have formed a national campaign to combat racism in football. SCARF (Supporters' Campaign Against Racism in Football) was formed in 1991 in response to an increase in far-right activity at Scottish grounds, mainly involving the British National Party. Most of the campaign consisted of leafleting the worst-affected grounds, Rangers and Hearts being two examples, but it has not been without its problems. As well as one female campaigner being threatened and others abused, SCARF say that they have had a problem in getting clubs and officials to recognize that there is a problem at all.

The government 'Football Task Force' set up in 1997 addressed the question of racism in its first report, entitled *Eliminating Racism from Football* (Department for Culture Media and Sport 1998). It made a large number of recommendations, the progress of which have been assessed by Steven Bradbury (2001). One of the main recommendations was that, 'The FA [Football Association], the FLA [Football Licensing Authority] and the Football Safety Officers' Association should ensure that football stewards are trained to deal with incidents of racism at football matches'. Subsequently, co-author Steve Frosdick worked with 'Kick it out' to write a new module – *Dealing With Racism and Disability Discrimination* – for the national Training Package for Stewarding at Football Grounds (see

Football League *et al.* 1996, 2003). The impact of this initiative has not been evaluated.

Fanzines started in the mid-1980s and have offered an alternative, positive view of football fans in the post-Heysel era. Almost every club has at least one fanzine and these are almost exclusively anti-racist. Some are actually produced by anti-racist groups themselves such as *Marching Altogether* (LFUARAF) – which is given away free – and *Filbo Fever* (Leicester City Foxes Against Racism). Other clubs whose fanzines actively support anti-racism campaigns include Everton, Celtic, Manchester United, Cardiff City, Leyton Orient and Chelsea. One criticism levelled at fanzines is that they are simply preaching to the converted as the fans who buy them will already be anti-racist. Nevertheless, fanzines have enjoyed increasing popularity over the years and this should be recognized as a positive sign.

Campaigners also believe that the 'civilization' of football grounds – through seating, family enclosures, executive boxes, etc. – will encourage more blacks and Asians to attend football matches. They may be right but this has not occurred yet in England. Every football ground in the Premier League is now all-seater yet, as mentioned before, white people constitute 99 per cent of the attendance.

Nevertheless, noting the various initiatives being undertaken, Moran concludes that 'there is reason to be optimistic about the levels of racism within football' (2000: 198). This does not mean that racism has been eliminated – far from it. For example, in December 2001, Everton Football Club began sending undercover stewards to away matches to try to identify those who were orchestrating racist chanting. The club also threatened to ban ticket sales to their own fans for away matches. In 2004, there were allegations that Sheffield Wednesday fans had racially abused Chesterfield's black players (*Daily Telegraph* 24 November 2004). Whilst a Blackburn Rovers fan was convicted of making monkey chants and gestures at Dwight Yorke – one of his own team's players – as he warmed up for a match against Birmingham City (*Daily Telegraph*, 25 November 2004).

The European dimension

Throughout Europe, racism figures prominently in football-related violence. Neo-Nazi and neo-Fascist groups target football grounds in Europe in the same way as their English equivalents did here. Amongst the worst-affected clubs are Lazio and AC Milan in Italy, Paris Saint-Germain in France and Real Madrid in Spain. In eastern Europe the problems are even more acute.

In Italy, a Jewish player, Ronnie Rosenthal, was unable to play even one game for Udinese because of massive pressure from neo-Fascist circles, and Aaron Winter, a native of Suriname of Hindustani extraction was subject to attacks at Lazio involving cries of 'Niggers and Jews out'. Paul Ince, a black English player for Inter Milan, has also expressed his anger at the way he was treated by the Italian fans.

Germany has a poor reputations for far-right influence amongst its fans, with frequent displays of Hitler salutes, particularly at international matches. Professor Volker Rittner of the Sports Sociology Institute in Cologne, however, believes that these are no more than provocative displays designed to get the fans into the papers, but some reports of right-wing activity in Germany have been disturbing. In 1990 there were reports of skinheads barracking the small number of black players in the Bundesliga and in 1992 similar reports were made of neo-Nazi groups in Germany using football matches as occasions to plan and organize attacks against local ethnic communities and east European refugees. An analysis of the political attitudes of German fans revealed that 20 per cent feel close to neo-Nazis.

Spain has suffered problems which received considerable publicity during 2004 and 2005. Spain's national coach was under investigation following a furore about racist comments he made about Arsenal's black French player, Thierry Henry. The Spanish Football Association was fined after several England players were racially abused during a Spain v. England 'friendly' in November 2004 in Madrid. A January 2005 match between Atletico Madrid and Real Madrid was marred by racist chanting and, to cap it all, 20 February 2005 saw the first time that a Spanish referee halted a match because of racist abuse. The game between Malaga and Espanyol was suspended after Malaga fans made repeated monkey chants at Espanyol's Cameroon goalkeeper. The referee insisted on the club making a public announcement to tell the fans to stop the abuse before he restarted the game. New regulations allowing referees to stop matches have also been invoked in Holland, where a Den Haag v. PSV Eindhoven match was abandoned with ten minutes remaining after the referee was taunted with repeated anti-semetic chants (*Daily Telegraph* 18 October 2004).

Neo-Nazi and neo-Fascist influences have been very marked in eastern Europe, with frequent complaints from English clubs playing in European competitions and from the England national team about the racist abuse suffered by black English players. For example, England players Emile Heskey and Ashley Cole had to put up with sustained monkey-chanting during a European Championship qualifier in Slovakia in October 2002.

Some European countries have initiated similar schemes to the British 'Let's kick racism out of football' campaign. The Netherlands uses the motto 'When racism wins, the sport loses', which is displayed on posters at train stations and at tram and bus stops. Players in the Netherlands even went on strike in protest against racism. Players have also led the way in Italy by threatening to walk off the pitch if black players continued to be abused by racists. This resulted in a day of action in December 1992 when all players in the top two divisions displayed the slogan 'No Al Razzismo!' ('No To Racism'). In Switzerland, footballers from the national team are involved in 'street football' competitions for young people, held in a different town each weekend.

A more general campaign was 'All different – all equal' against racism, xenophobia and intolerance, organized by the Council of Europe. Football players from many countries have been involved, most notably in Sweden where the national team appeared in a short video, shown several times on national TV, to promote the campaign.

Football Against Racism in Europe (FARE) is a pan-European campaign which 'aims to rid the game of racism by combining the resources of anti-racist football organisation throughout Europe. It helps to support and nurture groups and coordinates efforts on an European scale. By working together, FARE helps organisations share good practice and present a united front against racism in football'.

Prior to 1999, UEFA had not adopted any specific measures to combat racism in football. They argued that their 'Fair play' scheme was adequate in tackling the problem. In this, behaviour both on and off the field was evaluated, and negative marks were given for racist chanting or the display of racist slogans. At the end of the season the three national associations with the best records were awarded an extra place in the UEFA Cup for one of their clubs. Whilst this may have provided some sort of incentive for fans not to be racist, critics argued that this was not enough.

Subsequently, in December 2000, the UEFA Executive Committee adopted a new clause on racism in the UEFA Disciplinary Regulations. In March 2001, the Executive Committee approved the partner and sponsorship agreement with the FARE network, which began to receive funds from fines meted out in European competitions. In October 2002, UEFA launched its own ten-point action plan, and in December 2002, invited the 'European football family' to a 'Unite against racism' conference held at Chelsea FC on 5 March 2003. UEFA would now consider itself active against racism and a search for 'racism' on its website reveals numerous stories of clubs and national associations being fined because of racism by their supporters, although UEFA have been criticized for the derisory level of some of these punishments.

Conclusion

Although actual levels of racism are extremely hard to quantify and statistics thin on the ground, it seems apparent that there has been a reduction in the levels of racism at football matches in England. Garland and Rowe's survey in 1996 revealed that 84 per cent of the fanzine editors who responded felt that levels of racism had decreased since 1990, with over half these claiming a significant decline. Only 6 per cent felt that racism had increased during this time. Garland and Rowe also claim that this view was backed up by nearly all the administrators, players and officials interviewed in addition to the survey. The role of fan-based groups and the growth of fanzine culture were the two most cited reasons for the decline in racism, although this may not be surprising given that the respondents were all fanzine editors. Perhaps more important, therefore, is the fact that 57 per cent believed that the increase in the number of black players was a major factor for the decrease in racism. All respondents were aware of the 'Let's kick racism out of football' campaign and 44 per cent felt that it had raised public awareness of the problem.

As Garland and Rowe point out, however, less public forms of racism may still be present and support for the national team seems still to have distinct racist factions to it. In any case, the lack of support from ethnic minorities suggests that clubs, authorities and fans still need to go a long way in convincing people that they will not encounter racism at football grounds.

Racism in other parts of Europe does not look as if it is decreasing and in some parts may be increasing. In Germany, the neo-Nazi and neo-Fascist movements continue to increase their support and the Front National in France, led by Jean Marie Le Pen, holds public support across the board, football supporters being no exception. The issue of racism in football was raised in a report to the European Parliament (1996) on football hooliganism, drafted by the German Green Group MEP Claudia Roth. The committee was said to be 'shocked at the racist demonstrations and attacks perpetrated on players who are black or Jewish or come from different national or ethnic backgrounds' and 'concerned at the ways in which extremist organisations deliberately exploit violence connected with sport including the manipulation and infiltration of hooligan groups'. The report went on to suggest that players should take an active role in combating racism by refusing to play if 'violent, racist, xenophobic or anti-semitic behaviour' occurred. It also called for a Europe-wide ban on any racist or xenophobic symbols being displayed at football matches and for a European day of anti-racism and fair-play in sport to be held throughout Europe in 1997 (the European Year against Racism).

In an international context, the media, in particular the English tabloid press, play a part in encouraging racism and xenophobia at football matches and this was also recognized in the European Parliament report. In the report's explanatory statement the committee stated that the media frequently present international matches as 'warlike confrontations' which thus give rise to jingoism and sometimes acts of violence. The committee recommended that the media should endeavour to bring the sporting aspect back into sport. Whilst one must recognize that the problem of racism is different in each country, the Europe-wide initiatives we have outlined to combat the problem must surely be welcomed.

Further study

For a very full analysis of 'Racism and anti-racism in football', we would recommend Garland and Rowe's book of the same name (2001). For a succinct overview of the issues, see the University of Leicester fact sheet (Number 6) on *Racism and Football* (SNCCFR 2002) available to download from the Centre for the Sociology of Sport website.

Chapter summary

Writers on racism do not particularly refer to football hooliganism, neither do writers on football hooliganism particularly refer to racism as a causal factor. Yet racism has become a football hooliganism issue, particularly because of the increasing criminalization of 'hate speech' – in this context racist chanting. The true extent of racism amongst football supporters is almost impossible to quantify. Extensive speculation and debate on the subject are not supported by much reliable empirical data. For the media and public opinion, however, racism amongst football fans is a serious problem which is often blamed for outbreaks of violence, particularly at international matches.

Amongst academics and professionals involved with football, the role of racism and far-right groups in football violence is a contested issue. Some agencies, such as the National Criminal Intelligence Service, regard their influence as minimal, whilst others have directly blamed them for violent incidents. The balance of academic opinion seems to be that far-right groups have had little influence on British football hooliganism.

In Britain, racist chanting at matches still occasionally occurs, but at nowhere near the levels it reached in the 1970s and 1980s, when black players were often greeted with monkey-noises and bananas. The reduction may be due in part to campaigns designed to combat racism, such as the 'Let's kick racism out of football' campaign.

Elsewhere in Europe, there are some indications that the problem may be more persistent. The problem is certainly being taken seriously across Europe, and a number of initiatives have been launched, including the 'When Racism Wins, The Sport Loses' campaign in the Netherlands, 'No al Razzismo' in Italy and the Europe-wide initiatives, 'All different all equal' and 'Fans against racism in Europe'. The success of these initiatives is difficult to measure, but the UK has certainly seen a decrease in racist behaviour at football grounds.

Part IV

Tackling Football Hooliganism

Part IV begins by dealing with the methods of social control adopted by the police and other authorities. As it was with folk-football in the Middle Ages, most social policy in this area has been negative and focused on repression and suppression rather than prevention or cure. As we shall see, the various strategies and responses have been primarily reactive and, increasingly, have been influenced (if not entirely led) by technological developments, such as the use of closed-circuit television and computer databases. Such advances have certainly helped the flourishing collaboration between the member states of Europe in tackling hooliganism. The European Parliament, however, has expressed concern about the use of such technology, particularly in relation to the issue of the free movement of individuals across member state boundaries.

The UK is perceived by virtually all observers in Europe, and by football fans themselves, as having had the earliest and most severe problems with football hooliganism. Certainly, it is the only nation to have received a blanket expulsion from all European football competitions – a ban that was initially made for an indefinite period following the Heysel Stadium tragedy in which 39 Juventus fans died when a wall collapsed after clashes with Liverpool supporters. It is perhaps because of this unenviable record that the UK has taken the lead in the development of control measures to deal with hooliganism. The evolution of these measures is closely examined in Chapters 12 and 13.

The approach taken by the British authorities to reducing football hooliganism has been largely reactive – increasingly sophisticated policing, surveillance and monitoring techniques, segregation of fans, etc. Chapter 12 opens by looking at the historically negative attitude of the public police towards football fans and at the harsh containment policies adopted towards them. It then examines the contemporary policing style of reaction and, in some cases, over-reaction, to crime and disorder in football grounds.

Chapter 12 continues with an examination of 'intelligence-led' policing, outlining the nationwide system which evolved under the co-ordination of the National Criminal Intelligence Service. The impact of this intelligence system in reducing disorder inside grounds is noted; however, it is shown that there are limitations on using intelligence as a predictor for the future. We also see that this partial success had come at the price of considerable police-imposed restrictions, together with displacement away from the grounds.

The British government has also introduced specific legislation to cover acts of 'hooliganism'. Chapter 13 outlines the whole raft of football-specific criminal legislation, noting that much of it is an unnecessary and draconian 'political moral panic' response with serious implications for civil liberties. The restraining influences of new and refurbished grounds, together with their various technological systems such as CCTV, ticketing and access control, are then reviewed and it is noted that these represent a more subtle form of containment, but containment, none the less. The chapter then examines the 13 official government reports produced between 1924 and 2001, concluding that, in the context of disorder, these have been rather more concerned to be seen to be doing something than to tackle the underlying social roots of the violence.

Chapters 12 and 13 show how repeated and increasingly repressive social controls have met with limited success, yet the government seems determined to continue down the same road. Whilst such measures are evident elsewhere in Europe, the German, Dutch and Belgian authorities, in particular, have been more proactive in their approach to the problem. Chapter 14 begins by referring to the benefits of the 'friendly but firm' policing style adopted by the Dutch for the 2000 European Football Championships. It then looks at how preserving public order has been put back into balance with the maintenance of public safety within a broader risk management framework.

Chapter 14 then continues with a discussion on changing the culture of football supporting from within. In particular, we look at the phenomenon of the 'fan projects' and 'fan coaching' schemes, which originated in Germany in the 1970s and which have been swiftly imitated by many other countries in Europe, including Belgium and the Netherlands. These schemes, which involve social workers deployed with groups of fans, appear to have had an impact on levels of violence in certain areas. They thus provide useful models for other countries.

12. Policing football hooliganism

Introduction

Policing forms the major social control applied to football hooliganism. This chapter therefore examines such policing from both a historical and contemporary perspective. The chapter is in three main parts. The first part looks at the historically very repressive policing approach applied prior to the nadir of the Hillsborough stadium disaster in Sheffield in April 1989 and the subsequent English hosting of the European Championships in 1996. The second part examines policing at those championships, highlighting the co-ordinating role of the National Criminal Intelligence Service (NCIS) and the supporting police organization and network of 'spotters'. The final part of the chapter then discusses the evolution of policing since 1996, examining the role reversal of police and stewards and the police move to a more 'intelligence-led' policing style.

Policing prior to Euro '96

Containment

Historically, the principal difficulty for the police in dealing with football hooliganism has been in differentiating between the hooligan and the ordinary football supporter. This difficulty led to the police developing a system whereby all fans were contained, both inside the ground and in travelling to the ground. Frosdick and Sidney (1999: 209) have argued that:

> Throughout the 1970s and 1980s, football match days often resembled military operations. In terms of crowd management, the emphasis was firmly on public order. Huge numbers of police were employed

on tactics which achieved control, but at the expense of safety and comfort. This repressive policing style was generally coupled with hard engineering measures such as the high fences still seen in most continental stadia. And the grounds themselves were generally old, poorly maintained and with minimal facilities for the spectator.

The British police have had a very negative attitude towards sports fans – particularly football supporters. Officers regularly described fans as 'animals' – and treated them as such. A common sight in the 1970s (and for much of the 1980s) was that of the police escorting visiting supporters from railway and coach stations to and from the ground. Supporters – especially the away fans – were herded like cattle from their transport to the stadium, literally surrounded by police, some on horseback and others with police dogs.

In contrast, the 1990s saw the use of the less confrontational tactic of posting officers at specified points *en route* to the ground. This was, perhaps, more to do with the circumstances of away fans than with the police entirely changing their tactics. It has certainly been the case that travelling away support has dwindled and changed. The withdrawal of 'football specials' means that the familiar *en masse* arrival of football fans at stations around the country on a Saturday lunchtime is, perhaps, a sight of the past. Away fans more commonly travel on organized coach trips or by private car.

The police, however, have still been heavily criticized in some quarters for an overzealous approach in dealing with travelling supporters, such as conducting unnecessary searches of coaches for alcohol and even searching supporters' belongings in their absence, although in a 1993 fan survey (Middleham 1993), only 20.7 per cent of supporters disagreed with the use of police escorts, stressing their use as effective protection for away fans.

Historically, however, the policing style was often very harsh. Officers were aggressive, arbitrary and unjust, particularly towards away supporters. Co-author Steve Frosdick served as a police officer between 1979 and 1996 and has personal experience of throwing people out of the ground simply to show who was 'in charge'. On arrival at the ground, the visiting (or away) fans were invariably herded into grounds via separate turnstiles. They were shown into caged pens where they were carefully segregated from the home support. These isolationist operations were often emphasized by a line of police officers separating the home and away fans in a sort of 'no man's land' and by the high metal fences which surrounded these fan pens, an attempt to prevent fans from spilling on to the football pitch itself (Harrison 1974). At the end of the match, they were required to wait behind (the 'lock in') until the surrounding streets were clear and then quickly herded away back to their transport.

The police have also been commonly used at the turnstile. Traditionally, this has been a law enforcement role, with the emphasis on preventing illegal entry into the ground, enforcing exclusion orders and searching supporters for weapons and other prohibited articles. But they have also been used by clubs to enforce club policy and ground regulations, such as enforcing club bans and membership schemes and deterring fraud by turnstile operators. In the 1990s, the role of the steward came to the fore at football grounds, which partly relieved the responsibilities of the police in this area.

The undercover operation

In addition to the strategy of containment, the second primary strategy of the police was the undercover operation: an attempt to ascertain who exactly the hooligans were. The English Football Association recommended that plain-clothes officers be used in the domestic game as far back as the mid-1960s and requests for the police to infiltrate travelling supporters with plain-clothes officers were also made by the Football Association in 1981. The belief of the police (torridly supported by the media) by the 1980s was that football hooligans had transformed themselves from an ill-organized mob into highly organized forces with a complex network of hierarchies (see Home Affairs Committee 1991a, 1991b; Armstrong and Hobbs 1994).

Officers were given new identities and instructed to live the life of a hooligan and mingle with other hooligans. These tactics resulted in the launch of numerous early-morning raids on the homes of suspected football hooligans from around March 1986. Armstrong and Hobbs detail a familiar pattern in the arrest and charging of suspects in these raids. The suspects would generally be part of an organized gang that had apparently caused mayhem throughout the country; they would have a 'calling-card' which would normally be displayed on or left beside their victim; they would have used an array of weaponry (which the police nearly always displayed to the media in the post-arrest briefing); and they would often possess incriminating literature – although on one occasion, this included a copy of an academic book on football hooligans entitled *Hooligans Abroad* (Williams *et al.* 1984).

On most occasions, individuals arrested in these raids were charged with conspiracy to cause affray or conspiracy to commit violence, with what they had said to the police and what the police had found in their homes being used as the primary evidence against them. Many of the raids resulted in high-profile trials and convictions (e.g. the 18-week trial of four Chelsea fans which cost over £2 million and resulted in sentences including one of ten years). But many also failed in sometimes dramatic circumstances, with the reliability of evidence being intensely disputed and the behaviour of undercover officers severely condemned (see Armstrong and Hobbs 1994; Armstrong 1998).

Police tactics at grounds

While the use of *en masse* containment alongside covert detective operations has been the basic pattern of policing football hooliganism, police tactics can vary considerably at individual football grounds, as indeed they do on other matters. Such tactics can depend on various factors including the prospective size of the crowd, the relative profile of the particular match, the reputation of the supporters involved and the priorities of the local force involved (Home Affairs Committee 1991a, 1991b; Middleham 1993).

The inconsistencies between different police forces in their approach to dealing with football supporters were highlighted in the Home Office Affairs Committee report, *Policing Football Hooliganism* (1991a), which recognized that:

> different police forces and, within police forces, the different police Commanders were inconsistent. A variety of witnesses complained of these inconsistencies. The FSA [Football Supporters Association] told us that 'acceptable behaviour at one ground could be an arrestable offence at another' ... [and] different Ground Commanders had different approaches to policing the same ground.

The decline of the 'away' fan

In the Premier League in particular, demand for tickets rose considerably whilst ground capacities declined due to the introduction of all-seated stadiums. The expanding interest in football also led to an increasing commercial interest in the game and, subsequently, an increase in corporate facilities to the detriment of the traditional fan. For example, 14,000 corporate guests were present at the England v. Scotland match during the Euro '96 championships.

Thus, there was now less room for the away fans than ever before, with clubs obviously favouring their own home support above that of away fans. In 1995, six out of ten of a national sample of FA Premier League fans said that they would travel to more games if more tickets were made available to them (SNCCFR 1996).

It could be suggested that policing at football grounds had been made easier by the decline of away support. However, the past tendency of fans towards *en masse* travelling when away from home has been replaced by a proclivity towards independent travel, which is, perhaps, more difficult to police. Group travel still occurs and the police regularly escort away fans in coaches, via specified rendezvous points. Indeed, the

Traffic Commissioner has outlined specific guidelines to the police on dealing with the travel arrangements of fans, such as recommending that coaches should arrive at the ground no more than two hours before the designated kick-off time.

The steward

The 1990s also saw a shift away from using police to control fans inside the ground, with clubs relying more and more on stewards, employed by the clubs themselves or provided by private security companies. This is certainly the principal reason why the ratio of police to fans declined from 1:74 in 1985 to 1:132 in 1992 (Wilmot 1993). Some clubs, particularly in the lower divisions, played most of their home games without a single police officer inside the ground. Other more high-profile clubs increasingly relied on stewards to police the stadium.

Police officers could only eject individuals from grounds if they were breaking the law, whereas stewards could follow a particular club's agenda and eject people for breaking club rules and ground regulations. A report on policing football (Wilmot 1993) recommended that the police leave the task of ejecting supporters to the stewards. But the ability of stewards to deal with disorder inside grounds was severely questioned, not least by the Channel 4 programme *Dispatches* in October 1994. There was also evidence suggesting the bias of stewards towards the home fans. Garland and Rowe (1995) noted that stewards could occasionally provoke the away fans, for example by celebrating home goals in front of them.

The Taylor Report (Home Office 1990) highlighted the lack of training for stewards. There was at that time no national standard for the training of stewards in crowd control and spectator safety or, indeed, any legislative requirement that clubs should provide such training for stewards. Referring to the early 1990s, Garland and Rowe (2000) have suggested that stewards did not then have the traditional authority that the police possessed and would need proper training and briefing if future problems were to be avoided.

Closed-circuit television (CCTV) and hand-held cameras

CCTV was introduced into football grounds around the middle of the 1980s and, by 1996, was present in almost every Premier and Football League ground. The effectiveness of such camera surveillance has also been improved by the introduction of all-seater stadiums across the country (Garland and Rowe 2000). Certainly, the results of fan surveys suggested that the introduction of CCTV had, for the most part, been welcomed by supporters, who quickly became accustomed to CCTV surveillance.

Another technological feature of police tactics at football grounds was

– and remains – the use of hand-held video cameras, with police filming supporters, primarily in a bid to deter violence, gather intelligence and monitor the efficacy of crowd control (Middleham 1993). A further technological advance was the 'photophone' system that allowed the police to exchange photographs of football hooligans from CCTV and other sources via telephone and computer links, allowing vital information to be readily available to the police on match days.

The 'Hoolivan'

Advances in technology also aided the police in both overt and covert surveillance operations. The 'Hoolivan' was launched at the beginning of the season that followed the plethora of incidents in the spring of 1985. This hi-tech item of machinery enabled the police to maintain radio contact with all officers inside and outside the ground and to be linked with the CCTV cameras in and around the stadium. The Hoolivan tended to be used at high-profile matches or when the police were concerned about a particular set of supporters. During Euro '96, Greater Manchester police used a Hoolivan known as the 'skyhawk', which contained nine hydraulic cameras, each of which could be raised up to 30 feet in height.

European co-operation

It was really only after 1985 (after the Heysel Stadium tragedy) that a concerted effort had been made to establish cross-border co-operation in Europe between both police forces and football authorities to combat football hooliganism. The impact of the Heysel tragedy (where 39 Italian supporters were killed at the European Cup Final between Juventus and Liverpool) was such that three major European bodies addressed the issue of football violence. First, the Council of Europe (1985) adopted a *European Convention on Spectator Violence and Misbehaviour at Sports Events, and in Particular at Football Matches.* This made a good number of recommendations on measures that should be taken to prevent and punish violent behaviour in sport. The various measures have been well summarized by Rowlands (2001). The convention is monitored by a Council of Europe Standing Committee, which prepares periodic reports on the extent of compliance by member countries. Secondly, the European Council called on all member countries to deal with violence in and around sports stadiums and, finally, the European Parliament proposed a number of different measures to combat football hooliganism.

On 22 April 1996, the European Union issued guidelines on dealing with football hooliganism, many of which adopted UK proposals. These guidelines included using the EPI centre system (secure e-mail) to enable the swift exchange of police intelligence information, the seizure of racist material intended for distribution abroad and the training of club stewards in crowd safety and control techniques. It was also proposed that police forces participate in member states' relevant training courses to aid the exchange of information about the techniques that can be used to prevent hooliganism.

Whilst Europe was quick to adopt many strategies on hooliganism formulated in the UK, the European Parliament remained especially concerned about restrictions placed on the free movement of football supporters. The Parliament's Committee on Civil Liberties and Internal Affairs commissioned a report on football hooliganism, which was drafted by the MEP, Claudia Roth and adopted by the European Parliament (1996). The report contained some criticism of police databases and the new information exchange networks, stressing that such networks had led to the arrest and expulsion of innocent people. In the UK, this was certainly viewed as an attack on the work of the National Criminal Intelligence Service Football Unit, in particular. Any information thus exchanged between member states 'must be carried out in compliance with the criteria laid down by the Council of Europe for the protection of data of a personal nature'.

The report, however, supported the British Home Secretary's demands for increased co-operation between member states regarding the control of cross-border hooliganism. But it further stressed that nationality alone cannot be a basis on which to prevent access to sports stadiums and that 'only after a supporter has been convicted of an offence either of violence or an offence connected with football, can he/she legitimately be prevented from attending matches at home or abroad'. The report concluded by refuting the argument that restrictions imposed on the freedom of movement of football supporters were either a viable or a suitable means of controlling football hooliganism. As we shall see in Chapter 13, this refutation was not accepted by the British government.

Further study

For more detailed information on the convention and on the policing of football across Europe, visit the website created by Rowlands (2001) at http://www.ex.ac.uk/politics/pol_data/undergrad/rowlands/index.htm.

Policing Euro '96

The European Championships held in England in June 1996 highlighted both the expanding level of co-operation between European police forces since Heysel and the increased sophistication of safety and security techniques that had developed to deal with the football hooligan.

National Crime Intelligence Service Football Unit

The security campaign for Euro '96 was organized by the National Crime Intelligence Service Football Unit (see Drew 1999). The NCIS Football Unit in 1996 consisted of six full-time police officers led by a superintendent. Over six thousand names and photographs of individuals were held on computer files. Indeed, the information gathered by the Football Unit formed the basis of much of the evidence presented in the Home Affairs Committee reports (1991a, 1991b).

The head of the Football Unit (an assistant chief constable seconded from Greater Manchester police) was also in overall control of the police operation for Euro '96. The Football Unit worked in conjunction with an ACPO (Association of Chief Police Officers) steering group and a multi-agency working party. Pre-tournament estimates suggested over 10,000 police officers from nearly a dozen different police forces were involved in policing Euro '96, at a cost of approximately £25 million. The Football Trust provided 75 per cent of the funding required to update police technology for the tournament.

Police organization

A Police National Co-ordinating Centre was based at Scotland Yard in London for the duration of the competition and included police representatives from each of the 16 countries taking part. In addition to this, a police liaison officer travelled with each team and with each national football association throughout their stay in the competition. In addition, four principal subgroups were in operation throughout the competition. The Match Commander Group comprised the head of policing at each of the eight Euro '96 venues. The purpose of this group was to engender 'a common police philosophy' between the different police commanders.

Teams of police officers were also assigned to deal with other crimes as well as football hooliganism. The Senior Investigating Officers Group was instigated to enable information to be exchanged on outbreaks of crimes such as shop-theft and pick-pocketing. The Information Technology Group was responsible for maintaining the various computer links between the National Co-ordinating Centre and the match commanders at the eight venues. Essentially, all the police forces in the UK were included in the computer link-up, enabling the movement of fans between venues to be monitored at all times through the exchange of information between the forces. The task of the Press and Media Group was to avoid sensationalist reporting of any hooligan incidents by encouraging openness between the various police forces and the media. A more salient initiative of the group included issuing detailed advice packs to visiting supporters in four different languages.

Each of the eight venues in Euro '96 housed a police command centre, complete with intelligence co-ordinator. Intelligence could be passed between each of these centres via the EPI centre system. The EPI centre system is an electronic mail system developed by the Home Office Scientific Development Branch that enables large amounts of data to be transferred electronically at speed, and in a secure fashion. Ten 'photophones' were also provided, one for each of the Euro '96 venues and one each for the co-ordination centres at New Scotland Yard and the British Transport Police.

Hooligan hotline

A 'hooligan hotline' number was also established whereby supporters could phone in and report incidents of hooliganism and perhaps even identify perpetrators. Although this scheme was promoted as being entirely new, similar schemes had been in existence since 1988, when the West Midlands police set up a 24-hour hotline. An identical scheme was launched in 1990 before the World Cup Finals (even though these were taking place outside the UK, in Italy) in an attempt to deter disorder by English fans and, again, a purely domestic hotline was established at the beginning of the 1992/3 domestic season in August 1992. Two Premiership clubs (Manchester United and Leeds United) have also had telephone hotlines for people to ring in with information on hooligans.

Spotters

The 'spotter' system was also in operation at each venue. This is a system which is used throughout the season in the English Premier and Football Leagues, where a police liaison officer is attached to a particular club and has the responsibility of identifying and monitoring hooligans, usually travelling to away games and assisting the local force with the detection of hooligans. During Euro '96, this system was a primary example of co-operation between police from different European countries, with officers from each of the visiting countries providing spotters to work alongside the home country officers at the relevant stadiums. (At a previous European championship in Germany in 1988, the British police sent spotters to aid their German counterparts in the detection of English hooligans.)

Developments in policing since Euro '96

Stewarding

After Hillsborough, the Home Affairs Committee (1991a) recommendation for policing football was of 'higher-profile stewarding supported by lower-profile policing'. As we saw earlier, many matches at many clubs now take place with few or no police officers in the ground. Somewhat perversely, only being heavily involved in 'high risk' matches means that police are less experienced at policing football than they used to be. Meanwhile, football stewarding has advanced considerably, with national standards emerging in the form of a national 'Training Package for Stewarding at Football Grounds' and a 'Football Stewarding Qualification' (see Frosdick and Sidney 1999; Football League *et al.* 1995, 1996, 1998, 1999, 2003). We shall say something more about this in Chapter 14.

Policing style

Nowadays, the British 'policing' style of uniformed officers and stewards on duty in the ground is planned, reactive and assertive. Exuberant behaviours are tolerated up to a point. But once the threshold of tolerance has been breached, the culprits generally experience a swift 'no nonsense' ejection from the venue. Importantly, this style is supported by generally good operational and contingency planning, allowing careful deployment and pre-planned reactions by police and stewards (see Warne 1999: 197–9). The primary reactive role of the police service has evolved to focus on crime, disorder and major emergencies (see Wilmot 1993; ACPO 2002).

Stewards generally display more tolerance and guile than police officers. Take the case of someone using abusive language which merits ejection from the ground. Whereas the police might wish to steam straight in to the crowd, sometimes inflaming the situation, the stewards will wait until the miscreant goes to the toilet at half-time. Style is often the product of experience. When co-author Steve Frosdick took his students on a field visit to Portsmouth v. Millwall in 2002, it was found that the Hampshire Constabulary were all dressed up in their full riot gear and were inclined to draw their batons and react aggressively to the slightest hint that there might be trouble.

In continental Europe, with the exception of Holland, the style of policing remains reactive and aggressive. In 1996, for example, Nottingham Forest travelled to France for a UEFA cup match. At the security briefing, the French senior police officer was asked to outline his contingency plans. He answered: 'If there is a problem, we will deal with it.' Experience suggests that what we meant was 'We will get our sticks out and start beating everybody over the head'. There are many good examples of serious police over-reaction to football supporters, e.g.

in Belgium during the 2000 European Soccer Championships. In one notorious incident, Belgian police threw tear gas grenades into a crowded bar and indiscriminately arrested everyone inside. The deportees who arrived back in England included an American tourist and a Swiss businessman who just happened to be in the bar at the time.

There was some nervousness about the policing for the 2002 World Cup in Japan and South Korea. Early in the preparations, senior Japanese police officers visiting the UK were asked: 'What level of tolerance will you show to supporters?' They simply did not understand the question. According to Kevin Miles, the national co-ordinator of the Football Supporters Association:

> There's always a concern that policing of English fans could be based more on the stereotype than on the reality ... It doesn't bode well if you look at some of the exercises by the Japanese police in preparation for the tournament ... Our first impression has been that they have no clear concept of the culture of English football. We have to get across that what may seem loud and threatening to them can, to us, be entirely good natured (*Sunday Telegraph*, 2 December 2001).

Fortunately, the Japanese and Korean understanding moved on and, as it turned out, the fans behaved very well.

In some cases, police over-reaction – which has included firing live rounds into the crowd – has resulted in disastrous crowd stampedes. As Frosdick (2001a) concludes:

> in too many places, we still see high fences and draconian policing. We are still seeing injuries and deaths resulting from the indiscriminate and wholly inappropriate use of baton charges and tear gas. In too many countries, the policing of sports events is still about protection *from* the crowd rather than the protection *of* the crowd.

Intelligence-led policing

We saw earlier that the police undercover 'infiltration' operations undertaken during the 1980s were undermined by the failure of several prosecutions because of problems with the reliability of the police evidence. The subsequent 'intelligence-led' approach to football policing, as with many other safety and security initiatives, also has its origins in the 1989 Hillsborough disaster. Police forces appointed football liaison/intelligence officers to each club and these officers busied themselves gathering information on and getting to know their own 'hooligans'. They also set up reciprocal arrangements with other clubs so that the police 'spotters' from one club would travel away with their own supporters to point out potential trouble-makers to their police colleagues at the 'home' club.

The Metropolitan Police Service established a National Football Unit in 1989. This was shortly afterwards incorporated within the NCIS. The NCIS Football Intelligence Unit collates the work of the football liaison/ intelligence officers and has a number of other national functions. These include strategic planning for major events, acting as the UK central point for information on travelling fans abroad and providing an advisory service. The NCIS unit maintains a database of known and suspected hooligans, categorized as A (peaceful, *bona fide* supporters), B (possible risk of disorder, especially alcohol-related violence) and C (violent supporters or organizers of violence). The NCIS also houses the Football Banning Orders Authority. The NCIS is being subsumed within the new Serious and Organized Crime Agency (SOCA) and, at the time of writing, it is not clear whether the Football Unit and Football Banning Orders Authority will form part of SOCA or be moved into another organization.

In order to plan the number of police (if any) to deploy to a particular match, the police make an assessment of the risk of disorder and then categorize each match as either 'police free', category A (low risk), B (medium risk) or C (high risk). These assessments are usually done *en bloc* in conjunction with the local football club safety officer at the start of each season. The assessments are informed by the work of the football intelligence/liaison officers and the reports available from the NCIS, but are largely a matter of experience and judgement based on the 'history' between the two sets of fans. The intelligence/liaison officers seek to update the assessment as the date of each match approaches and the match categorization may sometimes be revised as a result.

For example, let's say that 'City' are playing 'United' in a League match next Tuesday night. There have been no previous problems between the fans and few visiting fans are expected to travel. The match is categorized as low risk (A). Imagine now that the two teams are drawn to play each other in the cup and that the intelligence/liaison officer has learnt from a source that groups of United and City fans are planning to meet for a fight. This makes the League match more significant. The police may thus recategorize the match as medium risk (B) and wish to deploy more resources.

Depending on their intelligence-led perceptions of the risk of disorder for a particular match, the police may also insist on the imposition of other control measures, particularly for category C games. These may include bringing the kick-off time forward so that fans have less opportunity to visit public houses or requiring the match to be 'all ticket' with no sales on the day. More extremely, the police and club may even ban other clubs' supporters from attending their ground. This can be a reciprocal arrangement, such as when Leeds United played Glasgow Rangers in the

European Cup in 1992, when each leg of the two-leg fixture was sold out to 'home' fans only – although a few of the more determined Rangers fans managed to get tickets to Leeds and got themselves ejected from the ground for their own safety. It can also be a unilateral initiative. Because of the problems which Millwall experienced with their fans during the 2001/2 season, 'stringent measures' were planned for 2002/3:

> No away supporters will be allowed at Millwall's fixtures against Wolves, Burnely, Nottingham Forest, Stoke City, Portsmouth, and Leicester City. Millwall fans will also be banned from travelling to the return games … A further four matches, against Coventry, Derby County, Reading and Crystal Palace, will be made all-ticket for away spectators and arranged with kick-off times that ensure they finish an hour before dusk … In order to buy a ticket for any Millwall game next season supporters will have to be season ticket holders or members of Millwall Supporters Club (*Daily Telegraph*, 12 June 2002).

It may be argued that the fans' experience of this 'intelligence-led' approach is sometimes just as repressive and controlling as its 'containment' predecessor. And just how effective has it been? As they do with CCTV, Garland and Rowe (2000) point out the successes yet limitations of the use of intelligence, arguing that 'the authorities might have successfully confronted orchestrated football violence, at least in the environs of football grounds, but that "unorganized hooliganism" is a significant issue and a form of disorder that is much more difficult to police'.

It is worth reflecting on the extent to which hindsight can be used as a predictor of future risks, and the relevance this could have for the 'intelligence-led' policing of football-related violence. The key point is that people's previous good behaviour is a somewhat unreliable guarantee about their future good behaviour. Similarly, people's previous bad behaviour may have been a one-off and does not necessarily mean they will behave the same way again. Nevertheless, the intelligence-led approach has enjoyed some success. As we saw in Chapter 3, football-related disorder is in long-term decline and has been displaced. But as Williams (2001) argues, the efforts the police make to keep the phenomenon in the headlines have tended to mask the progress which has been made – by police, clubs and fans alike.

Chapter summary

This chapter opened by looking at policing prior to the 1996 European Championships. We examined the historically negative attitude of the police towards football fans and the harsh containment policies adopted towards them. The failure of attempted undercover operations was noted, as were the inconsistencies in police tactics at grounds. We took a brief look at changes in 'away' supporting and at the emerging role of the steward. A number of technological developments, particularly CCTV, were then discussed. The first main section of the chapter then examined developments in European co-operation.

The chapter continued by looking at the policing of Euro '96, with particular reference to the organization and intelligence work of the police service at that time. The chapter then went on to examine developments in stewarding and in the contemporary policing style of reaction and, in some cases, over-reaction, to crime and disorder in sports grounds.

The chapter concluded with an examination of 'intelligence-led' policing, outlining the nationwide system which had evolved under the co-ordination of the NCIS. The impact of this intelligence system in reducing disorder inside grounds was noted; however, it was shown that there were limitations on using intelligence as a predictor for the future. We also saw that this partial success had come at the price of considerable police-imposed restrictions, together with displacement away from the grounds.

13. Repressive social controls

Introduction

Of course, policing is not the only form of social control applied to football hooliganism, and so needs to be located within a wider framework. Policing is underpinned by a set of repressive, even oppressive, legal provisions, including restrictions on the sale and consumption of alcohol, specific football-related offences and some quite draconian legislation which provides for the imposition of banning orders and travel restrictions on convicted and, uniquely in English criminal law, even on unconvicted persons whom the police believe may engage in football hooligan behaviour.

The alternative yet equally repressive containment offered by all seating monitored by closed-circuit television is examined, as is the obsession of previous governments with the control of fan behaviour, notwithstanding the true non-hooliganism causes of the crowd-related disasters in which many fans have died or been injured.

Legal provisions

Sports fans and spectators in general are subject to the general body of criminal law. They can be dealt with in the normal way for offences against the person, against property and against the state. What is unusual is that there is a whole raft of criminal legislation which is solely football related. A good summary of the various legal provisions is contained in Home Office Circular 34/2000, which is available to download from the Home Office website (see Home Office 2002).

Alcohol controls

The Sporting Events (Control of Alcohol) Act 1985 created restrictions on the possession and sale of alcohol, together with specific offences of drunkenness. As we saw in Chapter 10, such restrictions are not supported by the research evidence. They also, as we saw, create some bizarre situations. For example, if you attend a stadium for a rugby match or pop concert, you are subject only to the normal licensing laws and are at liberty to take a beer with you to consume in your seat as you watch the event. If you attend the same stadium for a football match, you face restrictions on when you can purchase and are not allowed to take your drink anywhere within sight of the pitch.

Specific football offences

The Football Offences Act 1991 created the three specific football offences of throwing things, indecent or racist chanting and pitch incursion. It can be argued that this legislation was quite superfluous. Brick (2000) cites Greenfield and Osborn (1998) and notes that the there was already 'ample provision in the existing criminal and common law to punish the specific acts criminalized under the Act'. Throwing missiles and indecent or racist chanting are already covered by other public order legislation, whilst pitch incursion can also be adequately dealt under the criminal law. For example, following problems with pitch incursions during the Pakistan tour in 2001, the English Cricket Board found that they could use the criminal offence of aggravated trespass to prosecute pitch invaders.

Banning orders and travel restrictions

Through the Football Spectator Act 1989, Crime and Disorder Act 1998, Football (Offences and Disorder) Act 1999 and Football (Disorder) Act 2000, the UK has seen increasingly draconian legislation involving restriction/banning orders and travel restrictions. These can be applied not only to convicted hooligans but also to fans without previous convictions whom the police suspect may cause trouble. Such measures are unprecedented in UK criminal law and, as the Football Industry Group (FIG) at the University of Liverpool note, 'obviously have serious civil libertarian consequences for innocent fans' (FIG 2002).

For example, the *Daily Telegraph* (16 April 2002) reported how about 1,200 English fans were to be stopped from travelling to the World Cup in Japan. Some 1,000 of these were the subject of international banning orders, either arising from a previous football-related conviction or from a police application to a court using a civil complaints procedure. Such police applications have been challenged under the Human Rights Act – but without success. Note the language used by Lord Justice Laws in dismissing the fans' applications: 'The purpose here is to prevent the public, here and abroad, from the evil of football violence and the threat of it ... The state was entitled to conclude that very firm measures were justified to confront the various sickening ills of football violence' (*Daily Telegraph*, 14 July 2001). This report also carried the response of Kevin Miles of the Football Supporters Assocation, who said:

> We cannot see why football fans should be the only people for whom criminal standards of evidence should not be required before a sanction is taken against them. We also feel that the way the law has been framed, allowing police to use old convictions, is imposing a second punishment on fans a long time after the original offence.

As if such an application in respect of an unconvicted person wasn't enough of an infringement of civil liberties, the *Daily Telegraph* (16 April 2002) also reported how 'Names of a further 200 potential trouble-makers against whom there is insufficient evidence for a ban will be handed to Japanese police and immigration authorities'. In other words, where the police are unable to satisfy a court that a person should be made subject of a banning order, they will anyway give his or her details to the Japanese, who will then simply refuse him or her leave to enter the country. This strikes us as nothing short of outrageous.

Contrast this UK approach with that of Germany. During the 1998 World Cup in France, a German supporter attacked a French gendarme (named Nivel) and almost killed him. After serving his prison sentence, the fan was free to go to the 2002 World Cup in Japan. The *Sunday Telegraph* (12 May 2002) interviewed a German police spokesman, whom they reported as saying:

> He can go to any football match he wants to. As far as the police are concerned he has served his sentence and that's it ... The fact that he was involved in the Nivel case is not enough for him to constitute a threat. As far as we are concerned there would have to be an indication that he was about to commit an act of violence.

Clearly the Germans do not consider that a previous conviction provides the whole predictive picture about likely future conduct. This raises the interesting question of the likely effectiveness of the UK legislation. Why was it introduced? And will it stop the disorder? The introductory paragraphs to the Bassam Report (Home Office 2001) and to Home Office Circular 34/2000 (Home Office 2002) can be construed as a government 'moral panic' response to media amplification of and diplomatic and political pressure about fan behaviour at the European Championships in Belgium. In the Foreword to his report, Lord Bassam states that

'A significant outbreak of xenophobia and racism was coupled with unpleasant violence by fans on the streets of Charleroi and Brussels. The Government was not prepared to tolerate this. We acted quickly and firmly with new legislation' (Home Office 2001: 2).

Whilst the Home Office claimed that: 'Sadly, the shameful and utterly reprehensible behaviour of some of the followers of the England football team competing in Euro 2000 this summer, obliged the government to introduce further legislation to deal with the particular menace of our home-grown football hooligans when abroad' (Home Office 2002), there was no mention of criticisms of Belgian police over-reaction. No mention of the mass indiscriminate arrests and deportations. No mention that only one England fan was convicted of anything at Euro 2000 and that even his conviction has been criticized as highly suspect.

Certainly there was some disorder, but it is instructive to note who appears to get involved. Reporting on arrest data for England fans at the 1998 World Cup, Garland and Rowe (2000) note that of the 286 fans arrested, only 52 (18 per cent) were known to the NCIS. The vast majority were not known to the police. So the nub of the problem is that these draconian restrictions may help stop known hooligans from travelling to engage in pre-planned violence, but they can't stop those who get involved for the first time, perhaps because the disorder is spontaneous, or perhaps simply because they get caught up in or carried away with it – sometimes, as we have seen, in response to inappropriate police tactics (see Stott and Reicher 1998).

New and refurbished grounds

One of the principal changes which followed the nadir of the 1989 Hillsborough disaster was the introduction of all-seated accommodation for spectators in the upper divisions of British Football Leagues (see Elliott *et al*. 1999). All-seated accommodation was introduced primarily as a safety measure to address the risks of crowd crushing, but it had the secondary effect of reducing disorderly behaviour in grounds. If fans are required to buy tickets and sit in numbered seats, instead of paying cash and standing where they like, then they have a lot less choice about where they sit and whom they sit with. Groups which might have congregated together thus get broken up.

The improved toilet, catering and other facilities which accompanied the many stadium renovations to introduce all-seating also brought about a change of mindset. The shift was from 'cage them up because they're animals' to 'encourage decent behaviour by providing decent facilities'. There are positive examples of where this has worked well, such as when Nottingham Forest hosted Bayern Munich in the UEFA Cup (see Frosdick *et al.* 1999). But there are also negative examples of where such facilities have been abused. For example, co-author Steve Frosdick attended one match between Wycombe Wanderers and Cardiff City where, immediately on their arrival, a group of the away fans systematically wrecked the toilet facilities in their 'end'.

Technology

Together with the introduction of seating, closed-circuit television (CCTV), which we mentioned in Chapter 12, is widely recognized as a major cause of reduced football hooliganism *inside* grounds (for example, see SNCCFR 2001: 13). The technology advanced considerably during the 1990s from the early black-and-white cameras with limited zoom and tilt producing grainy images to the crystal-clear, full-colour pictures from today's high-performance digital systems.

When fans are behaving in a way which requires an intervention from the police or stewards, they will often be tapped on the shoulder and their direction drawn to the cameras overhead. Sometimes, the fans will even be shown a digital photograph of themselves. The inference is clear – 'we can see what you're doing'. Where serious disorder takes place, the police are then able to use the video footage to support a post-incident inquiry to identify the perpetrators and arrest them.

Sounding a cautionary note to the general perception of CCTV as a panacea for crime in general, Garland and Rowe (2000) suggest that, whilst CCTV has been an effective deterrent against *organized* violence, it has done little to deter *spontaneous* outbreaks in grounds.

As part of their 'evidence-gathering' process, the police often deploy officers with hand-held video cameras to film the fans. Quite often, the officers are wearing their full riot gear – no doubt on the grounds of the perceived risks to their own health and safety. Such filming can be both intimidating and provocative. The authors have seen many 'negative spiral' instances where groups of fans react to the camera by chanting aggressively. The temperature being raised, the police then deploy more officers to the vicinity to deal with the perceived threat.

Ticketing technology also contributes to the repression of disorderly behaviour in grounds. Many Premier League clubs are sold out for every match, often with a very large proportion of season ticket holders. Some clubs, such as Newcastle United, have large waiting lists of people who want to become season ticket holders. Knowing the name and address of the occupier of almost every seat, and knowing that there is a queue of people waiting for a ticket, puts the stadium manager in a very powerful position. One stadium manager explained how he was able to call fans in for a dressing-down and had seen men in tears at the prospect of having their season ticket withdrawn.

Whilst paying cash to 'the man on the gate' persists for many minor grounds, access control for football and other major sports has become much more sophisticated, with 'smart' tickets, cards and turnstiles used to control entry. It is now possible to know from the access control system that a named individual has entered the ground and to use the CCTV to see whether he or she is in his or her seat. Thus the crude containment offered by the caged pen and hostile police has been replaced by the more subtle containment of the designated seat and sophisticated technical monitoring.

Government reports

We have seen how the media, academics and the police responses to football hooliganism have tended to be disproportionate to the nature and extent of the phenomenon. Something similar might be said for successive governments, since no less than 13 official reports have been commissioned into safety and order at British football grounds. Here, though, the key point is the repeated overemphasis on public order, which was less of a problem, and the repeated neglect of public safety, which was disastrously compromised (see Elliott *et al.* 1999).

The Shortt Report (Home Office 1924) followed a near-disaster at Wembley in 1923 and included recommendations about responsibility, licensing, stewarding and fire safety – all largely ignored. The Moelwyn Hughes Report (Home Office 1946) arose from an overcrowding disaster in Bolton. Recommendations about calculating maximum capacities and co-ordinated counting of numbers admitted were not pursued.

The growth of football hooliganism prompted the Chester Report (Department of Education and Science 1968), the Harrington Report (1968) and Lang Report (Ministry of Housing and Local Government 1969). Harrington reviewed previous reports and noted that their helpful suggestions had often been ignored. He went on to comment on the lack of legislation covering standards of safety and amenity at grounds. Lang included references to the benefits of CCTV and the impact of alcohol on behaviour. The Wheatley Report (Home Office 1972) was prompted by the 1971 Ibrox disaster in Scotland and resulted in legislation requiring safety certificates at designated grounds – 50 years after Shortt first recommended such action.

The McElhorne Report (Scottish Education Department 1977) was concerned with spectator misbehaviour in Scotland. Recommendations included legislation to control alcohol, spectator segregation, perimeter fencing, CCTV, improved amenities, stewarding, club membership and club community involvement. Set up following disorder at England matches abroad, the Department of the Environment Working Group (1984) repeated similar recommendations for English clubs.

The Popplewell Reports (Home Office 1985, 1986) dealt with disasters at Bradford and Birmingham and the Heysel tragedy in Belgium. Many recommendations echoed the 1977 and 1984 reports. The Football Trust funded the installation (at last) of CCTV and there was considerable legislative activity. Exclusion and restriction orders were introduced to keep convicted hooligans both away from British grounds and unable to travel to matches abroad.

Following the fatal crushing of 95 Liverpool supporters at Hillsborough Stadium on 15 April 1989, the Taylor Reports (Home Office 1989; 1990) proved to be the catalyst for radical change. There was swift implementation of changes in planning, responsibilities, testing and improving the fabric of stadiums, involving considerable energy and expense for clubs, local authorities, police and others. Other key areas of change included the scrapping of a proposed national fan membership scheme and the establishment of the Football Licensing Authority (FLA). New criminal offences of pitch invasion, racist chanting and missile throwing were created. The police role shifted to concentrate on crime, disorder and major emergencies (Wilmot 1993), whilst the clubs appointed safety officers and began to improve the quality of their stewarding schemes (see Football League *et al.* 1995, 1996, 1998, 1999, 2003). As we saw earlier, the most notable change involved the elimination of standing accommodation at all Premier and Football League stadiums, although the all-seater requirement was subsequently relaxed for the lower division clubs.

Whilst the Taylor Reports had a primary focus on safety, the government also undertook a Home Affairs Committee (1991a, 1991b) investigation into the policing of football hooliganism. This coined the concept of 'higher-profile stewarding supported by lower-profile policing' which we shall be looking at further in Chapter 14.

Following the disturbances in Marseilles during the 1998 World Cup, a Home Office consultation document (Home Office 1998) proposed 29 new control measures (see also SNCCFR 2001: 16), some of which resulted in legislation. Finally in 2001, the Bassam Report (Home Office 2001) proposed a further 54 recommendations. Some have resulted in further legislation and other action, whilst others (at the time of writing) do not appear to have progressed. We suggested earlier that the Bassam Report could be taken as a government 'moral panic' response to media amplification of and diplomatic and political pressure about fan behaviour at the European Championships in Belgium. Worse still, as Williams (2001) suggests, the Bassam Report can be seen as quite shoddy work. Describing the work of the study group, Williams explains:

This body promised to study some of the underlying causes and producing [*sic*] a comprehensive package of proposals. I sat in on some of these meetings, which involved fans' representatives, academics, practitioners, people from football and government – and Billy Bragg. A good start, a suitably Big Tent. But after a few early throat-clearing exchanges of views, a general election loomed and so game Home Office civil servants were swiftly instructed to somehow turn these loose, often contradictory, unscripted exchanges into a tidy report with 54 (count 'em) recommendations. This strikes me as an incredible – and incredibly bad – way of making policy (2001: 29).

As Elliot *et al.* (1999) conclude in respect of disasters, all these government reports have served the political purpose of being seen to be doing something. The same seems equally valid in respect of disorder. 'Legislation by crisis' applies a sticking plaster but it doesn't heal the wound. *When Saturday Comes* magazine (2002) argues that 'none of the measures introduced, even taken together, really did away with hooliganism'. What successive governments have failed to do is to get to grips with the underlying issues. As Garland and Rowe (2000) conclude: 'The crime prevention approaches outlined above assume that football hooliganism will occur and address how it might be thwarted, whilst paying relatively little attention to social, political, economic or cultural factors that underpin such behaviour.' Perryman (2001: 24) concludes that 'The initiatives concerned with football violence since Euro 2000 have been largely concerned with control, mixed with a dose of demonisation'.

And there is little sign of any willingness to engage with the wider issues. In a letter dated 15 July 2002 (to Assistant Chief Constable Ron Hogg, the national police spokesperson on football intelligence), Home Office Minister John Denham outlined the need for a post-World Cup football disorder strategy which further exploited what was already the toughest legislation in the world. Subsequently, the Home Office made £5 million available to police forces for police intelligence operations aimed at increasing the number of football banning orders (see Home Office 2003a). As we saw in Chapter 3, the Home Office (2004) figures show that these have indeed increased dramatically from 1,794 on 14 August 2003 to 2,596 on 18 October 2004. Thus a continued ratcheting up of the controls seems much more likely than an attempt to treat the root causes.

Chapter summary

This chapter opened outlining the whole raft of football-specific criminal legislation, noting that much of it was an unnecessary and draconian 'political moral panic' response with serious implications for civil liberties. The restraining influences of new and refurbished grounds, together with their various technological systems such as CCTV, ticketing and access control, were then reviewed and it was noted that these represented a more subtle form of containment, but containment, none the less. The chapter then examined the 13 official government reports produced between 1924 and 2001, concluding that, in the context of disorder, these were rather more concerned to be seen to be doing something than to tackle the underlying social roots of the violence.

We have seen in this chapter how repeated and increasingly repressive social controls have met with limited success, yet the government seem determined to continue down the same road. But repression is not the only solution and there is good evidence of more proactive and preventive measures – and it is to these that we now turn.

14. More proactive and preventive measures

Introduction

Whilst British writers might have taken the lead in expounding theories of football hooliganism, and have historically been considered the world leaders in policing public disorder, we cannot claim a monopoly on the more proactive and preventive work which has emerged across Europe over recent years. This chapter will examine the Dutch concept of 'friendly but firm' policing, now adopted to good effect for all major football championships. It will also look a 'fan coaching' and similar fan-based initiatives, which again have their origin in continental Europe. The main area of the British contribution is in the appreciation that crowd disasters have arisen from allowing safety and security to get out of balance and thus in seeing football hooliganism as one risk to be dealt with within a holistic view of risk and safety management.

'Friendly but firm' policing

The concept of 'friendly but firm' policing has its origins in the work of Otto Adang of the Dutch Police Academy (see, for example, Adang and Cuvelier 2000; Adang 2001) and was first demonstrated in the arrangements adopted by the Dutch police for the 2000 European Championships, jointly hosted by Belgium and Holland. The Dutch set out to create a carnival atmosphere in which fans could enjoy themselves rather than to confront, contain and repress them. The Dutch police removed objects that might be thrown (such as tables and chairs) from town squares and arranged for local bars to serve low-alcohol beer in plastic glasses. They set up large sound systems to play popular music and, when fans became boisterous, they simply turned the volume up until it was so deafening that it drowned other noise out and people quietened down. There were even reports of Dutch pornographic film stars parading the streets in their underwear to fraternize with and 'welcome' the fans! The police presence was unobtrusive, friendly but firm if needed. This carefully planned approach resulted in no reports of serious problems. The Dutch policing style contrasted markedly with the Belgian over-reaction we discussed in Chapter 12. And it is perhaps significant to note that, of the two countries, it was Belgium and not Holland which experienced the public disorder.

The Belgian experience is in line with the research findings of Stott *et al.*, which we briefly mentioned in Chapter 6. A boisterous crowd may consider that its behaviour is acceptable, perhaps engaging in the kind of ritual displays of aggression described by Marsh. Yet if the police perceive the crowd as hooligan and so intervene, often with inappropriate use of force, then the crowd may turn on the police and thus 'real' violence may break out, with people who were not previously disposed to violence now joining in to protest against the police over-reaction.

The work of both Adang and Stott, who have been collaborating on a major research project, has been highly influential in the evolution of policing style for international matches, particularly for European Championships (for example, see Stott 2003; Adang and Stott 2004). The Bassam Report noted the success of the 'friendly but firm' approach, encouraged its more widespread adoption in tournament preparations, and recommended that further research should be done on its potential usefulness (Home Office 2001: 25–6). Subsequently, the British authorities were able to point to the Dutch experience to persuade the Japanese and Koreans to soften their own policing style for the 2002 World Cup. Most recently, the Portugese police successfully adopted the 'friendly but firm' approach for the 2004 European Championships.

However the approach is not yet universally accepted by the police in continental Europe. Notwithstanding the extensive preparations made for England's visit to Spain for an international match in 2004, junior police commanders ignored the agreements reached on policing style and there were serious allegations of police brutality. The *Sunday Telegraph*, (28 November 2004) reported that 'The Football Supporters Federation will this week pass to the Home Office a 70 page dossier of around 100 eye-witness accounts of police brutality before and during the match'. Deputy Chief Constable David Swift was quoted as saying that 'On this occasion, the policing style was not what English fans have become used to … There was little engagement with the fans and little discussion and negotiation. It was quite confrontational with the obvious incidents that materialise as a result'.

Risk and safety management

Control of violence has also become a subset of more general risk and safety management, within which disorder is just one of the risks to be dealt with. This is particularly so in the UK where there has been a post-Hillsborough paradigm shift from the management of public order to the management of public safety; from 'protection from the crowd' to 'protection of the crowd'. There is a balance to be maintained between public safety and public order so sometimes the club safety officer will choose to live with minor disorder in order not to compromise public safety. Thus some obscene chanting or a minor fracas may be overlooked if dynamic risk assessment suggests that sending the stewards into the crowd may inflame the situation and result in public safety being compromised. The reverse is also true, such as when the safety officer chooses to preserve public order by overlooking the safety risks posed by a volatile crowd persistently standing in a seated area.

It was a government committee in 1991 (Home Affairs Committee 1991a, 1991b) which recommended that 'higher-profile stewarding supported by lower-profile policing' represented the way forward in sports grounds. The police had become concerned about their exposure to civil and even criminal liability in the event of another disaster – they did not want to take responsibility for safety just to fill the void left by nobody else accepting the responsibility. They did not want to be sued for negligence or face criminal charges for manslaughter. The police were faced with burgeoning demands for their services and public events offered one area where they could cut back on their involvement to free up resources to service new demands elsewhere. And although they could charge clubs for their services, often they could not recover all their costs. So the police refocused their role. They appointed intelligence liaison officers for each club, established a network of 'spotters' to monitor hooligans and set up a national football intelligence co-ordinating unit. They drew up statements of intent with clubs to clarify who was responsible for what – the club for safety and the police for order and emergencies. So clubs had primacy for 'policing' functions and called in the police to help when serious disorder or a major incident took place (see Frosdick and Sidney 1999).

Thus we have seen the police and stewards change places. Take the example of Nottingham Forest. In 1989 they used to have 150 police in the ground, supported by 75 stewards. For their UEFA Cup run in 1996 they had 250 stewards supported by just 22 police. And many clubs have no police officers at all in the ground. Portsmouth, for example, had only two matches during 2001/2 at which there were police in the ground. However, there were usually police officers on duty outside the ground whom the club could call on if needed. A good number of clubs also invite the visiting club to send their own stewards so that the 'away' fans are then policed by people who know them.

Revised and updated guidelines for stewarding have been produced, together with a national training package and assessment scheme (Football League *et al*. 1996, 1998, 1999, 2003). The training package covers the general duties of stewards; their work to keep the stadium safe; caring for the spectators; giving medical first aid; preventing and dealing with fires; emergency evacuation; and dealing with racism and disability discrimination. Conflict management is being added in 2005. The training package is used at almost every ground in the UK and has also been drawn on by other countries hosting major championships.

The change from policing to stewarding is well illustrated by the following two examples witnessed by co-author Steve Frosdick. At one point during a match between Wycombe Wanderers and Cardiff City, the Cardiff fans became fairly aggrieved by a refereeing decision and stood up, shouting aggressively. A police inspector quickly deployed a line of officers to stand in front of the fans. The steward supervisor said to the police inspector: 'I'm in charge here and there's no need for your officers. Withdraw them.' The police inspector (grudgingly) complied. In the post-match debrief, the club safety officer told the stewards: 'I'm proud of you all. The Cardiff was hard work but we done it ourselves [*sic*].'

At a 2005 match between Millwall and Coventry City, there were no police officers deployed in the ground. A Millwall fan in the home end was observed on CCTV drinking lager from a plastic glass (it is an offence to consume alcohol within sight of the pitch). Two stewards (one of whom was black) made their way into the crowd, recovered the lager and arrested the man, who followed them out with only a little protest. Notably, there was no adverse reaction from the Millwall crowd – who have a historical reputation for violence and racism which is quite undeserved today. The safety officer commented: 'That shows how far we have come – a few years ago that would have caused a riot.'

Following government recommendations (Department of National Heritage and Scottish Office 1997), ground management assumed full responsibility for the safety of their customers. Football led the way with the appointment of ground safety officers. In the early days, these were often the retired local police chief working part time. Increasingly, however, we have seen the emergence of full-time, younger personnel with a health and safety rather than police background. The Football Safety Officers' Association (FSOA) was set up in 1992. Almost all safety officers are members. The FSOA has slowly grown in stature and influence and its national officers have worked with the various regulatory bodies on various developments such as stewards training and assessment. Other sports have also begun to appoint safety officers and sports such as rugby union and rugby league have set up their own safety officers' associations.

There is a growing debate about the competence of safety officers and there is a trend – painfully slow – towards greater professionalization. Safety officers should assume full responsibility for all health and safety functions – staff and banqueting guests as well as the match-day crowd – and they need to demonstrate their competence through continuing professional development and qualifications (see Frosdick 2001b). Since 2003, the FSOA have run their own training courses leading to the award of a 'Certificate in Event and Matchday Safety Management'. The course is accredited by the University of Portsmouth and provides much of the underpinning knowledge needed to obtain a Level 4 National Vocational Qualification on Spectator Management. This in turn provides 80 of the 360 higher education credits needed to obtain a BSc honours degree in risk and security management, although by 2005 only a handful of people had entered university via this route.

The paradigm shift we have referred to is not only about maintaining a balance of safety and order but also a balance between four competing demands (see Frosdick 1998b). Safety and order needs to be located within a broader risk management framework in which managers strike an appropriate balance between safety and security and three other competing demands. Commercial pressures mean they must optimize the commercial viability of the venue and its events. Spectator demands for excitement and enjoyment require credible events staged in comfortable surroundings, whilst any negative effects which the venue and event may have on the outside world must be kept to a minimum. So the control of football hooliganism is only part of a more complex risk management picture.

Fan culture and coaching

We saw in Chapters 12 and 13 how the imposition of repressive control from without has had only a limited impact on football-related violence. There is, however, good evidence of initiatives which seek to change the culture of football supporting from within. Over ten years ago, Williams (1991a) suggested that it was the fans themselves who would be central to football's efforts to become a more modern and peaceful sport.

England

The supporters' clubs attached to each football club play a part in discouraging bad behaviour through members-only areas of grounds and arranging away coach travel. 'Football in the Community Schemes' encourage young fans to have a stake in clubs through coaching and teaching schemes, although there have been criticisms of the token nature of many of these. There is also evidence of efforts to change the culture of

English football supporting. We saw in Chapter 5 how Scotland's 'Tartan Army' reinvented themselves as the 'friendly' fans in order to beat the English off the pitch, becoming cultural tourists rather than invading hordes (Giulianotti 1991, 1995a). There are now strong initiatives amongst England supporters to change the culture of following the national team abroad. Mark Perryman led the 'Football yes, violence no' campaign for England fans attending the 2000 European Championships and has set out a full analysis of the changes needed (Perryman 2001).

Further study

If you want to know more about changing the culture of England supporters abroad, read the introductory chapter in Mark Perryman's book, *Hooligan Wars* (Perryman 2001).

Europe

Whilst the UK has certainly taken the lead in the development of highly sophisticated techniques to prevent and monitor football hooligans, an enlightening movement from Europe has been the evolution of the 'fan projects'. These involve clubs and municipalities employing social workers to liaise with fan groups to facilitate atmosphere but discourage violence.

Germany were the first to introduce the fan projects, which began in Bremen in 1981, though detached youth workers in Munich had previously worked with football fans back in 1970. The projects were an attempt to take preventative measures against football hooliganism by detailing youth or social workers to work amongst football supporters. The project workers established a link between football supporters and the football and police authorities, creating lines of communication that had previously not existed, although critics suggested that the project workers were simply informers working at the behest of the authorities, discovering information about hooligans and what plans they might have for particular matches. The primary function of the fan projects was to turn supporters away from hooliganism 'by means of concrete street-work activities … to help the adolescent fan find his personal identity and to show various possibilities of coping with life'.

Löffelholz *et al.* (1994) detailed a complex network of activities undertaken by the fan workers (alternatively known as 'fan coaches'), including individual guidance to fans, intervention in critical situations (e.g. when arrested), educational and careers advice and recreational activities, such as organizing travel to matches and producing fan magazines.

By 1996, there were over 25 fan projects in Germany. Each individual fan project was based around a particular club, from the highest echelons of the Bundesliga, through to the German Second Division and even the amateur football leagues, which attract a extremely high following in Germany. Funding was mainly drawn from the individual clubs, who themselves obtained funds from a pool organized and funded by Deutscher Fussball Bund (the German equivalent of the Football Association). Finance was also available to projects from the local authorities and from 'social sponsorship' (as opposed to commercial sponsorship).

The Bundesarbeitsgemeinschaft der Fan-Projekte (Federal Study Group of Fan Projects) was formed in May 1989 and represented the fan projects on a national and international level. The group were responsible for fan project activities at the World Cup in Italy in 1990 and in the European championship finals in Sweden in 1992. The organization of the projects was further cemented by the formation of the Koodinationstelle Fanprojekte (Federal Department Co-ordinating Fan Projects) in August 1993, who co-ordinated the expanding network of projects and their various initiatives throughout Germany.

Eight representatives from the Koodinationstelle Fanprojekte were at the Euro '96 championships in England and were available at the Football Supporters' Association fan embassy in Manchester where the German team was based for the majority of the tournament. The German Euro '96 project printed eight thousand fan guides which provided a variety of information including arrangements for accommodation, entertainment and ticket allocations. The project workers were a vital link between the Euro '96 organizers and German fans, as well as between Deutscher Fussball Bund and the supporters.

Similar (if not identical) fan projects have also functioned in the Netherlands. Learning from the German model, the Dutch fan projects began in 1986 following government-sponsored research on football hooliganism that indicated a need for a preventative approach to the problem. Initially, the projects were financed by a three-year government grant, which was extended for a further five years to 1994. Subsequently, the financing for the projects came under the auspices of individual clubs and city councils, who were responsible for the payment of the youth workers. Funding was also available from Koninklijke Nederlandsche Voetbalbond (KNVB – the national football association), particularly for the projects organized around international matches and tournaments. For example, the KNVB funded project workers at Euro '96, who spent two weeks on a reconnaissance mission in England prior to the tournament.

The emphasis within the Dutch fan projects has been very much on a multi-agency approach, with project co-ordinators constantly liaising with the police, football clubs, local authorities and the various supporters' organizations. Like the German model, the fan projects were based around particular football clubs such as Ajax, Feyenoord, PSV Eindhoven and Utrecht. As in Germany, the project workers (commonly known as 'fan coaches') attempted similar socio-pedagogical guidance to fans, helping them to obtain employment or places on educational courses. They also provided purely pragmatic advice, such as details of travel and ticket arrangements for games. However, the project workers also admitted to relaying information to the police on the strategy of hooligans for particular matches.

The Belgian fan projects officially began only in 1993, although some fan coaches have been sporadically working with football supporters since 1989. As with the German and Dutch examples, the Belgian project workers are qualified social and youth workers. François Goffe, one of the co-ordinators of the Belgian fan coaches, commented: 'Our fan coaches are certainly not to be compared with the stewards prevalent in the English game. We work purely as social workers and we work with the fans every day of the week, not just on the day of a particular football match' (fieldwork interview).

In contrast to the German and Dutch models, however, the Belgian projects received no financial help from Union Royale Belge des Sociétés de FA (the Belgian football association) or any of the football clubs. Neither did they receive monetary assistance from local authorities. Instead, financial assistance was obtained from central government funds only. The Belgian fan-coaching projects liaise closely with the football clubs, police and the Union Royale Belge des Sociétés de FA on various matters, including security arrangements and ticket allocation. Because they do not receive any financial backing from these organizations, they remain independent and are often openly critical of individual clubs, the police and the football authorities.

A number of other countries have followed the lead from Belgium, Germany and the Netherlands by introducing similar fan projects or fan coaching. These include Switzerland and Sweden, where the Project Battre Lakter Kulture ('Project for a Better Culture') has worked alongside the Swedish Football Association in running a variety of anti-hooligan initiatives. As with German and Dutch models, the Swedish fan projects are based at football league clubs such as AIK Stockholm and Hammerbee FC.

From about 2000, the University of Liege in Belgium have been running a European Commission-funded 'fan coaching' project to facilitate exchanges of information and good practice across Europe. This initiative resulted in the publication of a Council of Europe booklet on the prevention of violence in sport (Comeron 2002). Comeron argues that 'In order to supplement conventional security measures and to ensure that they are balanced, the overall international policy on hooligan management must place a greater emphasis on prevention and step up its efforts in this field' (2002: 13). Comeron emphasizes the 'need for improved club–supporter relations and for strengthening of club's social roles' (p. 17). He offers a menu of preventive initiatives, including 'fan coaching', 'fan embassies', 'accompanying persons', 'relations between clubs and supporters', 'the club's role in its social environment' and 'the role of local authorities'.

'Fan coaching' staff have an educational and social support role during the week, working both through structured activities such as organized adventure trips and through street work, hanging out with groups of fans. On match days, staff provide a point of mediation between the fans and the police. It is thus important that they maintain neutrality and do not become perceived as working as police 'spotters'.

'Fan embassies' have been a feature of major championships since Euro '96 and offer a friendly place where fans can go for help and support whilst away from home. Comeron recommends that 'During any international tournament, each host city should have its own fan embassy scheme. Various formats are possible: a single embassy, or two embassies – one for each of the countries concerned – possibly even with a third information centre for other foreign fans in transit' (p. 28).

On the question of relations between clubs and supporters, Comeron refers to the value of supporters' charters, such as have been adopted by most English clubs, and to the need for clubs to support the various fans' associations which exist for their own club. Here it is noticeable how English clubs have allowed a formal voice to independent fan associations as well as the 'official' club supporters' clubs, for example, through a notes page in the match-day programme. The club's social role is also emphasized, through local community and education schemes. Finally, Comeron advocates proactive involvement by local authorities in the prevention of violence in sport in their local area.

Further study

For further details on the concept of 'fan coaching', read the Council of Europe booklet on *The Prevention of Violence in Sport* by Manuel Comeron (2002).

New directions in tackling football hooliganism

Our overview of approaches to tackling football violence reveals a distinct gulf between that of the British philosophy and the line taken in other European countries. Whilst the German, Belgian and Dutch authorities, in particular, have engaged in proactive initiatives to reduce the problems, the British continue to employ control strategies involving more intensive policing of football fans, sophisticated surveillance and intelligence measures and new legislation.

This more reactive approach is also the line taken to some extent by the Italian authorities, and the police presence at certain games in their country can be intimidating in the extreme, with water cannon, tear gas and automatic weapons often in evidence. The Decreto Maroni in 1994, which followed the fatal stabbing of a Genoa fan, introduced further restictions on the movement of football fans and controls on their behaviour in the stadiums:

> The chief constable ['questore'] of the province in which the sporting events take place, can forbid people, who have been reported to the police for or convicted of taking part in violent incidents during or because of sporting events, or to people who in the same event have encouraged violence in such with symbols or posters/banners, access to places where sporting events are taking places, and can oblige the same people to report to the police during the days and hours in which the sporting events are taking place ... The person who infringes the above regulations will be punished with a minimum jail sentence of three months and a maximum of eighteen months. People who have ignored a caution can be arrested in flagrante.

Whilst the British and the Italian authorities favour the increased use of penal approaches, the trend must be towards tackling football violence at its roots. Despite the clear limitations of the 'fan coaching' schemes developed in the European mainland, they do provide a basis for a more satisfactory treatment of the problems than has existed since the late 1960s in Britain and from the early 1980s in many other countries. The German football clubs have also been much more willing to support and assist such schemes than their English and Scottish counterparts. Whilst a few British clubs (for example, Watford, Oxford United, Millwall, etc.) have introduced schemes to enable closer contact between fans and club officials, the large majority seem reluctant to take responsibility for the behaviour of their fans. Even those who have received government grants under the 'Football in the Community' scheme have largely instituted fairly token football coaching and school visit programmes.

Whilst football hooliganism appears to be on the decline, at least in the UK the problems that remain are unlikely to be eradicated simply through additional – and in some people's view, oppressive – controls on the movement of fans, curbs on the availability of alcohol or similarly simplistic 'solutions' to a complex phenomenon. In line with the views of many researchers in this area, and with the opinions of representatives of formal and informal fans' groups throughout Europe, we see a continuing need for stronger involvement of the football clubs themselves in helping to redirect and curb the occasionally disruptive and violent behaviour of a small minority of their fans. This might best be achieved through the increasing involvement of fans in the running of their clubs.

There are two clear ways in which this can happen. First are the local fans' forums found at various clubs, through which supporters and club directors have a regular and much stronger channel of communication. Secondly is through the appointment or co-option of fans to the board of directors. This practice has its origins in the 'Supporters Direct' initiative whereby fans were encouraged to form supporters' trusts which would take a financial stake in – and in some cases mount a financial rescue of – their own clubs (see Hamil *et al.* 2001). These measures, allied to fan-coaching schemes run by clubs and local authorities along the lines suggested by Comeron (2002), might succeed in changing fan behaviour on the simple presumption that they are less likely to damage the reputation of a club in which they feel they have a genuine involvement.

Chapter summary

This chapter began by referring to the benefits of the 'friendly but firm' policing style adopted by the Dutch for the 2000 European Football Championships. It then looked at how preserving public order had been put back into balance with the maintenance of public safety within a broader risk management framework. Noting that oppressive policing and repressive social controls have failed to tackle the problems of football hooliganism, the chapter then continued with a discussion on changing the culture of football supporting from within, including the efforts being made in respect of England fans abroad and the benefits of the fan-coaching projects found particularly in Germany, Belgium and the Netherlands. These more proactive and preventive measures represent a much better way forward since they offer the chance to tackle football hooliganism at its roots.

References and selected bibliography

ACPO (2002) *Manual of Guidance on the Policing of Football Events*. Bramshill: Centrex National Crime and Operations Faculty.

Adang, O. (1987) 'Football violence and police measures' in T. O'Brien (ed.) *Proceedings of the European Conference on Football Violence*. Preston: Lancashire Polytechnic.

Adang, O. (1990) *Geweld en Politie–Optreden in Relsituaties*. Utrecht: Universiteit Utrecht.

Adang, O. (1999) 'Systematic observations of violent interactions between football hooligans' in K. Thienpont and R. Cliquet (eds) *In-group/Out-group Behaviour in Modern Societies: An Evolutionary Perspective*. Brussels: Vlaamse Gemeenschap.

Adang, O. (2001) 'Friendly but firm: the maintenance of public order.' Paper prepared for delivery at the *2001 Annual Meeting of the American Political Science Association*, San Francisco, 29 August to 2 September 2001.

Adang, O. and Cuvelier, C. (2000) *Policing Euro 2000*. Apeldoorn: Dutch Police Academy.

Adang, O. and Stott, C. (2004) *Preparing for Euro 2004: Policing International Football Matches in Portugal*. A Report for the Portuguese Public Security Police.

Allan, J. (1989) *Bloody Casuals: Diary of a Football Hooligan*. Glasgow: Famedram.

Andersson, T. (2001) 'Swedish football hooliganism 1900–1939', *Soccer and Society*, 2: 1–18.

Andersson, T. and Radmann, A. (1996) 'Fans in Scandinavia.' Paper given at the *Fanatics! Conference*, Manchester, 11–13 June.

Archetti, E. (1992) 'Argentinian football: a ritual of violence? '*International Journal of the History of Sport*, 9: 209–35.

Archetti, E. (1994) 'Death and violence in Argentinian football' in R. Giulianotti *et al.* (eds) *Football, Violence and Social Identity*, pp. 37–72. London: Routledge.

Armstrong, G. (1998) *Football Hooligans: Knowing the Score*. Oxford: Berg.

Armstrong, G. and Giulianotti, R. (eds) (2001) *Fear and Loathing in World Football*. Oxford: Berg.

Armstrong, G. and Harris, R. (1991) 'Football hooligans: theory and evidence', *Sociological Review*, 39: 427–56.

Armstrong, G. and Hobbs, D. (1994) 'Tackled from behind', in R. Giulianotti *et al.* (eds) *Football, Violence and Social Identity*, pp. 196–228. London: Routledge.

Ateyo, D. (1979) *Blood and Guts, Violence in Sports*. New York, NY: Paddington Press.

Back, L., Crabbe, T. and Solomos, J. (1999) 'Beyond the racist/hooligan couplet: race, theory and football culture', *British Journal of Sociology*, 50: 419–442.

Bailey, P. (1978) *Leisure and Class in Victorian England*. London: KRP.

Bale, J. (1993) *Sport, Space and the City*. London: Routledge.

BBC (2002) 'Hooligans: troublespots', retrieved 18/03/05 from http://news.bbc. co.uk/hi/english/static/in_depth/programmes/2002/hooligans/diary.

Blain, N., Boyle, R. and O'Donnell, H. (1993) *Sport and National Identity in the European Media*. Leicester: Leicester University Press.

Blain, N. and O'Donnell, H. (1990) 'Games across frontiers: issues of national identity and the reporting of Italia '90 in the European press.' Paper presented at the *5th International Conference on Public Communication*, University of Navarre, Pamplona, 8–9 November.

Blain, N. and O'Donnell, H. (1994) 'The stars and flags: individuality, collective identities and the national dimension in Italia '90 and Wimbledon '91 and '92' in R. Giulianotti and J. Williams (eds) *Game without Frontiers: Football, Identity and Modernity*. Aldershot: Arena.

Boyes, W. and Faith, R. (1993) 'Temporal regulation and intertemporal substitution: the effect of banning alcohol at college football games', *Public Choice*, 77: 595–609.

Boyle, R. (1994) '"We are Celtic supporters...": questions of football and identity in modern Scotland', in R. Giulianotti and J. Williams (eds) *Game without Frontiers: Football, Identity and Modernity*. Aldershot: Arena.

Bradbury, S. (2001) *The New Football Communities*. Leicester: Sir Norman Chester Centre for Football Research.

Bradley, J. (1994) '"Ethnicity": the Irish in Scotland – football, politics and identity', *Innovation*, 7: 423–439.

Brick, C. (2000) 'Modern moralities and the perception of the football fan', *Soccer and Society*, 1: 158–172.

Bromberger, C. (1987) 'L'Olimpique de Marseille, la Juve et la Torino', *Espirit*, 4.

Broomhead, R. (2004) 'To What extent is English football hooliganism motivated by racism and xenophobia?' Unpublished BSc dissertation, University of Portsmouth.

Brown, A. (ed.) (1994) *The United Colours of Football*. Liverpool: Football Supporters' Association.

Brown, M. (ed.) (1995) *Kick it Again: Uniting Football against Racism*. London: Commission for Racial Equality.

Brug, H. van der (1986) *Voetbalvandalisme, Een Speurtocht naar Verklarende Factoren*. Haarlem: De Vrieseborch.

Brug, H. van der (1987) *Voetbalvandalisme en Beleid: Een Onderzoek naar de Mogelijkheden en Onmogelijkheden om het Voetbalvandalisme te Bestrijden*. Haarlem: De Vrieseborch.

Brug, H. van der (1989) *Voetbalvandalisme in Nerderland*. Amsterdam: Stichting Het Persinstut.

Brug, H. van der (1994) 'Football hooliganism in the Netherlands' in R. Giulianotti *et al.* (eds) *Football, Violence and Social Identity*, pp. 174–95. London: Routledge.

Brug, H. van der and Meijs, J. (1988) 'Voetbalvandalisme en de Media', *Tijdschrift voor Criminologie*, 4: 336–47.

Brug, H. van der and Meijs, J. (1989) *Effectevaluatie Voetbalvandalisme en Jeugdwelzijn*. Amsterdam: Stichting Het Persinstituut.

Brug, H. van der and Meijs, J. (1991) *Dutch High-risk Supporters at the World Championship Football in Italy*. Amsterdam: Stichting Het Persinstituut.

BTP (2002) 'Press release 22 July 2002', retrieved 13/08/02 from http://www.btp. police.uk/press_july02.htm#annualreport.

Buford, B. (1991) *Among the Thugs*. London: Secker & Warburg.

Bull, D. (1992) *We'll Support you Evermore: Keeping Faith in Football*. London: Duckworth.

Cachet, A. and Muller, E. (1991) *Beslissen over Voetbalvandalisme: een Permanent Probleem*. Gouda: Quint Arnhem.

Cameron, A. (1976) *Circus Factions; Blues and Greens at Rome and Byzantium*. Oxford: Clarendon Press.

Canter, D., Comber, M. and Uzzell, D. (1989) *Football in its Place: An Environmental Psychology of Football Grounds*. London: Routledge.

Carnibella, G. Fox, A., Fox, K., McCann, J., Marsh, J. and Marsh, P. (1996) *Football Violence in Europe*. Oxford: Social Issues Research Centre.

Carroll, R. (1980) 'Football hooliganism in England', *International Review of Sport Psychology*, 15: 77–92.

Cassell, C. and Rea, J. (1996) 'Short but sweet?', *When Saturday Comes*, August: 26.

Centre for Leisure Research (1984) *Crowd Behaviour at Football Matches: A Study in Scotland*. Edinburgh: Centre for Leisure Research.

Chalmers, J. (2004) 'What impact does the lack of published statistical data of spectator ejections at Premier and Football League clubs in England and Wales have on our current understanding of spectator behaviour inside football stadia?' Unpublished BSc dissertation, University of Portsmouth.

Chapman, L. (2002) 'Aggro business', *When Saturday Comes*, July: 20–1.

Chapman, R. (2004) 'Hard copy', *When Saturday Comes*, March 2004: 24–5.

CJS Online (2002) 'Practical Guide to Crime Prevention: Alcohol and Drugs', retrieved 31/05/05 from http://www.cjsonline.org.uk/access/citizen/crimeprev/guides. htm#alcohol

Clarke, J. (1973) *Football Hooliganism and the Skinheads*. Birmingham: Centre for Contemporary Cultural Studies.

Clarke, J. (1978) 'Football and working class fans: tradition and change' in R. Ingham *et al.* (eds) *'Football Hooliganism': The Wider Context*, pp. 37–60. London: Inter-action Imprint.

Coalter, F. (1985) 'Crowd behaviour at football matches: a study in Scotland', *Leisure Studies*, 4: 111–7.

Cohen, P. and Robins, D. (1978) *Knuckle Sandwich: Growing up in the Working Class City*. Harmondsworth: Penguin Books.

Cohen, S. (1971) *Folk Devils and Moral Panics*. London: Paladin.

Cole, T. (1988) 'Football hooliganism', *New Society*, 83: 41.

Coleman, C. and Moynihan, J. (1996) *Understanding Crime Data: Haunted by the Dark Figure*. Buckingham: Open University Press.

Comeron, M. (2002) *The Prevention of Violence in Sport*. Strasbourg: Council of Europe Publishing.

Costa, P., Perez, T. and Tropea, F. (1996) *Tribus Urbanas: el Ansia de Identidad Juvenil: Entre el Culto a la Imagen y la Autofirmacion a Travers de la Violencia*. Barcelona, Spain: Ediciones Paidos.

Council of Europe (1985) *European Convention on Spectator Violence and Misbehaviour at Sports Events and in Particular Football Matches*. Strasbourg: Council of Europe.

Dal Lago, A. (1990) *Descrizione di una Battaglia: I Rituali del Calcio*. Bologna: Il Mulino.

Dal Lago, A. and de Biasi, R. (1994) 'Italian football fans: culture and organisation', in R. Giulianotti *et al.* (eds) *Football, Violence and Social Identity*. London: Routledge.

Dal Lago, A. and Moscati, R. (1992) *Regalateci un Sogno: Miti e Realtà del Tifo Calcistico in Italia*. Milano: Bompiani.

Davies, H. (1972) *The Glory Game*. London: Weidenfeld & Nicholson.

Davies, H. (1990) *My Life in Football*. Edinburgh: Mainstream.

Davies, P. (1991) *All Played Out: The Full Story of Italia '90*. London: Mandarin.

Department for Culture Media and Sport (1998) *Eliminating Racism from Football: A Report of the Football Task Force*. London: DCMS.

Department of Education and Science (1968) *Report of the Committee on Football (Chairman D.N. Chester CBE)*. London: HMSO.

Department of National Heritage and Scottish Office (1997) *Guide to Safety at Sports Grounds* (4th edn). London: HMSO.

Department of the Environment (1984) *Report of an Official Working Group on Football Spectator Violence*. London: HMSO.

Drew, B. (1999) 'Policing Euro '96,' in S. Frosdick and L. Walley (eds) *Sport and Safety Management*, pp. 239–251. Oxford: Butterworth-Heinemann.

Duke, V. (1990) 'Perestroika in progress? The case of spectator sports in Czechoslovakia, *British Journal of Sociology*, 41: 145–56.

Duke, V. (1991a) 'The politics of football in the new Europe', in J. Williams and S. Wagg (eds) *British Football and Social Change: Getting into Europe*, pp. 187–200. Leicester: Leicester University Press.

Duke, V. (1991b) 'The sociology of football: A research agenda for the 1990s', *Sociological Review*, 39: 627–45.

Dunning, E. (1971) 'The development of modern football', in E. Dunning (ed.) *The Sociology of Sport: A Selection of Readings*, pp. 133–149. London: Frank Cass.

Dunning, E. (1989) 'The economic and cultural significance of football', in *Football into the 1990s*. Proceedings of a conference held at the University of Leicester, 29–30 September 1988. Leicester: Sir Norman Chester Centre for Football Research, University of Leicester.

Dunning, E. (1994) 'The social roots of football hooliganism: a reply to the critics of the "Leicester School"', in R. Giulianotti *et al.* (eds) *Football, Violence and Social Identity*, pp. 128–57. London: Routledge.

Dunning, E. (2000) 'Towards a sociological understanding of football hooliganism as a world phenomenon', *European Journal on Criminal Policy and Research*, 8: 141–62.

Dunning, E. *et al.* (1981) 'Ordered segmentation and the socio-genesis of football hooligan violence: a critique of Marsh's "ritualised aggression" hypothesis and the outline of a sociological alternative' in A. Tomlinson (ed.) *The Sociological Study of Sport: Configurational and Interpretive Studies*. Eastbourne: Brighton Polytechnic, Chelsea School of Human Movement.

Dunning, E., Maguire, J., Murphy, P. and Williams, J. (1982) 'The social roots of football hooliganism. *Leisure Studies*, 1: 139–56.

Dunning, E., Murphy, P. and Waddington, I. (1991) 'Anthropological versus sociological approaches to the study of soccer hooliganism: some critical notes', *Sociological Review*, 39: 458–78.

Dunning, E., Murphy, P. and Williams, J. (1988) *The Roots of Football Hooliganism: An Historical and Sociological Study*. London: Routledge & Kegan Paul.

Dunning, E., Murphy, P. and Williams, J. (1986) 'Spectator violence at football matches: towards a sociological explanation', *British Journal of Sociology*, 37: 221–244.

Dunning, E., Murphy, P., Waddington, I. and Astrinakis, A. (eds) (2002) *Fighting Fans: Football Hooliganism as a World Phenomenon*. Dublin: University College Press.

Dunning, E., Murphy, P., Williams, J. and Maguire, J. (1984) 'Football hooliganism before the First World War', *International Review for the Sociology of Sport*, 19: 215–40.

Dwertmann, H. and Rigauer, B. (2002) 'Football hooliganism in Germany: a developmental sociological study', in E. Dunning *et al.* (eds) *Fighting Fans: Football Hooliganism as a World Phenomenon*, pp. 75–87. Dublin: University College Press.

Edensor, T. and Augustin, F. (2001) 'Football, ethnicity and identity in Mauritius: soccer in a rainbow nation' in G. Armstrong and R. Giulianotti (eds) *Fear and Loathing in World Football*, pp. 91–104. Oxford: Berg.

Eichberg, H. (1992) 'Crisis and grace: soccer in Denmark', *Scandinavian Journal of Medicine and Science in Sports*, 2: 119–28.

Elias, N. and Dunning, E. (1971) 'Folk football in medieval and early modern Britain', in E. Dunning (ed.) *The Sociology of Sport: A Selection of Readings*, pp. 116–32. London: Frank Cass.

Elias, N. and Dunning, E. (1986) *Quest for Excitement*. Oxford: Blackwell.

Elliot, D. and Smith, D. (1993) 'Football stadia disasters in the United Kingdom: learning from tragedy?', *Industrial and Environmental Crisis Quarterly*, 7: 205–29.

Elliott, D., Frosdick, S. and Smith, D. (1999) 'The failure of legislation by crisis', in S. Frosdick and L. Walley (eds) *Sport and Safety Management*, pp. 11–30. Oxford: Butterworth–Heinemann.

European Parliament (1996) *Report on Hooliganism and the Free Movement of Football Supporters*. Committee on Civil Liberties and Internal Affairs. European Parliament Session Document, 25 April.

Evans, R. (2001) 'Call for contribution to costs of policing football games'. *Police Review*, 24 August: 9.

Fabrizio, F. (1976) *Sport e Fascismo*. Rimini: Guaraldi.

Fabrizio, F. (1977) *Storia Dello Sport in Italia*. Rimini: Guaraldi.

Faulkner, K. (2004) 'Football hooliganism: theories, commonalities and police stereotyping.' Unpublished BSc dissertation, University of Portsmouth.

FIG (2002) *FIG Fact Sheet Four: Football Hooliganism*. Liverpool: University of Liverpool Football Industry Group.

Finn, G. (1994) 'Football violence – a societal psychological perspective', in R. Guilianotti *et al.* (eds) *Football, Violence and Social Identity*, pp. 90–127. London: Routledge.

Finn, G. and Giulianotti, R. (1996) 'A sense of Scotland: Scottish identities, Scottish football and England.' Paper presented to the *Fanatics! Conference*, Manchester, 11–13 June.

Football League, Football Association and FA Premier League (1995) *Stewarding and Safety Management at Football Grounds*. Lytham St Annes: Football League.

Football League, Football Association and FA Premier League (1998) *Safety Management at Football Grounds*. Lytham St Annes: Football League.

Football League, Football Association and FA Premier League (1999) *Football Stewarding Qualification*. Lytham St Annes: Football League.

Football League, Football Association, FA Premier League and Football Safety Officers' Association (1996) *Training Package for Stewarding at Football Grounds.* Stafford: Staffordshire University.

Football League, Football Association, FA Premier League and Football Safety Officers' Association (2003) *Training Package for Stewarding at Football Grounds* (2nd edn). Preston: Football League.

Football Safety Officers' Association (2004) 'Match reports', retrieved 26/03/04 from http://www.fsoa.org.uk.

Forsyth, R. (1990) *The Only Game: The Scots and World Football.* Edinburgh: Mainstream.

Frankenberg, R. (1991) 'Cultural aspects of football: introduction', *Sociological Review,* 39: 423–4.

Frosdick, S. (1998a), 'Drink or dry?', *Stadium and Arena Management,* August 1998: 20–4.

Frosdick, S. (1998b) 'Strategic risk management in public assembly facilities' in P. Thompson *et al.* (eds) *Stadia, Arena and Grandstands: Design Construction and Operation,* pp. 65–76. London: E. and F.N. Spon.

Frosdick, S. (1999) 'Introduction: beyond football hooliganism' in S. Frosdick and L. Walley (eds) *Sport and Safety Management,* pp. 3–10. Oxford: Butterworth–Heinemann.

Frosdick, S. (2001a) 'Switch to safety', *Stadium and Arena Management,* October: 2001: 9–10.

Frosdick, S. (2001b) 'Completely safe', *Panstadia International Quarterly Report,* January: 70–2.

Frosdick, S. (2004) 'Tale of two cities – Part I', *Stadium and Arena Management,* August: 23–4.

Frosdick, S., Holford, M. and Sidney, J. (1999) 'Playing away in Europe', in S. Frosdick and L. Walley (eds) *Sport and Safety Management,* pp. 221–38. Oxford: Butterworth–Heinemann.

Frosdick, S. and Newton, R. (2004) 'The nature and extent of football hooliganism', Paper presented at the *Criminology, Governance and Regulation Conference,* British Society of Criminology, 8 July.

Frosdick, S. and Sidney, J. (1999) 'The evolution of safety management and stewarding at football grounds', in S. Frosdick and L. Walley (eds) *Sport and Safety Management,* pp. 209–20. Oxford: Butterworth–Heinemann.

Frosdick, S. and Walley, L. (1999) *Sport and Safety Management.* Oxford: Butterworth–Heinemann.

Fynn, A. and Guest, L. (1994) *Out of Time: Why Football Isn't Working.* London: Simon & Schuster.

Fynn, A., Guest, L. and Law, P. (1989) *The Secret Life of Football.* London: Queen Anne Press.

Garland, J. and Rowe, M. (1995) 'Pitch battles', *Police Review,* 20 October: 22–4.

Garland, J. and Rowe, M. (1996) 'Racism and anti–racism in English football', in U. Merkel and W. Tokorski (eds) *Racism and Xenophobia in European Football.* Germany: Meyer & Meyer.

Garland, J. and Rowe, M. (2000) 'The hooligan's fear of the penalty', *Soccer and Society,* 1: 144–57.

Garland, J. and Rowe, M. (2001) *Racism and Anti-racism in Football*. Basingstoke: Palgrave.

Gehrmann, S. (1994) 'Football and identity in the Ruhr: the case of Schalke 04' in R. Giulianotti and J. Williams (eds) *Game without Frontiers: Football, Identity and Modernity*. Aldershot: Arena.

Giulianotti, R. (1991) 'Scotland's tartan army in Italy: the case for the carnivalesque', *Sociological Review*, 39: 503–27.

Giulianotti, R. (1993) 'Soccer casuals as cultural intermediaries: the politics of Scottish style' in S. Redhead (ed.) *The Passion and the Fashion*. Aldershot: Avebury.

Giulianotti, R. (1994a) 'Social identity and public order: political and academic discourses on football violence', in R. Giulianotti *et al.* (eds) *Football, Violence and Social Identity*, pp. 9–36. London: Routledge.

Giulianotti, R. (1994b) 'Scoring away from home: a statistical survey of Scotland football fans at international matches in Romania and Sweden', *International Review for the Sociology of Sport*, 29: 171–200.

Giulianotti, R. (1995a) 'Football and the politics of carnival: an ethnographic study of Scottish fans in Sweden', *International Review for the Sociology of Sport*, 30: 191–223.

Giulianotti, R. (1995b) 'Participant observation and research into football hooliganism: reflections on the problems of entree and everyday risks', *Sociology of Sport Journal*, 12: 1–20.

Giulianotti, R., Bonney, N. and Hepworth, M. (eds) (1994) *Football, Violence and Social Identity*. London: Routledge.

Giulianotti, R. and Williams, J. (eds) (1994) *Game without Frontiers: Football, Identity and Modernity*. Aldershot: Arena.

Govaert, S. and Comeron, M. (1995) *Foot et Violence: Politique, Stades et Hooligans. Heysel 85*. Brussels: De Boeck.

Greenfield, S. and Osborn, G. (1998) 'The legal regulation of football and cricket: "England's dreaming"', in M. Roche (ed.) *Sport, Popular Culture and Identity*. Aachen: Meyer & Meyer.

Guttman, A. (1986) *Sport Spectators*. New York, NY: Columbia University Press.

Hahn, E. (1987) 'Politics and violence in soccer in Europe and the Federal Republic of Germany' in T. O'Brien (ed.) *Proceedings of the European Conference on Football Violence*. Preston: Lancashire Polytechnic.

Hall, S. (1978) 'The treatment of football hooliganism in the press' in R. Ingham *et al.* (eds) *'Football Hooliganism': The Wider Context*, pp. 15–36. London: Inter-action Imprint.

Hall, S., Clarke, J., Critcher, C., Jefferson, T. and Roberts, B. (1978) *Policing the Crisis*. London: Macmillan.

Hall, S. and Jefferson, T. (eds) (1976) *Resistance through Rituals*. London: Hutchinson.

Hamil, S., Michie, J., Oughton, C. and Warby, S. (eds) (2001), *The Changing Face of the Football Business: Supporters Direct*. London: Frank Cass.

Hargreaves, J. (1986) *Sport, Power and Culture*. Cambridge: Polity Press.

Harré, R. and Secord, P. (1972) *The Explanation of Social Behaviour*. Oxford: Blackwell.

Harrington, J. (1968) *Soccer Hooliganism: A Preliminary Report*. Bristol: John Wright.

Harrison, P. (1974) 'Soccer's tribal wars', *New Society*, 29: 692–4.

Hart, P. and Pijnenburg, B. (1988) *Het Heizeldrama: Rampzalig Organiseren en Kritieke Beslissingen*. Alpen aan den Rijn: Samson.

Haynes, R. (1995) *The Football Imagination: The Rise of Football Fanzine Culture*. Aldershot: Arena.

Heitmann, H. (1983) *Samstag ist Feiertag. Rebellion in den Stadien – zum Phanomen Jugendlicher Fußballfans*. Berlin: Diplomarbeit.

Heitmeyer, W. and Heitmeyer P. (1988) *Jugendliche Fußballfans. Soziale und Politische Orientierungen, Gesellungsformen, Gewalt*. Weinheim: München.

Hill, D. (1989) *Out of his Skin: The John Barnes Phenomenon*. London: Faber & Faber.

Hobbs, D. and Robins, D. (1991) 'The boy done good: football violence, changes and continuities', *The Sociological Review*, 39: 551–79.

Holt, R. (1990) *Sport and the British: A Modern History*. Oxford: Oxford University Press.

Home Affairs Committee (1991a) Policing Football Hooliganism. Volume One. *Report together with the Proceedings of the Committee*. London: HMSO.

Home Affairs Committee (1991b) *Policing Football Hooliganism. Volume Two. Memoranda of Evidence, Minutes of Evidence and Appendices*. London: HMSO.

Home Office (1924) *Committee of Inquiry into the Arrangements Made to Deal with Abnormally Large Attendances on Special Occasions, Especially at Athletic Grounds – Report by the Rt Hon. Edward Shortt KC*. London: HMSO.

Home Office (1946) *Enquiry into the Disaster at the Bolton Wanderers Football Ground on 9 March 1946 – Report by R. Moelwyn Hughes KC*. London: HMSO.

Home Office (1972) *Report of the Inquiry into Crowd Safety at Sports Grounds (by the Rt Hon. Lord Wheatley)*. London: HMSO.

Home Office (1985) *Committee of Inquiry into Crowd Safety and Control at Sports Grounds – Chairman Mr Justice Popplewell – Interim Report*. London: HMSO.

Home Office (1986) *Committee of Inquiry into Crowd Safety and Control at Sports Grounds – Chairman Mr Justice Popplewell – Final Report*. London: HMSO.

Home Office (1989) *The Hillsborough Stadium Disaster 15 April 1989 – Inquiry by the Rt Hon. Lord Justice Taylor – Interim Report*. London: HMSO.

Home Office (1990) *The Hillsborough Stadium Disaster 15 April 1989 – Inquiry by the Rt Hon.Lord Justice Taylor – Final Report*. London: HMSO.

Home Office (1998) *Review of Football-related Legislation*. London: Home Office.

Home Office (2001) *Working Group on Football Disorder Chaired by Lord Bassam: Report and Recommendations*. London: Home Office.

Home Office (2002) 'Home Office Circular 34/2000: Home Office guidance on football-related legislation', retrieved on 18/03/05 from http://www.homeoffice.gov.uk/docs/hoc3400.html.

Home Office (2003a) *Targeted Help to Tackle Football Hooliganism*. Home Office press release 222/2003, 18 August. London: Home Office.

Home Office (2003b) 'Home Office statistics on football-related arrests and banning orders: season 2002/2003', retrieved 12/01/05 from http://www.homeoffice.gov.uk/docs2/arrestbodata2002–3.pdf.

Home Office (2004) 'Home Office statistics on football-related arrests and banning orders: season 2003/2004', retrieved 12/01/05 from http://www.homeoffice.gov.uk/docs3/football_stats2004.pdf

Horak, R. (1990) 'Fussballkultur in Österreich von den Englischen Anfängen zum Österreichischen Ende', *SWS – Rundschau*, 3.

Horak, R. (1991) 'Things change: trends in Austrian football hooliganism from 1977–1990. *Sociological Review*, 39: 531–48.

Horak, R. (1994) 'Austrification as modernization: changes in Viennese football culture' in R. Giuilianotti and J. Williams (eds) *Game Without Frontiers: Football, Identity and Modernity*, Aldershot: Arena.

Horak, R., Reiter, W. and Stocker, K. (1987) 'Football violence in Austria: a report on a study of fan subculture and soccer hooliganism', in T. O'Brien (ed.) *Proceedings of the European Conference on Football Violence*. Preston: Lancashire Polytechnic.

Hutchinson, J. (1975) 'Some aspects of football crowds before 1914', in *The Working Class*. University of Sussex Conference Report.

Ingham, R. *et al.* (1978) *Football Hooliganism: The Wider Context*. London: Inter-action Imprint.

Inglis, S. (2002) 'All gone quiet over here', in M. Perryman (ed.) *Hooligan Wars: Causes and Effects of Football Violence*, pp. 87–94. Edinburgh: Mainstream Publishing.

Jary, D., Horne, J. and Bucke, T. (1991) 'Football "fanzines" and football culture: a case of successful "cultural contestation"', *Sociological Review*, 39: 581–97.

Kerr, J. (1994) *Understanding Soccer Hooliganism*. Buckingham: Open University Press.

King, A. (1995) 'Outline of a practical theory of football violence', *Sociology*, 29: 635–51.

Lanfranchi, P. (1994) 'Exporting football: notes on the development of football in Europe' in R. Giuilianotti and J. Williams (eds) *Game Without Frontiers: Football, Identity and Modernity*. Aldershot: Arena.

Le Bon, G. (1896) *The Crowd. A Study of the Popular Mind*. London: T. F. Unwin.

Lindström, P. and Olsson, M. (1995) *Det Obegripliga Våldet*. Forskninggsrådsnämnden.

Löffelholz, M. *et al.* (1994) *Sociale Arbeit mit Fussbollfans – Deutschlands Fanprojekte im Portrait*: Frankfurt/main:Kos Fan-Projekte beider Deutschen Sportjugend

Lowles, N. (2001) 'Far out with the far right' in M. Perryman (ed.) *Hooligan Wars: Causes and Effects of Football Violence*, pp. 108–21. Edinburgh: Mainstream.

Maguire, J. (1986) 'The emergence of football spectating as a social problem: 1880–1985: a figurational and developmental perspective', *Sociology of Sport Journal*, 3: 217–44.

Marivoet, S. (2002) 'Violent Disturbances in Portugese football', in E. Dunning *et al.* (eds) *Fighting Fans: Football Hooliganism as a World Phenomenon*, pp. 158–73. Dublin: University College Press.

Marples, M. (1954) *A History of Football*. London: Secker & Warburg.

Marques, M. *et al.* (1987) 'Youth commitment in football fan associations: the Juve Leo case', in T. O'Brien (ed.) *Proceedings of the European Conference on Football Violence*. Preston: Lancashire Polytechnic.

Marsh, P. (1975) 'Understanding aggro', *New Society*, 32: 7–9.

Marsh, P. (1977) 'Football hooliganism: fact or fiction?', *British Journal of Law and Society*, 2: 256–9.

Marsh, P. (1978a) *Aggro: The Illusion of Violence*. London: Dent.

Marsh, P. (1978b) 'Life and careers on the soccer terraces', in R. Ingham *et al.* (eds) *'Football Hooliganism': The Wider Context*, pp. 61–81. London: Inter-action Imprint.

Marsh, P. (1982a) 'Social order on the British soccer terraces', *International Social Science Journal*, 2: 257–66.

Marsh, P. (1982b) 'Rhetorics of violence' in P. Marsh and A. Campbell (eds) *Aggression and Violence*. Oxford: Blackwell.

Marsh, P. (1983) 'Rules in the organization of action: empirical studies', in R. Harré and M. von Cranach (eds) *The Analysis of Action: Some Recent Theoretical and Empirical Studies*. Cambridge: Cambridge University Press.

Marsh, P. (1988) *Tribes*. London: Pyramid.

Marsh, P. and Campbell, A. (eds) (1982) *Aggression and Violence*. Oxford: Blackwell.

Marsh, P. and Fox, K. (1992) *Drinking and Public Disorder*. London: Portman Group.

Marsh, P. and Harré, R. (1978) 'The world of football hooliganism', *Human Nature*, 1: 62–9.

Marsh, P. and Harré, R. (1981) 'The world of football hooligans', in M. Hart and S. Birrell (eds), *Sport in the Sociocultural Process*. Dubuque, IA: William C. Brown.

Marsh, P., Rosser, E. and Harré, R. (1978) *The Rules of Disorder*. London: Routledge & Kegan Paul.

Mason, T. (1980) *Association Football and English Society 1863–1915*. Brighton: Harvester.

Mathias, P. (1991) 'Football fans: fanatics or friends?', *Journal of Community and Applied Psychology*, 1: 29–32.

Melnick, M. (1986) 'The mythology of football hooliganism: a closer look at the British experience', *International Review for the Sociology of Sport*, 21: 1–19.

Middleman, N. (1993) *Policing the Supporter*. London: Home Office Police Research Group.

Mignon, P. (1994) 'New supporter cultures and identity in France: the case of Paris Saint-Germain', in R. Giuilianotti and J. Williams (eds) *Game without Frontiers: Football, Identity and Modernity*. Aldershot: Arena.

Ministry of Housing and Local Government (1969) *Report of the Working Party on Crowd Behaviour at Football Matches (Chairman John Lang)*. London: HMSO.

Moorhouse, H. (1984) 'Professional football and working class culture: English theories and Scottish evidence', *Sociological Review*, 32: 285–315.

Moorhouse, H. (1987) 'Scotland against England: football and popular culture', *International Journal of the History of Sport*, 4: 189–202.

Moorhouse, H. (1991a) 'Football hooligans: old bottle, new whines?', *Sociological Review*, 39: 498–502.

Moorhouse, H. (1991b) 'On the periphery: Scotland, Scottish football and the new Europe' in J. Williams and S. Wagg (eds) *British Football and Social Change: Getting into Europe*, pp. 201–19. Leicester: Leicester University Press.

Moorhouse, H. (2000) Book review of 'Football hooligans: knowing the score' (Armstrong 1998). *Urban Studies*, 37: 1463–4.

Moran, R. (2000) 'Racism in football: A victim's perspective', *Soccer and Society*, 1: 190–200.

Morris, D. (1981) *The Soccer Tribe*. London: Jonathan Cape.

Murphy, P., Dunning, E. and Williams, J. (1988) 'Soccer crowd disorder and the press: processes of amplification and de-amplification in historical perspective', *Theory, Culture and Society*, 5: 645–73.

Murphy, P., Williams, J. and Dunning, E. (1990) *Football on Trial: Spectator Violence and Development in the Football World*. London: Routledge.

Murray, W. (1984) *The Old Firm: Sectarianism, Sport and Society in Scotland*. Edinburgh: John Donald.

Murray, W. (1988) *Glasgow Giants: A 100 Years of the Old Firm*. Edinburgh: Mainstream.

National Heritage Committee (1996) *Press Coverage of the Euro '96 Football Competition* (HC532). London: HMSO.

NCIS (1992) *Summary of Statistics 1991/2 Season Showing Comparison with the 1990/1 Season*. London: National Criminal Intelligence Service Football Unit.

NCIS (2000a) 'NCIS press release 26/00', retrieved 17/03/03 from http://www.ncis.gov.uk/press/26_00.html.

NCIS (2000b) *Football Disorder Log for Season 1999/2000*. London: NCIS.

NCIS (2001a) *Football Disorder Log for Season 2000/2001*. London: NCIS.

NCIS (2001b) 'NCIS press release 29/01', retrieved 17/03/03 from http://www.ncis.gov.uk/press/29_01.html.

Newton, R. (2004) 'Fight, fight wherever you may be: a critical analysis of the nature and extent of football hooliganism.' Unpublished BSc dissertation, University of Portsmouth.

O'Brien, T. (ed.) (1987) *Proceedings of the European Conference on Football Violence*. Preston: Lancashire Polytechnic.

O'Kelly, D. and Blair, S. (eds) (1992) *What's the Story? True Confessions of Republic of Ireland Soccer Supporters*. Dublin: ELO.

Pearson, G. (1973) *The Profession of Violence*. London: Panther.

Pearson, G. (1983) *Hooliganism, a History of Respectable Fears*. London: Macmillan.

Peitersen, B. and Skov, H. (1990) *Herliger Tider: Hitorien om de Danske Roligans*. Copenhagen.

Peitersen, B., Toft, J., Langberg, H. and Saarup, J. (1991) 'Det er Svært at Være Fodboldfan i Danmark', in *Allsvenskan Genom Tiderna*. Stockholm: Strömbergs/Brunnhages Förlag.

Perryman, M. (2001) 'Hooligan wars', in M. Perryman (ed.) *Hooligan Wars: Causes and Effects of Football Violence*, pp. 13–33. Edinburgh: Mainstream.

Pilz, G. (1996) 'Social factors influencing sport and violence: on the problem of football hooliganism in Germany', *International Review for the Sociology of Sport*, 31(1): 49–68.

Porro, N. (1992) 'Sport, political system and sociology in Italy', *International Review for the Sociology of Sport*, 27: 329–40.

Poulton, E. (2001) 'Tears, tantrums and tattoos', in M. Perryman (ed.) *Hooligan Wars: Causes and Effects of Football Violence*, pp. 122–38. Edinburgh: Mainstream.

Pratt, J. and Salter, M. (1984) 'A fresh look at football hooliganism', *Leisure Studies*, 3: 201–30.

Raspaud, M. (1994) 'From Saint–Etienne to Marseilles: tradition and modernity in French soccer and society', in. R. Giulianotti and J. Williams (eds) *Game without Frontiers: Football, Identity and Modernity*. Aldershot: Arena.

Redhead, S. (1986) *Sing When You're Winning*. London: Pluto.

Redhead, S. (1991a) 'Some reflections on discourses on football hooliganism', *Sociological Review*. 39: 479–86.

Redhead, S. (1991b) *Football with Attitude*. Manchester: Wordsmith.

Redhead, S. (1991c) *No Violence Please We're Fans*. Manchester: Wordsmith.

Redhead, S. (1991d) 'An era of the end or the end of an era: football and youth culture in Britain', in J. Williams and S. Wagg (eds) *British Football and Social Change: Getting into Europe*, pp. 145–59. Leicester: Leicester University Press.

Redhead, S. (ed.) (1993) *The Passion and the Fashion*. Aldershot: Avebury.

Richardson, W. (1993) 'Identifying the cultural causes of disasters: an analysis of the Hillsborough Football Stadium disaster', *Journal of Contingencies and Crisis Management*, 1: 27–35.

Roadburg, A. (1980) 'Factors precipitating fan violence: a comparison of professional soccer in Britain and North America', *British Journal of Sociology*, 31: 265–76.

Robins, D. (1984) *We Hate Humans*. Harmondsworth: Penguin Books.

Robson, G. (2000) *No One Likes Us, We Don't Care: The Myth and Reality of Millwall Fandom*. Oxford: Berg.

Roversi, A. (1991) 'Football violence in Italy', *International Review for the Sociology of Sport*, 26: 311–32.

Roversi, A. (1994) 'The birth of the "ultras": the rise of football hooliganism in Italy', in R. Giuilianotti and J. Williams (eds) *Game without Frontiers: Football, Identity and Modernity*. Aldershot: Arena.

Roversi, A. and Balestri, C. (2000) 'Italian ultras today: change or decline?', *European Journal on Criminal Policy and Research*, 8: 183–99.

Rowlands, J. (2001) 'Policing European football hooliganism', retrieved 12/01/05 from http://www.ex.ac.uk/politics/pol_data/undergrad/rowlands/index.htm.

Russell, G. (1995) 'Personalities in the crowd – those who would escalate a sports riot', *Aggressive Behavior*, 21: 91–100.

Russell, G. and Goldstein, J. (1995) 'Personality differences between Dutch football fans and non-fans', *Social Behavior and Personality*, 23: 199–204.

Ryan, M. (2003) *Penal Policy and Political Culture in England and Wales*. Winchester: Waterside Press.

Salvini, A. (1988) *Il Rito Aggressivo. Dall'Aggressivita Simbolica al Compartamento Violento: Il Casa dei Tifoso Ultras*. Florence: Giunti.

Salvini, A., Biondo, R. and Turchi, G. (1988) 'Aspetti Interattivo–Aggressivi Nel Comportamento dei Tifosi: Rilievi Teorici ed Empirici', in M. Guicciardi and A. Salvini (eds) *La Psicologia dell'Atleta*. Milano: Giuffrè.

Sande, J. van de (1987) 'Football and violence in Holland', in T. O'Brien (ed.) *Proceedings of the European Conference on Football Violence*. Preston: Lancashire Polytechnic.

Scottish Education Department (1977) *Report of the Working Group on Football Crowd Behaviour (The McElhone Report)*. London: HMSO.

Siekmann, R. van. (ed.) (1982) *Voetbalvandalisme*. Haarlem: De Vrieseborch.

Sim, M. (1983) *Violence and Sport*. Toronto: Butterworths.

Smith, T. (2000) 'Bataille's boys: postmodernity, fascists and football fans', *British Journal of Sociology*, 51: 443–60.

SNCCFR (1996) *FA Premier League Fan Survey 1995/96*. Leicester: Universityof Leicester, Sir Norman Chester Centre for Football Research.

SNCCFR (2001) *Fact Sheet 1: Football and Football Hooliganism*. Leicester: University of Leicester, Sir Norman Chester Centre for Football Research.

SNCCFR (2002) *Fact Sheet 6: Racism and Football*. Leicester: Leicester University, Sir Norman Chester Centre for Football Research.

Social Science Research Council/Sports Council (1978) *Public Disorder and Sporting Events: A Report by a Joint Council of the Sports Council and the Social Science Research Council.* London: Sports Council/SSRC.

Solomos, J. (1989) *Race and Racism in Contemporary Britain.* Basingstoke: Macmillan Education.

Solomos, J. (2003) *Race and Racism in Britain* (3rd edn). Basingstoke: Palgrave Macmillan.

Spracklen, K. (1997) Book review of 'Understanding Soccer Hooliganism (Kerr 1994)', *Reviewing Sociology*, 10, retrieved 05/05/2000 from http://www.rdg.ac.uk/RevSoc/archive/volume10/number2/10–2v.htm.

Stott, C. (2003) 'Police expectations and the control of English soccer fans at "Euro 2000"', *Policing: An International Journal of Police Strategies and Management*, 26: 640–55.

Stott, C., Hutchinson, P. and Drury, J. (2001) '"Hooligans" abroad? inter-group dynamics, social identity and participation in collective "disorder" at the 1998 World Cup finals', *British Journal of Social Psychology*, 40: 359–84.

Stott, C. and Reicher, S. (1998) 'How conflict escalates: the inter-group dynamics of collective football crowd disorder', *Sociology*, 32: 353–77.

Sugden, J. (2001) 'We are Leeds!', in M. Perryman (ed.) *Hooligan Wars: Causes and Effects of Football Violence*, pp. 95–107. Edinburgh: Mainstream.

Sugden, J. and Bairner, A. (1988) 'Sectarianism and football hooliganism in Northern Ireland', in T. Reilly *et al.* (eds) *Science and Football.* London: E. & F.N. Spon.

Sugden, J. and Tomlinson, A. (eds) (1994) *Hosts and Champions, Soccer Cultures, National Identities and the USA World Cup.* Aldershot: Arena.

Sumner, M. and Parker, H. (1995) *Low in Alcohol: A Review of International Research into Alcohol's Role in Crime Causation.* Manchester: University of Manchester.

Taylor, I. (1971a) '"Football mad": A Speculative Sociology of football hooliganism' in E. Dunning (ed.) *The Sociology of Sport: A Selection of Readings*, pp. 352–77. London: Frank Cass.

Taylor, I. (1971b) 'Soccer consciousness and soccer hooliganism' in S. Cohen (ed.) *Images of Deviance.* Harmondsworth: Penguin Books.

Taylor, I. (1976) 'Spectator violence around football: the rise and fall of the "working class weekend"', *Research Papers in Physical Education*, 4: 4–9.

Taylor, I. (1982a) 'Class, violence and sport: the case of soccer hooliganism in Britain', in H. Cantelon and R. Gruneau (eds) *Sport, Culture and the State.* Toronto: University of Toronto Press.

Taylor, I. (1982b) 'On the sports violence question: soccer hooliganism revisited', in J. Hargreaves (ed.) *Sport Culture and Ideology.* Cambridge: Polity.

Taylor, I. (1984) 'Professional sport and the recession: the case of British soccer', *International Review for the Sociology of Sport*, 19: 7–30.

Taylor, I. (1987) 'Putting the boot into a working class sport: British soccer after Bradford and Brussels', *Sociology of Sport Journal*, 4: 171–91.

Taylor, R. (1991) 'Walking alone together: football supporters and their relationship with the game', in J. Williams and S. Wagg (eds) *British Football and Social Change: Getting Into Europe*, pp. 111–29. Leicester: Leicester University Press.

Taylor, R. (1992) *Football and its fans: supporters and their relations with the game 1885–1985.* Leicester: Leicester University Press.

Taylor, R. and Ward, A. (1995) *Kicking and Screaming: An Oral History of Football in England*. London: Robson Books.

Trivizas, E. (1980a) 'Offences and offenders in football crowd disorders', *British Journal of Criminology*, 21: 276–88.

Trivizas, E. (1980b) 'Sentencing and the football hooligan', *British Journal of Criminology*, 21: 342–49.

Trivizas, E. (1984) 'Disturbances associated with football matches', *British Journal of Criminology*, 24: 361–83.

Turner, R. (1990) *In your Blood: Football Culture in the Late 1980s and Early 1990s*. London: Working Press.

UEFA (2004) *Binding Safety and Security Instructions*. Nyon: Union of European Football Associations.

Vamplew, W. (1988) *Pay Up and Play the Game*. Cambridge: Cambridge University Press.

Veugelers, W. (1981) 'Wie Zijn de Echte Voetbalsupporters? Oorzaken en Achtergronden van het Voetbalvandalisme', *Psychologie en Maatschappij*.

Vreese S. de (2000) 'Hooliganism under the statistical magnifying glass: a Belgian case study', *European Journal on Criminal Policy and Research*, 8: 201–23.

Vuddamalay, S. (2002) Personal communication by the Secretary General of the Mauritius Football, 6 May.

Waddington, D., Jones, K. and Critcher, C. (1989) *Flashpoints*. London: Routledge.

Wagg, S. (1984) *The Football World: A Contemporary Social History*. Brighton: Harvester Press.

Walgrave, L., Colaers, C. and Limbergen, K. van (1987) 'After Heysel: a Belgian research project on the societal and socio-psychological backgrounds of football hooliganism', in T. O'Brien (ed.) *Proceedings of the European Conference on Football Violence*. Preston: Lancashire Polytechnic.

Walker, G. (2000) 'The challenges facing managers in modern sport: a European perspective.' Keynote paper, Management Commission, *6th World Leisure Congress*, Bilbao, Spain, July.

Walvin, J. (1986) *Football and the Decline of Britain*. Basingstoke: Macmillan.

Walvin, J. (1994) *The People's Game: The History of Football Revisited*. Edinburgh: Mainstream.

Wann, D. (1993) 'Aggression among highly identified spectators as a function of their need to maintain a positive social identity', *Journal of Sport and Social Issues*, 17: 134–43.

Wann, D. (1994) 'The "noble" sports fan: the relationships between team identification, self-esteem and aggression', *Perceptual and Motor Skills*, 78: 864–6.

Ward, C. (1989) *Steaming In: Journal of a Football Fan*. London: Simon & Schuster.

Warne, C. (1999) 'Crowd risks in sports grounds', in S. Frosdick and L. Walley (eds) *Sport and Safety Management*, pp. 186–200. Oxford: Butterworth-Heinemann.

Watt, T. (1993) *The End: 80 Years of Life on Arsenal's North Bank*. Edinburgh: Mainstream.

Whannel, G. (1979) 'Football, crowd behaviour and the press', *Media Culture and Society*, 1: 327–342.

When Saturday Comes (2002) 'Object Lessons', *When Saturday Comes*, March: 4.

Williams, J. (1980) 'Football hooliganism: offences, arrests and violence – a critical note', *British Journal of Law and Society*, 7: 104–11.

Williams, J. (1991a) 'Having an away day: English football fans and the hooligan debate', in J. Williams and S. Wagg (eds) *British Football and Social Change: Getting into Europe*, pp. 160–84. Leicester: Leicester University Press.

Williams, J. (1991b) 'When violence overshadows the spirit of sporting competition: Italian football fans and their sports clubs – commentary on paper by Zani, B. and Kirchler, E.', *Journal of Community and Applied Psychology*, 1: 23–8.

Williams, J. (1992a) *'Lick My Boots...' Racism in English Football*. Leicester: Leicester University Press.

Williams, J. (1992b) *Football Spectators and Italia '90: A Report on the Behaviour and Control of European Football Fans at the World Cup Finals, 1990'. Report to the Council of Europe*. Leicester: Sir Norman Chester Centre for Football Research.

Williams, J. (2001) 'Aggro phobia', *When Saturday Comes*, August: 28–9.

Williams, J. (2002) 'Who are you calling a hooligan?', in M. Perryman (ed.) *Hooligan Wars: Causes and Effects of Football Violence*, pp. 37–53. Edinburgh: Mainstream.

Williams, J., Dunning, E. and Murphy, P. (1984) *Hooligans Abroad: The Behaviour and Control of English Fans in Continental Europe*. London: Routledge & Kegan Paul.

Williams, J., Dunning, E., Murphy, P. and Bucke, T. (1989) *Football and Football Supporters after Hillsborough: A National Survey of Members of the Football Supporters Association*. Leicester: Sir Norman Chester Centre for Football Research.

Williams, J. and Wagg, S. (eds) (1991) *British Football and Social Change: Getting into Europe*. Leicester: University of Leicester Press.

Wilmot, D. (1993) *Policing Football Matches*. Manchester: Greater Manchester Police.

Zani, B. and Kirchler, E. (1991) 'When violence overshadows the spirit of sporting competition: Italian football fans and their clubs', *Journal of Community and Applied Social Psychology*, 1: 5–21.

Useful Websites

European Convention on Spectator Violence and Misbehaviour at Sports Events and in Particular Football Matches (http://conventions.coe.int/Treaty/en/Treaties/Word/120.doc).

University of Liverpool Football Industry Group Fact Sheet Four: Football Hooliganism (http://www.liv.ac.uk/footballindustry/hooligan.html).

Football Safety Officers' Association (http://www.fsoa.org.uk).

Home Office Working Group on Football Disorder Chaired by Lord Bassam: Report and Recommendations (http://www.homeoffice.gov. uk/docs/ftblwgrp.pdf).

Home Office Statistics on Football-related Arrests and Banning Orders: Season 2001/2002 (http://www.homeoffice.gov.uk/docs2/arrestdata2002pdf).

Home Office Statistics on Football-related Arrests and Banning Orders: Season 2002/2003 (http://www.homeoffice.gov.uk/docs2/arrestbodata2002-3.pdf).

Home Office Statistics on Football-related Arrests and Banning Orders: Season 2003/2004 (http://www.homeoffice.gov.uk/docs3/football_stats2004.pdf).

Home Office Circular 34/2000: Home Office Guidance on Football-related Legislation (http://www.homeoffice.gov.uk/docs/hoc3400.html).

National Criminal Intelligence Service (http://www.ncis.gov.uk).

Policing European Football Hooliganism (http://www.ex.ac.uk/politics/pol_data/undergrad/rowlands/index.htm).

University of Leicester: Sir Norman Chester Centre for Football Research Fact Sheet 1: Football and Football Hooliganism (http://www.le.ac.uk/snccfr/resources/factsheets/fsl.html).

Kick Racism out of Football (http://www.kickitout.org).

Index

abuse, racist 43, 139
academic explanations 82–4
access control 174
Adang, Otto 178
adventure-oriented fans 57
advice packs, for supporters 163
Advisory group against racism and
  intimidation (AGARI) 144
age
  Italian militant supporters 59
  Swedish football hooligans 66
aggression, working-class behaviour
  95
aggressive nature, of football 12
aggro 82
Albania, football violence 55
alcohol
  bans
    at UEFA matches 125
    unexpected consequences of
      132–4
  controls
    anomalies in 128–9
    effectiveness 129–30
    legislation 170
  and culture 130–1
  football violence 125–37
    connection between 125–8
    perceived as contributing factor
      to 80, 96
    police view 132
  roligan behaviour 131–2
  Scottish fan behaviour 134–5

alcohol stewards 135
alcohol-free lager 130
'All different – all equal' campaign
  148
all-seated accommodation 172
American football, spectator violence 4
amplification spiral 19, 44, 92–3, 113,
  115–16
  see also de-amplification
anti-racist initiatives 138–9, 142–6
anti-republican chanting 141
anti-semitic chants 139
anti-semitism, Italy 146–7
anti-social tendencies 109
Ape Mountain 69
Armstrong, Gary 82, 97
Arnold, Dr Thomas 14
arrest statistics 32–3, 34–6, 48, 64
Athletico Bilbao 53–4
attendance statistics 35t
Australia, spectator violence 4
Austria
  fan profiles/behaviour 65
  football violence/hooliganism 53,
    109, 121
'away' fans, decline of 158–9

banners, messages to journalists 120
banning orders 36, 170–2
Barnes, John 139
Bassam Report 43, 112, 171–2, 175–6
Beattie, John 133
Bedouin syndrome 104

Belgium
  fan coaching/projects 185
  football violence/hooliganism
    49–50, 109
biological perspective 83
black players 138, 139, 147
Black and White News 140
Blue Saints 67
Bordeaux Devils 62
Boulogne kop 52
breaches of the peace 33
Britain
  extent of football hooliganism
    34–43
  historical examples of football
    violence 20–2
  theoretical perspectives
    in detail 86–101
    overview 77–85
  see also England; Scotland
Britannia stadium 129–30
British National Party 140, 145
British Transport Police (BTP) 42
British Union of Fascists 140
Broomhead, Robert 142
Brug, H. Van der 108, 120
Bulldog 140
Bundesarbeitsgemeinschaft der
  Fan-Projekte 184
Buford, Bill 83

calendrical rituals, folk-football
  violence 10
cannabis, increased use of 133
career structure, football terraces as
  alternative 93
carnival style, supporting 68, 83, 124,
  178
casuals 16, 62
Category C fans 58
cautions, Italian football fans 48
Certificate in Event and Matchday
  Safety Management 182
Chalmers, Jim 40–1

chanting, racist 139–40
Charlton Athletic 145
Chester Report (1968) 18, 174
claques 54
Clarke, John 82, 90, 91–2
closed-circuit television (CCTV)
  159–60, 173
club level problems 67, 68, 69
Combat 18 141
commercial interests 122–3, 158
Commission for Racial Equality
  (CRE) 138, 142, 144
compensatory drinking 133–4, 137
consumer-oriented fans 57
containment 155–7
corporate facilities 158
COTASS (Club-oriented Ticketing and
  Authorization System for Stadiums)
  51
Council of Europe
  anti-racist campaign 148
  booklet on violence prevention 185
  convention on spectator violence
    127, 160
Council of Europe Standing
  Committee 160
counter-culture youth protest
  movements 18
covert police tactics 98
crews, football violence 16
cricket, spectator violence 4
Crime and Disorder Act (1998) 170
Criminal Justice (Scotland) Act (1980)
  126, 134–5
criminal law 169
cross-national differences, football
  violence 46–7
cross-national similarities,
  development of football violence
  69–70
culture
  and alcohol 128, 130–1
  change, and Scottish fan behaviour
    98–9
  difference between Italian and
    English 59
  of laughter 68

see also fan culture
cup matches, arrest rates 38
Czech Republic, football hooliganism 54–5

data sources *see* statistics
de-amplification 44, 122–3
  see also amplification spiral
de-ritualization 105
  see also ritualized behaviour
Dealing with Racism and Disability Discrimination 145–6
Dean, Dixie 139
deaths, football-related 23
Decreto Maroni (1994) 187
democratization of football 90
Denham, John 176
Denmark
  adoption of British sporting values 14
  football fans, profiles/behaviour 67–8
  football violence/hooliganism 53, 109, 121
  see also roligans
Department of the Environment Working Group 127
Derby County, anti-racist scheme 144–5
detention statistics, Italian football 48
discourses, football violence hooliganism 99
disorder, construing 43–4
displacement, football hooliganism 42
domestic research, Europe 110
double standards, in tabloid press 118
downward mobility, football hooligans 65, 108
dress, French fans 62
driving accidents, alcohol-related 134
drugs, as substitute for lager 132–3
drunkenness, violent disorder 125–6
Dunning, Eric 83, 94, 95, 96, 111

Eastern Europe, racism 147
ecstasy (MDMA), increased use of 133
'editing for impact' 116
Eichberg, H. 109, 131

ejection statistics 40–1
Eliminating Racism from Football 145
embourgeoisement, of football 89
England
  disorder overseas 43–5
  fan culture and coaching 182–3
English disease 3
English sporting values, European adoption 14
EPI centre system 160
ethnographic approaches 97–101
ethogenic approach 93–4, 110
Euro '96, policing 161–3
Europe
  concern about fan behaviour 3
  cross-border police cooperation 160–1
  export of English football to 14–15
  fan culture and coaching 183–6
  football violence 18–20
    cross-national differences 46–7
    historical examples 22
    lack of data 46
    levels of 47–8
    rival explanations for 46
    stages of development 69–70
    theoretical approaches 102–12
  racism 146–8
  spectator violence 5
  style of policing 164–5
  see also individual countries
European Conference on Football Violence (1987) 54
European Convention on Spectator Violence, and Misbehaviour at Sports Events, and in Particular at Football Matches 127, 160
European Parliament, report, football hooliganism 124, 149, 161
European Union, guidelines on dealing with football hooliganism 160–1
Everton Football Club 146
expressive behaviour, football fans 102–3

'Fair play' scheme 148
fan coaching 185–6, 187, 188

fan culture 182–6
fan embassies 186
fan projects 106, 183–5
Fan-Treff 58
fans' forums 188
fanzines 146
far-right groups 140–1
Farndon, Nicholas 11
fault-lines hypothesis 111–12
fear, hooliganism 33
Federal Supporters Association (FSA) 138
fights, at Italian football matches 103
figurational sociology 94–5
Filbo Fever 146
firm rivalries 20
firms, football violence 16
'flag carriers' 55
flash-points model 83
folk-football, origins of violence 10–12
Fontana, Christine 106
football
    commercial interests 122–3, 158
    democratization of 90
    development of
        at public school 13–14
        as English working-class pastime 15
        export to Europe 14–15
    embourgeoisement of 89
    proclamation forbidding 11
Football Against Racism in Europe (FARE) 144, 148
Football Association (FA) 114, 145, 157
Football Banning Orders Authority 166
football clubs
    ban from European competitions 43
    English-style, in Europe 15
    erosion of democracy in 89
    fanzines 146
    French 63
    German 187
    intelligence liaison officers 180
    relations between supporters and 186
    tackling disruptive behaviour 187–8

see also club level problems
'Football in the Community' schemes 182, 187
football disasters 23
Football (Disorder) Act (2000) 170
Football Disorder Logs (NICS) 38
Football Factory, The 81
football fans
    behaviour
        as cause for concern 3
        expressive 102–3
    far-right groups
        influence on support 141
        targeting by 140
    lack of black and Asian 138
    police control as incitement to violence 106
    profiles/behaviour
        Austria 65
        Denmark 67–8, 72, 131–2
        France 52, 61–3
        Germany 57–8
        Italy 58–61, 103, 104, 120
        Netherlands 51, 63–5, 108, 120
        Norway 69
        Scotland 72, 83, 98–9, 120, 134–5
        stages of development 69–70
        Sweden 66–7
    sense of alienation from teams 89
    subject to criminal law 169
    see also fan coaching; fan projects; fans' forums; hooligans; supporters
Football Foundation 144
football grounds
    access control 174
    civilization of 146
    government reports on safety at 174–6
    new and refurbished 172–3
    safety officers 181–2
    see also stadiums
Football Hooliganism: The Wider Context 122
football hooliganism
    British theories
        in detail 86–101
        overview 77–85

definitional problems 27–8
  range of variables 28–9
  social context 29–30
EU guidelines on dealing with
  160–1
in Europe *see* Europe
European Parliament' report on
  124, 149, 161
European theories 102–12
extent of 34–43
  a changing problem 42–3
  data sources 31–3, 34–9
  a declining problem 39–42
fear of 33
lack of objective facts in theory and
  research 31–4
media *see* media
policing *see* policing
populist terms 3
proactive and preventive measures
  178–88
racism 141–2
repressive social controls *see* social
  controls
see also football violence; hooligans
Football Industry Group (FIG) 39, 40,
  170
football intelligence 31
Football Intelligence Unit (NCIS) 166
football intelligence/liaison officers
  166, 180
Football Licensing Authority (FLA)
  145, 175
football matches
  alcohol bans 125
  attraction to far-right groups 141
  medieval 24
  opportunity for ritual confrontation,
    Italy 103
  police risk assessments 166
  policing Euro '96 161–3
  tabloid build up to international
    118
  see also cup matches; international
    matches
football offences
  specific 170
  statistics 36

Football (Offences) Act (1991) 139, 170
Football (Offences and Disorder) Act
  (1999) 170
football players
  alienation from fans 89
  black 138, 139, 147
Football Safety Officers' Association
  (FSOA) 38, 145, 181–2
football specials, withdrawal of 156
Football Spectators Act (1989) 34, 170
Football Supporters Association (FSA)
  138, 142, 171
Football Supporters Federation (FSF)
  138, 142, 179
Football Task Force 145
football terraces, as alternative career
  structure 93
Football Trust 78, 95, 143, 144, 175
Football Unit (NCIS) 162
football violence
  and alcohol *see* alcohol
  in Europe *see* Europe
  folk football, origins of violence
    10–12
  history of 16–23
    before the First World War 16–17
    British examples 20–2
    calm between the wars 17–18
    European examples 22
    new hooligans 18
  see also football hooliganism
Football, Violence and Social Identity 46
'Football yes, violence no' campaign
  183
football-oriented fans 57
France
  adoption of British sporting values
    14
  fan profiles/behaviour 60, 61–3
  football as an 'allegory of
    liberalism' 15
  football violence 52
  racism 149
'friendly but firm' policing 178–9
Front National 149

German Green Group 149
Germany

fan profiles/behaviour 57–8
fan projects 183–4
football clubs 187
football violence 51–2
   theoretical approaches 106–7
police categorization of fans 58
racism 147, 149
Giulianotti, Richard 79–80, 83, 98–100
glorification, football hooliganism 117
Goffe, François 185
Goffman, Erving 99
government reports
   alcohol and football violence
      126–8
   safety at grounds 174–6
Greece, football violence 55
groups, of troublemakers 19–20

Hall, Stuart 90, 92, 115–16, 116–17
Harrington Report 87–8, 174
hate speech 43, 139
Heysel disaster 23, 160
higher-profile stewarding 175, 180
Hillsborough disaster 23, 175
historical parallels, Italian football
   hooliganism 103
Home Office statistics 31, 34–6
hooligan hotline 163
hooligan porn 81
hooligans
   downward mobility 65, 108
   emergence of new 18
   enjoyment of press coverage 121–2,
      124
   firm rivalries 20
   identity 84
   lack of criminological data on 84–5
   neo-Nazi image 107
   suspected
      early morning raids on 157
      NCIS database of 166
Hooligans Abroad 96, 130, 157
hooliologists 81
Hoolivan 160
Horak, Roman 65, 109, 121, 122

identity, football hooligans 84, 93
identity rituals, working-class

hooliganism 82
Ince, Paul 147
independent travel, increase in 158
inequalities, violence as an indication
   of 107
Information Technology Group, Euro
   '96 162
Ingham, Bernard 23
Ingham, Robert 122
Inglis, Simon 41–2
injuries, football-related 23
injury statistics, Italian football 48
intelligence liaison officers 180
intelligence-led policing 165–7
international matches
   aggressive reporting 118–19
   policing style 179
   see also Euro '96
Internet, log of football-related
   disorder 37
'intertemporal' substitution, alcohol
   bans 133–4
interwar period
   media reporting 114
   nationalist sentiment, public
      enthusiasm for football 15
Italy
   fan profiles/behaviour 58–61
   football hooliganism, role of media
      119–20
   football violence 19, 48–9
      theoretical approaches 102–6
   intimidating presence of police at
      games 187
racism 146–7

journalists, banners with messages to
   120

Kerr, John 83
Kick It! 143
'Kick it Out' 144, 145
King, Anthony 83
Klaphat 68
Koninklijke Nederlandsche
   Voetbalbond (KNVB) 184
Koordinationstelle Fanprojekte 184
kops 52, 62

Lago, Alessandro dal 60, 102–3, 119–20
Lang Report 88–9, 126, 174
laughter, Danish football 68
'law and order' problem, football violence as 107
Laws, Lord Justice 170–1
League matches, arrest and attendance 34, 35t
league tables, hooligan notoriety 117–18
Leeds Fans United Against Racism and Fascism (LFUARAF) 145
legislation, football-related 43, 169–72
Leicester School 83, 86, 94–7, 98
'Let's kick racism out of football' campaign 142–4
Leuven University study 71
licensing conditions, ten-point plan 135–6
lower-profile policing 175, 180
Lowles, Nick 141

McElhone Report (1977) 32–3, 39, 174
management controls, at stadiums 133
Marching Altogether 146
Marsh, Peter 82, 93, 94
Marxist perspective 82, 89
masculine proletarian norms 65, 95
Match Commander Group, Euro '96 162
media
    encouragement of racism and xenophobia 149–50
    football hooliganism 113–24
        amplification of 44, 92–3, 113
        concern, out of proportion 39
        de-amplification 44
        as easy target for 113
        history 114–15
        hooligans enjoyment of press coverage 121–2, 124
        reporting as contributory factor to 114, 116
        role, European countries 119–21
        sensationalism 3, 113, 123
        theory 115–19

see also television
medieval knights, fans contrasted to 103
medieval origins, football violence 10–11
Metropolitan Police 140, 166
middle classes, adoption of football, France 15
Miles, Kevin 165, 171
Millwall fandom 82
modern sports, folk-football and violence in 12
mods 90–1
Moorhouse, H. 82, 100
moral panic 44, 127, 175
municipalism, football culture as extended 58–9
Murphy, Patrick 83, 116

National Council for Crime Prevention (1985) 66
National Criminal Intelligence Service (NCIS)
    football intelligence 31, 166
    Football Unit 162
    football-related disorder logs 37, 38
    organized gangs as cause of violence 80
    statistics, football hooliganism 31–2, 36, 40
National Football Unit, Metropolitan Police 166
National Front 140
National Socialist Alliance 141
nationalist sentiment, public enthusiasm for football 15
NCIS see National Criminal Intelligence Service
neo-Fascism 147, 149
neo-Nazism 58, 65, 107, 147, 149
Netherlands
    anti-racist initiatives 147–8
    fan profiles/behaviour 63–5
    fan projects 184–5
    football hooliganism, role of media 120
    football violence 50–1
        theoretical approaches 108–9
    'friendly but firm' policing 178–9

Norway
  fan profiles/behaviour 69
  lack of football violence 53
Nottingham Forest Football club
  135–6, 180

organized gangs 16, 80

parental control, violence due to lack
  of 64–5, 108
personality variables, football
  violence 110
Pilz, Gunter 106–7
police
  categorization of fans, Germany 58
  control, as counter-productive 106
  data, alcohol-related driving
    accidents 134
  intimidating presence, Italy 187
  negative attitude towards sports
    fans 156
  over-reaction to minor incidents 44
  planning numbers at matches 166
  recommendation for plain-clothes
    officers 157–8
  tactics
    at grounds, prior to Euro '96 158
    as cause of football-related
      violence 83–4
    legitimation of covert 98
    statistics as reflection of 37
  used at turnstiles 157
  view on alcohol-related violence 132
  see also Metropolitan Police;
    Strathclyde police analysis
Police Football Intelligence Officers 37
Police National Co-ordinating Centre
  162–3
policing 155–68
  prior to Euro '96
    CCTV and hand-held cameras
      159–60
    containment 155–7
    European co-operation 160–1
    Hoolivan 160
    stewards 159
    tactics at grounds 158
    undercover operation 157–8

Euro '96 161–2
  hooligan hotline numbers 163
  police organization 162–3
  security campaign 162
  spotters 163
developments since Euro '96
  intelligence-led policing 165–7
  policing style 164–5
  stewarding 164
friendly but firm 178–9
peaceful behaviour of fans, Norway
  69
see also lower-profile policing
Policing Football Hooliganism 158
policy-making
  driven by populism and moral
    panic 127
  media role 116
political extremists
  ultras seen as a continuation of 60, 104
  see also neo-Fascism; neo-Nazism;
    right-wing groups
Popplewell Reports 127, 175
populist explanations, football
  hooliganism 80–1, 125
populist terms, football hooliganism 3
Portugal, football hooliganism 54
predictive style, press reporting 116
Premiership
  arrest and attendance statistics
    34, 35t
  scarcity of black or Asian fans 138
Press and Media Group, Euro '96 162
Professional Footballers Association
  (PFA) 138, 142, 144
Project Battre Lakter Kulture 185
psychological perspectives 83, 104–5,
  106, 110
psychologically-mediated effects,
  alcohol 130
psychopathic tendencies 109
Public Order Act (1986) 31, 139–40
public schools, development of
  football 13–14
public transport
  displacement of hooliganism on to
    19, 42
  herding of travelling supporters
    from 156

publicity-seeking, of football fans 124
punishment, media calls for tougher
115, 117

race relations, fault-lines hypothesis
112
racism 138–51
European dimension 146–8
football hooliganism 138, 141–2
forms of 139–41
media encouragement of 149–50
statistics 138
see also anti-racist initiatives
racist abuse 43, 139
radio contact, inside and outside
grounds 160
raids, on suspected hooligans 157
'Rams against racism' 144
'Red, white and black at the valley'
144, 145
Report on Public Disorder and Sporting
Events 113
repressive social controls 169–77
research, football violence
alcohol-related 136
British theories
in detail 86–101
overview 77–85
European and other theories 102–12
revenue risk, ban on alcohol sales 133
right-wing groups
Denmark 68
see also far-right groups
risk assessments
for alcohol controls 129
football matches 166
risk management 180–2
Rittner, Volker 107, 147
ritualized behaviour
violence as 82, 93, 102, 103
see also de-ritualization
rivalries
French fans 63
scoring systems 20
Robins, Dave 141
roligans 67–8, 72, 131–2
Roots of Football Hooliganism, The 111
Rosenthal, Ronnie 146–7
Rossonere, Brigate 59–60

Roth, Claudia 149
Roversi, Antonio 60, 102, 104
Roversi Report 19
rugby, spectator violence 4

safety, government reports 174–6
safety management 180–2
safety officers 181–2
Salvini, Alessandro 104–5
Scandinavia
castigation of football violence 17
fan profiles/behaviour 65–6
see also Denmark; Norway; Sweden
SCARF (Supporters' Campaign
Against Racism in Football) 145
Schneider, Thomas 58
school careers, violence due to
problematic 64, 108
scoring systems, hooligan 'firm'
rivalries 20
Scotland
17th century football violence 11
alcohol-related controls 126
fans
alcohol 134–5
anti-racist campaign 145
research on 98–9
Tartan Army 72, 83, 120
football hooliganism 5
role of media 120
see also Strathclyde Police
analysis
self-fulfilling prophecy, hooliganism
as 84
Senior Investigating Officers Group,
Euro '96 162
sensationalist reporting 3, 113, 116, 123
Serious and Organized Crime Agency
(SOCA) 166
Shortt Report 174
siders 51, 64, 108, 120
Sir Norman Chester Centre for
Football Research 40
skinhead groups
Austria 53, 65
France 61–2
parody of working-class traditions
90

Smith, T. 79
soccer casuals 16, 62
social anthropological perspective 82
social behaviour, working-class 95
social class
    Dutch fans 64
    fault-lines hypothesis 111
    French fans 61–2
    Italian fans 59
social construction, statistics 36
social controls 169–77
    government reports 174–6
    legal provisions 169–72
    new and refurbished grounds
        172–3
    roligan behaviour 68
    Sweden 67
    technology 173–4
social historical perspective 83
social learning theory perspective 105
social psychological perspective 82
songs, Italian ultras 60
Spain
    football violence/hooliganism 5, 53,
        109
    racism 147
Sparta fans 55
spectator violence
    EU convention on 127, 160
    as historical problem 3
    incidents at sports 4
    television and rise of 18
    see also football violence
spectators
    criminal law 169
    see also football fans
Sporting Events (Control of Alcohol)
    Act (1985) 127, 170
sporting values, European adoption
    of English 14
'spotter' system 163
stadiums
    deviancy as changing problem 42–3
    disasters 23
    fights outside 103
    management controls at 133
    as symbolic stage for ritual
        confrontation 103

    see also football grounds
statistics, nature and extent of
    hooliganism 31–3, 34–9
stewarding
    since Euro '96 164
    training package 145, 164, 181
    see also higher-profile stewarding
stewards
    club reliance on 159
    see also alcohol stewards
Stoke City football club 129
storico 103
Stott, Clifford 83
Strathclyde Police analysis 32–3, 39,
    174
subcultural perspectives 82, 90–2, 106
subnationalist politics, hooliganism
    bound up with 53–4
supporters
    anti-racist campaigns 145
    change in culture 182–3
    police' negative attitude towards 156
    relationship between clubs and 186
    see also football fans; travelling
        supporters; visiting supporters
supporters' charters 186
'Supporters Direct' initiative 188
Sweden
    fan profiles/behaviour 66–7
    fan projects 185
    football violence 53
    unruly spectator behaviour 14
Swift, David 179
Switzerland
    football hooliganism 54
    street football competitions 148
sworn enemies 52, 54

tabloid press, criticisms of 118
'taking ends' 20
Tartan Army 72, 83, 120
Taylor, Ian 82, 87–8, 89–90
Taylor Reports 127, 129, 159, 175
technology, control of hooliganism 173–4
telephone hotlines 163
television
    amplification spiral of violence 19
    rise of spectator violence 18

ten-point plans
  licensing conditions 135–6
  to combat racism 142–3
Terror On Our Terraces 145
theatrical style, support 60, 62–3, 63–4
ticketing technology 173
'tifo' 63
tolerance, of football violence 11
tough action/punishments, media
  calls for 115, 117
training, spectator management 182
training package, for stewarding 145,
  164, 181
travel arrangements, guidelines for
  police on dealing with 159
travel restrictions 170–2
travelling supporters
  criticism of police attitude to 156
  decline of 158–9
  herding from transport to stadiums
    156
Trivizas, Eugene 33, 84
Turkey, football violence 19
turnstiles
  alcohol bans, and last-minute
    rushes 133
  use of police at 157

ultras
  French 52, 61–2, 63
  Italian 59–60, 103, 104, 120
undercover operation 157–8
Union of European Football
  Associations (UEFA)
  anti-racist initiatives 148
  ban on alcohol sales at matches 125

'Unite against racism' conference 148
United Colours of Football 143
United States, spectator violence 4

Vålerenga 69
video cameras, hand-held 159–60
violent supporter behaviour *see*
  football hooliganism; football
  violence
visiting supporters, advice packs 163

water polo, spectator violence 5
Wharton, Arthur 138
Wheatley Report 174
When Saturday Comes 81
White Defence League 140
Wiener Hooligans 53
Williams, John 83, 96–7, 130, 132–3,
  175–6
Winter, Aaron 147
working-class
  football as Victorian pastime 15
  football violence
    as male identity ritual 82
    as a result of decline in traditional
      values 89
social behaviour 95

xenophobia 118, 123, 142, 149–50

youth protest movements 18
Yugoslavia, Zusism 19

Zani, Bruna 105
zealous patriotism 18
Zusism 19